When a seasoned theologian accepts the task of communicating the gospel in a non-Western setting, unexpected benefits may follow. The cross-cultural perspective provided both the occasion and the tools for Norman Kraus to examine many of the accretions of Western orthodoxy. In a rigorous quest for biblical authenticity, Kraus challenges us to rethink many of our conventional assumptions and definitions.

Along with the needed critique of traditional formulations, Kraus develops his own distinctive themes: the fundamental importance of agape, the advantages of the personal metaphor and the parent-child analogy, a theodicy of the cross, sin as shame, and salvation as solidarity *(koinonia)* with Christ.

Jesus Christ Our Lord is the impressive fruit of doing theology in a missionary context. It cuts across the usual theological categories to bring new insights to the ongoing task of understanding the meaning of Jesus the Christ.

> —J. R. Burkholder
> Adjunct Professor of Religion
> Goshen College

This is a fine book! It certainly should be read by anyone who wants to know what a systematic Anabaptist Christology ought to look like. And the fact that Kraus brings classic and not-so-classic themes to bear on issues that arise out of an Asian context is an added bonus. His study advances the scholarly discussion of Jesus' person and work. But more important, it advances the cause of Christian discipleship.

> —Richard J. Mouw
> Professor of Christian Philosophy and Ethics
> Fuller Theological Seminary

In *Jesus Christ Our Lord* C. Norman Kraus presents a thoughtful and creative Christological proposal informed by three guiding intentions. First, it seeks to be solidly grounded in the Scriptures and includes exegetical as well as systematic considerations. Second, it attempts to express the doctrine of Christ in a way which provides the basis for Christian discipleship in an Anabaptist perspective. Third, it aims to make missionary witness across cultural boundaries a high priority for speaking about the person and work of Christ.

Any one of these intentions is hardly usual in contemporary theology. The combination of all three is a highly unusual, but a welcome approach to Christology.

Kraus makes the case for couching Christology in historical and social-psychological categories, rather than in metaphysical concepts. He does this in a way which avoids the pitfalls of historicism and subjectivism and generally implements his three guiding intentions in consistent fashion.

The conversation with mission and Asian perspectives enables the author to articulate a more comprehensive understanding of the work of Christ. Most traditional Western doctrines of salvation have been preoccupied with the problem of guilt. Kraus enlarges the field of vision to include the reality of shame. This amounts both to recovering a frequently forgotten biblical category and to complementing and correcting the predominant attention given guilt in much Western soteriology.

Because *Jesus Christ Our Lord* does not fit readily into the ready slots of a particular school or direction of theological thought, it will doubtless elicit both support and criticism from a gamut of readers. But in any case, it merits careful study and discriminating discussion by missionaries, ministers, students, and teachers.

> —Marlin E. Miller
> President and Professor of Theology
> Goshen Biblical Seminary

JESUS CHRIST OUR LORD

Christology
from a Disciple's Perspective

C. Norman Kraus

HERALD PRESS
Scottdale, Pennsylvania
Kitchener, Ontario

Library of Congress Cataloging-in-Publication Data
Kraus, C. Norman (Clyde Norman), 1924-
  Jesus Christ our Lord.

  Bibliography: p.
  Includes index.
  1. Jesus Christ—Person and offices.   2. Christian
life—Mennonite authors.   I. Title.
BT202.K69   1987   232   87-14956
ISBN 0-8361-1289-X

JESUS CHRIST OUR LORD
Copyright © 1987 by Herald Press, Scottdale, Pa. 15683
  Published simultaneously in Canada by Herald Press,
  Kitchener, Ont. N2G 4M5. All rights reserved.
Library of Congress Catalog Card Number: 87-14956
International Standard Book Number: 0-8361-1289-X
Printed in the United States of America
Design by David Hiebert

    88 89 90 91 92 93 94 95 96 10 9 8 7 6 5 4 3 2

To Takio Tanase,
colleague and friend,
whose skill and dedication
both as oral interpreter and as translator
helped immeasurably to clarify my presentation.

CONTENTS

PART ONE
WHO IS JESUS, THE MESSIAH?

Approaching Christology

Attempting a Definition

PART TWO
THE MISSION OF JESUS,
THE MESSIAH

What Did He Do?

Defining the Mission

How Jesus' Life and Death Make a Difference   *So What?*

Participating in Jesus' Salvation "For Us"

Preface

A preface gives the author an opportunity to say what he has tried to do, and why. In that spirit I must begin by explaining why I, an American on loan to the church in Japan, should be writing a theology in the Japanese context. It did not just happen.

During several leaves of absence from Goshen (Indiana) College where I was teaching in the Bible and Religion Department I taught theology and Bible in Asia and Africa. In each culture the perspectives and questions differed. Those experiences awakened me to the significance of the cultural context for doing theology.

After many years of teaching theology in America I knew many of the questions to which Western theology was addressing itself. But the question that my cross-cultural experiences raised was whether these were the only—or even the best—questions. Perhaps the biblical meanings could be better understood through the medium of a different cultural setting.

Orthodoxy, of course, has assumed that there is only one perspective and set of questions which will correctly illuminate the meaning of Scripture. And liberalism (broadly defined) has worked largely as a response-reaction to orthodoxy. Thus it has dealt with the same set of questions and assumptions but with a different methodology and critical norm. Indeed, after viewing the theological scene from Asia, I am amazed how similar the perspectives of Western theologies look!

In the light of these experiences I pondered whether the stimulation of a new cultural context and the perspectives it would bring might be worth the dislocation and effort which would be involved in a move from comfortable and familiar haunts with excellent library resources. I had said for a long time that Anabaptist theology ought to be missionary theology.

Now that I was seriously interested in writing a theology, I had a chance to put these convictions to the test. Accordingly, we came to Japan to help the church here with the training of a new generation of leaders.

I considered that doing theology in this context might have advantages in several directions. It certainly would give the writer a fresh perspective, and if the writing were done in a missionary context in conversation with the emerging church, it might be helpful to the church of the author's adopted culture. And last, I dared hope that it might have a fresh and stimulating effect in its Western setting by raising the questions from a different angle of vision.

The first two of these possible advantages have proved in fact to be so. I have been disciplined to learn how to read the Bible from the perspectives of a new culture. Different cultural assumptions, surprising questions and responses, and different definitions and conceptualizations have time and again forced me to reexamine what was simply taken for granted in my Western orientation. In doing so I discovered new dimensions of meaning and application in the Scriptures themselves. After all, the Scripture is an Eastern book!

For the Japanese church the conversation has proven fruitful, but I must hasten to explain that I have no illusions that my work is a "Japanese theology." At best it is a kind of bridge which I hope will help the Japanese to move beyond a repetition of the Western theological dialogue to a fresh examination of the scriptural tradition for themselves.

I have given the subtitle "Christology from a Disciple's Perspective" to this essay as an indication of the approach I intend to take. But a further word or explanation may be in order.

For the past 300 years Western theology has been written in the maelstrom of the philosophical transition from rational metaphysics to empiricism. It has been a stormy passage. Besides absorbing the rush of historical and scientific discoveries into the theological discussion—a difficult enough task!—theologians have been almost totally involved in the critical issues of rational methodology. This was quite understandable and unavoidable, but as a result, theology has been done largely as polemics and apologetics, and it has been largely a university discipline.

By way of contrast to this rational polemic and apologetic stance this theological essay attempts to address the disciple church and propose a theological position that will undergird its life and work. It does not primarily commend itself either as a defense of dogma against liberalism or empiricism or as a polemic against the orthodox Protestant or Roman Catholic traditions. It does, however, attempt to relate to the historical and contemporary theological discussion. It is the author's contention that already in the sixteenth century the Anabaptist leaders began to enunciate an alternative to the Protestant repristination of Augustinianism (see also Klaassen, 1981). This present work is an attempt to present such an alternative in the contemporary situation, and this inevitably necessitates the analysis and evaluation of various theological positions that contribute to clarification of the author's own exposition.

From a disciple's perspective, then, I propose to begin with the witness of the original disciples to understand our contemporary experience with Christ. Thus we will attempt to keep firmly in view the original Christ event and its original meaning as our normative point of reference. On the other hand, with modern disciples in view we will attempt to communicate in the thought patterns and languages of the various modern cultures. A disciple's theology will be oriented to a time and place rather than attempt a universal statement. And last, it will be oriented to the message and strategy of the church in making disciples of all nations. (For further explanation, see Kraus, 1976:103-17.)

By way of theological introduction, two things need to be said concerning this volume. First, this is a "peace theology" in the Anabaptist tradition. For many years it has seemed to me that the biblical peace position does not fit well on the traditional Protestant theological foundation. What is needed is a more comprehensive theological perspective that will undergird and more consistently explain the implications of the cross and resurrection as God's way of dealing with evil. A peace theology should be a cross and resurrection theology.

Liberal Protestant pacifism caught something of the spirit and example of Jesus as peacemaker, but its theological rationale was different from the martyr theology of either the biblical or Anabaptist tradition. Protestant orthodoxy has from the beginning interpreted the cross in a way that justifies religious imperialism and the use of violence to achieve the ends of God's kingdom. This is not simply the interpretation of a few key passages which a peace theology might challenge. It involves the fundamental definitions of love and justice, the nature of the biblical witness and authority, and the meaning of incarnation itself.

The second theological note is that Jesus Christ himself must be the "Alpha and Omega" of a peace theology. "He is our peace" (Eph. 2:14). If we take this statement seriously, it has radical implications for doing theology.

If we say that Jesus himself is the normative criterion for theology, that means that—speaking formally—neither creation, general revelation, nor even special revelation prior to Jesus furnishes the norm for our theological statements. A theology of creation, for example, must be about creation as understood in light of the disclosure in Jesus. We seek to understand the word spoken at creation (Gen. 1:1-2) in light of the Word spoken in him (John 1:1-2). We seek to understand God in light of Jesus. That means, of course, that we will critique the great variety of theological interpretations in light of their faithfulness to the disclosure that has come in him.

We will deal with the doctrine of Scripture in detail at a later point, but here we should note that our understanding of Jesus' normativeness will also necessarily affect our understanding and use of Scripture. Of course Scripture, and especially the New Testament, remains the authoritative source as the apostolic witness to the pattern and meaning of Jesus as the Christ. But formally speaking we must say that Jesus himself is the hermeneutical norm for the reports about him. Thus we look for a composite apostolic witness—a *Gestalt*, a unified configuration or portrait—of the crucified and risen Lord as the criterion for theological interpretation, and we determine the use of any given text in the light of that normative *Gestalt*.

Making Jesus Christ of apostolic confession the normative criterion does not necessarily imply that all systematic theologies must begin with Christology as a topic, but it does open that intriguing possibility. Why not begin with an account of Jesus as "the Christ of God" and discuss the whole range of theological questions in relation to the self-revelation of God in him? Why not make explicit what is formally implicit in all authentically Christian theologies? Why, for example, should we assume that the Trinitarian principle is prior to and more comprehensive than the christological principle? To begin with Jesus as the Christ does not necessarily imply a sectarian or non-Trinitarian position. After all, in the historical development of theology it was the orthodox Christology of the third and fourth centuries which necessitated a doctrine of the Trinity.

This volume on the meaning of Jesus as Christ and Lord is in fact intended as the introductory volume to a full systematic theology, and it should be read in that light. Many theses that I hope can be developed more fully in a later volume are touched on here insofar as they reflect the meaning of God's self-disclosure in Jesus.

Further, since these chapters were written for and in cultures where the students are often first-generation Christians, I have given relatively more attention to the biblical terminology and background than might have been necessary in the seminaries of the West. For example, such concepts as covenant, forgiveness, sin, and even salvation cannot be taken for granted in Asian cultures.

Also since the Anabaptist theological position has not to my knowledge been presented systematically as an alternative to its Protestant counterparts, I have given relatively more attention to the classical Protestant position than to strictly modern positions. I have tried to be fair in my presentations and criticism of positions with which I do not agree; but since this is not a historical theology, my characterizations are of necessity brief and to the immediate point at hand, and I may at times have overlooked finer distinctions made by some of the theologians. For this I can only ask the reader's indulgence in advance.

While the above is the theological reason for beginning with Jesus, I should say in closing that there was a more existential missionary reason also. The first serious theological question I was asked after we arrived in Hokkaido, Japan, in 1981 was "Why did Jesus have to die?" This volume has grown out of extended discussions of the biblical answer to that question in the Japanese context as well as reflection upon my previous thirty years of reading and teaching at Goshen College and Seminary.

I have drawn on my memory from many sources such as B. B. Warfield and William Adams Brown whose theology was the subject for my doctoral dissertation and from earlier theologians like James Orr, E. Y. Mullins, P. T. Forsyth, Adolph Schlatter, as well as Karl Barth, Emil Brunner, G. C. Berkhouwer, Reinhold and Richard Niebuhr, and Paul Tillich. A special word of gratitude is due Donald Baillie whose essay, *God Was in Christ* (1948), first opened my eyes to broader perspectives in Christology. However, most of these names do not appear often, if at all, in the footnotes. The major reason for this is that their works often were not immediately available for reference at the time of writing and I have simply drawn on my memory and earlier notes. I owe them and others a great debt which I here inadequately acknowledge.

In its present scope the material was first presented as lectures to students at Eastern Hokkaido Bible School and at Union Biblical Seminary in Pune, India. After that, portions were used in class at Associated Mennonite Biblical Seminaries in Elkhart, Indiana. To my many students over the years who have challenged me with their interest and questions I owe a great debt. And to my colleagues both at Mennonite Board of Missions and at Goshen College and Seminary who encouraged me and helped by giving the manuscript a critical reading I am deeply grateful. And last, to Merlin Becker-Hoover who was responsible for getting the manuscript onto the word processor in the present good order, many thanks!

—*C. Norman Kraus*
Sapporo, 1986

Part One

WHO IS JESUS, THE MESSIAH?

Approaching
Christology

Chapter 1

Christology or Jesusology? [1]

"To Know Christ"

Here and there in the Bible, phrases such as "faith working through love" (Gal. 5:6) or "speaking the truth in love" (Eph. 4:15) catch the essence of the faith with such clarity that one needs hardly to explain further. One such phrase that has become a guiding text for this theological essay is found in Ephesians 4:20-21: "Christ . . . as the truth is in Jesus."

Christology begins with the faith conviction that the man Jesus can be rightly understood only in the unique categories of biblical messianism and attempts to explain how and why this is so. But it also begins with the firm conviction that this messianic image must be understood in light of the fact that the Christ is none other than Jesus of Nazareth. Christology moves beyond the biographical categories of a historical Jesus in its attempt to assess his significance, but it must never abandon its historical referent. The historical revelation in Jesus remains the norm for defining the authentic Christ image and the Christian's experience of God.

The Christocentric nature of the Ephesian epistle is well-known, and this is the only text in it that uses the name "Jesus" without adding an accompanying title. The entire text reads: "You did not so learn Christ!—assuming that you have heard about him and were taught in him, as the truth is in Jesus." The Christ of the Ephesian letter is not a mystical figure, a

---

1. Jesus, of course, was the given name of the man from Nazareth. Many biographies and "lives of" or "stories about" have been written in which he has been variously represented as martyr, religious visionary, prophet, or social reformer. On the basis of one such picture Charles Sheldon wrote his famous *In His Steps: What Would Jesus Do . . .?* (1897). And for many this more "down to earth" and humane picture is both satisfying and sufficient. Our question is whether this is an adequate representation, or whether it is necessary to speak of him in *theological* terms as the "Christ." And if so, how these two are related.

mythical symbol, or a philosophical principle, but precisely the one who is identified with and known in Jesus, the historical figure of apostolic tradition. He is our "Lord Jesus" (1:15), or "Lord Jesus Christ" (1:2, 3, 17; 5:20; 6:23). However, it is obvious that the resurrected Christ Jesus (1:20-21) who is "the Beloved" (1:6) "through whose blood we have redemption" (v. 7), "the head [of] the church" (1:22), and "Son of God" who shares kingdom authority (4:13; 5:5) is not simply identified as the "prophet great in word and deed" who raised messianic expectations in the hearts of some of his followers (Luke 24:19; Acts 2:22). He is now understood as the universal Lord and Savior (Eph. 1:20-21), the living Spirit who dwells in the hearts of his followers (3:7), and "Son of God" who is the true image of God (4:13ff.).

Attempting to understand this "Christ . . . as the truth is in Jesus" is not a purely speculative or theoretical task. Rather, it is a quest to "know the love of Christ which surpasses knowledge" (Eph. 3:19) and "to grow up in every way into Christ who is the head" (4:15) . . . "until we all attain to the unity of the faith and of the knowledge of the Son of God, to the maturity of the stature of the fulness of Christ" (4:13). Or again, in the words of Paul, it is part of the disciple's life quest to know "Christ Jesus my Lord" (Phil. 3:8).

The Need for a Theological Image of Jesus

Perhaps at first thought this seems like a fairly simple and straightforward task. Can we not simply read the New Testament Gospels for an account of the historical Jesus and the epistles for an interpretation of him as the Christ? Why must we theologize about Jesus at all? However, a moment's reflection will remind us that in fact there are a number of different pictures of Jesus in the Gospels. Which one shall we use?—the loving savior blessing the children and calling the weary to find rest? the healer and miracle worker? the eschatological prophet in sharp debate with the contemporary religious leaders? the social protester cleansing the temple? the rabbi-prophet of the new age delivering a new Torah? or the nonresistant "suffering servant" dying on the cross?

Further, it is generally recognized that the Gospels are already "theological" presentations of Jesus, the man from Nazareth. They do not give us a standardized, autobiographical account as eighteenth- and nineteenth-century "harmonies" of the Gospels suggested. The Epistles, which say almost nothing about the actual life and teaching of Jesus, compound the problem, for they present a multiplicity of Christ images and metaphors. Is the Christ to be understood as "the man Christ Jesus" who mediates between God and humans (1 Tim. 2:5)? Is he "great God and Savior Jesus Christ" (Tit. 2:13)? Is he the resurrected Lord reigning at God's right hand (1 Cor. 15:25) or the heavenly high priest (Heb. 4:14)? Is he "first-born of all creation" for and through whom all was created (Col. 1:15) or "second Adam," the "heavenly man" in God's true image (1 Cor. 15:45-49)? More images could be added, but these suffice to make the point.

The suggestion is not that these different images are contradictory or cancel out each other. Indeed, they are complementary and probably already represent attempts to give an authentic presentation of Jesus as the Christ of God in differing cultural settings. But they do differ significantly, and at least they require some selection and normative arrangement. Or if they are varying attempts to point to a form or *Gestalt* that lies behind them all, the theological task will be to construct that *Gestalt*.

Complicating our task still further is the confused multiplicity of interpretations and concepts of Christ in our modern world. Many of these are presented to us over the pulpit in popular guise. Nevertheless, they have clear theological import. For example, there are the liberal images of a popular teacher-prophet, a heroic social worker, and jovial associate of the lower classes; or the Roman Catholic image of the suffering Jesus hanging limp and lifeless from the cross; or the conservative Protestant image of the sacrificial victim, the one who pays the penalty of our sins.

This Christ may come in the semblance of an American savior whose image merges into that of the Statue of Liberty welcoming the distressed of the world to a land of freedom and opportunity.[2] Or he may be presented as the 900-foot-high miracle worker which Oral Roberts claims to have seen in his vision. Indeed, the multiplicity of individual nuances are as numerous as individual needs and the ingenuity to picture a "personal" savior.

The Christ which is presented in the standard evangelical theologies is the Christ of the substitutionary sacrifice for the guilt of sin. This image has dominated the world missionary enterprise. It is well-known in Japanese theology at least from the time of Uchimura Kanzō (1861-1930) who fervently maintained this orthodoxy even while he protested other aspects of conservative Protestant theology. Until recently it has simply been considered the normative biblical image in evangelical circles of every national culture. Now as we have become more conscious of the role that the cultural context plays in the communication of the gospel, we are realizing

---

2. The so-called Moral Majority's picture of Christ has him standing at attention flanked by American military servicemen with the U.S. flag unfurled above them, rather than Jesus hanging limp on a cross between two criminals under a mocking sign, "King of the Jews." However, in an almost ironic twist, this one who personifies the nineteenth-century American ideals is the victim who pays the penalty for our personal transgressions. He suffers as divine hero, martyr, and sacrificial victim all in one image. In an earlier era more liberal leaders like Josiah Strong (1845-1916) pictured Jesus as the great American ideal, his kingdom as the perfection of a free democratic society, and pressed for missions as an imperialistic duty of the American churches!

that this image alone is inadequate to communicate the full meaning of Jesus Christ.[3] Younger evangelical theologians from South America, Africa, and South and East Asia have begun to wrestle with this problem. Some of them met in Bangkok (1982) to share perspectives on Christology, and the editors of the conference papers reported that

> Many participants felt unable to give a definitive evangelical Christology in their context at this point in time. To be true to their situations, they felt that so many new areas were only now being opened up which contribute to formulating such Christologies, that they felt able only to set directions and agendas for the process of discerning the meaning of Jesus Christ of the Scriptures in their context. They could only share with us the milestone they had reached. (Samuel and Sugden, 1983:x)

The liberal image of Schleiermacher's Jesus as the one in whom the perfected consciousness of God "is supposed to have become a perfect being of God" (Welch, 1965:184) is well-known. He is the one through whom this genuinely original "God-consciousness" becomes a new possibility for those who will follow him. And Albert Schweitzer's picture of him as the eschatological martyr who was crushed in his attempt to usher in the kingdom of God has had influence in scholarly circles. But probably Albrecht Ritschl's image of him as a prophetic moral reformer who died as a martyr for his cause has been the most widely influential in liberal circles. In America this image has been popularized in the "Social Gospel."

More recently theologians from South America have pictured Jesus as liberator and friend of the powerless and oppressed. They begin with Jesus of Nazareth who was friend of sinners and social outcasts and who identified with their cause even to the extent of suffering their fate. He calls for a more radical change in the historical order than was suggested by the moral reformer of the Social Gospel. Thus we must think of him as liberator and revolutionary although not necessarily a violent one.

For Jon Sobrino, Jesuit priest and professor of theology in El Salvador, Jesus' person and mission are directly related to the historical situation of injustice and oppression which is caused by sin. He achieves his self-identity as Son of God in the achievement of his mission to be God's agent of liberation from sin. Jesus was not a divine Son of God who descended to earth temporarily to provide a cultic sacrifice for sins. His relation to God as Son must be defined in developmental personal terms. He "becomes" Son of God, not in the old sense of adoption but in the dynamic sense of achieving full self-awareness as God's Son through total obedience—even to death on the cross.[4]

Sobrino has been strongly influenced by Jürgen Moltmann, who emphasizes Jesus' total involvement in a historical salvation. Moltmann pictures him as "the crucified God." Jesus totally identified himself with God's cause of salvation, and in the process he suffered the fate of execution on the cross. Because he was totally identified with God, the cross can only represent his abandonment by God. Thus Moltmann pictures him as "the god-forsaken one" who in his abandonment by God on the cross reveals the very nature of God and God's involvement in the sin and suffering of humanity. In Jesus God suffered and died for the salvation of the world (Moltmann, 1974).

In the light of even this brief review of the existing variety of christological interpretations it must be obvious that we cannot simply avoid theological language in our attempt to understand Jesus' significance for history. If we are to answer the question "Who do you say that I am?" which he posed to his disciples, we must use more than biographical categories unless, of course, we answer that he is only another man who died for his mistaken beliefs. If we answer with Peter, "You are the Christ" (Mark 8:29), the theological implications of that response are clear, as Matthew's wording of the reply makes explicit. The Christ is "Son of the living God" (Matt. 16:16).

We need a theological description that will provide a norm for using the New Testament images in shaping the message of the gospel for the many cultures of the world. It must also give us a clue to our own self-

---

3. This problem is more acute in some cultures than in others. For example, the similarity of dealing with social transgression through confession and sacrificial rituals in the traditional societies of east Africa makes the biblical imagery of Jesus as sacrificial lamb readily understandable. But in Irian Jaya the concept of the "peace child" was more useful. And in Japan, where the use of blood sacrifice is almost unknown and sheep are uncommon, the image is quite unhelpful. In his *Life of Jesus* (1978) Christian novelist Shusaku Endo has maintained the image of sacrificial lamb but with a modification that might make it more understandable to the Japanese at the gut level. He portrays Jesus as the "do nothing" and "weakling" messiah in the eyes of those who think in terms of wonders and worldly success. It was precisely Jesus' weakness that made him the prime target for scapegoating. He became literally the substitute for Barabbas and his own disciples who also were liable to arrest by the authorities as collaborators. "They [the eleven] had avoided arrest and had saved their hides by deserting Jesus and denying him" (1978:168). And he had borne their desertion and betrayal without a glance or word of resentment. "No matter what happened, he was the man of sorrows, and he had prayed for nothing but their salvation" (1978:173).

Endo's earlier novel, *Wonderful Fool* (1974), had portrayed a similar Jesus figure. The fool is a bumbling, clown-like figure who is used by God in spite of himself to bring healing and peace.

4. Sobrino has clearly been influenced by Pannenberg and especially by Moltmann, for whom, he says, theology has become "a political theology of the cross" (1978:31). He himself begins with a historicized Jesus for whom the basic moral value was "re-creative justice" (1978:122) and in whom "the new form that love should take today" is embodied. He says, "In the history of Jesus himself we find love taking the form of effective action at first and then the form of accepted suffering" (1978:135).

understanding as followers of Christ and guide us into a relevant disciple-ship.

Normative Patterns for Christology

But a further question must be raised in light of the confusing variety of positions that we have noted. If there is neither one standard picture of the earthly Jesus nor one uniform christological interpretation in the New Testament, and much less so in Christendom at large, what shall we take as our norm for constructing a theological image? Who or what is the Jesus of history which informs our understanding of Christ? And is there any chris-tological pattern to which we may appeal as normative for faith? Or will each person's Christ be his or her own private existential response to the im-pressions received from reading the Bible and hearing the preaching of the churches? If there is a normative pattern, what is its nature and how does one arrive at it? We cannot discuss this question exhaustively here, but we should indicate at the outset what our approach will be.

The older post-Reformation orthodoxy which is still represented in the theology of Evangelicalism has maintained that the whole New Testament is a verbally inspired, inerrant record and witness to Jesus as the Son of God. Further, it holds that the Gospels' accounts of Jesus' words and actions are to be understood as literal history. It follows that since God cannot contradict himself, all the historical accounts of the New Testament are true and should be harmonized. No variant reading should be interpreted in a way that contradicts any other passage. With this hermeneutical assump-tion as their guide, they painstakingly and with great scholarly effort constructed a harmonious interpretation that for them became the norm. Indeed, for all practical purposes this theological construction was simply equated with the biblical text.[5]

This rationalistic orthodoxy was countered by a liberal rationalism in the eighteenth and nineteenth centuries and has its representatives among the empiricists and humanistic rationalists of our own day. Rationalism insisted on human reason as the final norm for interpreting the Bible as well as any other book. The accounts of Jesus must be understood in such a way that they square with human rationality. Thus they freely ruled out those aspects of the New Testament record which they considered irrational. Ra-tionalism pictured Jesus as a great religious teacher whose morals and re-ligious principles represent the pinnacle of human excellence. There were and are many variations within this general position, but the normativeness of a rationalized historical Jesus is common to them all.

In the twentieth century this conception of the norm was effectively challenged within the ranks of liberalism itself. Soren Kierkegaard (1813-55) was the forerunner of this challenge, claiming in effect that faith itself is the norm. Karl Barth (1886-1968) and Rudolf Bultmann (1884-1976) are its twentieth-century champions.

For a brief review of representative positions we can use Bultmann's more radical existentialist norm.[6] He understands the New Testament as a witness of faith to faith. It is in no sense a scientific historical report and should not be used as such. The kerygmatic norm is a purely confessional one. The picture of Jesus as the Christ is contained in the proclamation of the church (*kērugma*) which offers a faith interpretation of Jesus. According to Bultmann we have no way of constructing a picture of the historical Jesus that could serve as a norm for modern Christologies. Indeed, we have no way of knowing whether there is any material continuity between the Christ of the *kērugma* and the Jesus of history. Thus the *kērugma* itself is the only reference for faith, and faith is an existential decision, not a rational conclusion. In the *kērugma* Jesus is understood as the crucified one who calls us to existential understanding and decision about life under the rule of God.

Bultmann was trying to free faith in Jesus as the Christ from the

---

5. The appeal to verbal inspiration of the text does little to resolve the difficulties of interpreting the texts. It does not in itself indicate that a given text should be historicized or taken literally. However, *inerrancy* implies a literal meaning of the text. Otherwise, for example, what is the reason for arguing whether there were one or two blind men healed on the way to Jericho (Mark 10:46; Matt. 20:30)? What is at issue in such a question is not the *truth* of a sermonic representation of Jesus but the *accuracy* of a literal historical report. The harmonization process thus becomes essential for arriving at *truth*. This theologically harmonized image (truth) is a critical reconstruction of the texts just as surely as any other historical reconstruction. And the norm appealed to by those holding this position is that of a traditional orthodox consensus. The New Testament itself does not formulate such a harmonized consensus.

6. Bultmann's writings represent a radical wing of biblical criticism called "form criticism," which concentrates its attention on the homiletical forms in which the stories and sayings of Jesus were transmitted. I have used Bultmann as a representative of this position both because of his enormous influence on modern theological discussion and because of his radical consistency in following the logic of his position. It should be needless to say that his position does not provide an option for those who believe in the historical trustworthiness of the Gospels. Indeed, few—even among the liberal critics—accept his more radical conclusions.

Bultmann held that the Gospel accounts are almost entirely creations of the early church which reflect the church's understanding of Jesus but do not give us firm historical data from Jesus himself. Further, he held that the kerygmatic picture is given in the mythological categories of the first century; therefore, they must be *demythologized* for our use today. From the few authentic sayings and the account of Jesus' fate on the cross we can be fairly certain of Jesus' basic "understanding of existence," and the proclamation of the New Testament calls us to share this self-understanding or faith of Jesus. That is, the message of Jesus must be *existentially* and not mythically or historically understood.

The influence of Bultmann has been so pervasive and the literature so abundant and easily accessible that we shall list only one or two representative sources here: *Theology of the New Testament* (1951, 1955) and *Existence and Faith, Shorter Writings of Rudolf Bultmann* (1964). This latter is an excellent selection of his essays on various topics.

constantly changing picture of the historical Jesus as portrayed by the historical critics. It has been pointed out by his critics, however, that the New Testament itself gives far more weight to the work and words of Jesus as a norm for the kerygmatic interpretation than Bultmann's position allows.

In the post-Bultmannian period of debate, roughly 1960 to the present, some of his own former students have challenged the more extreme conclusions of Bultmann. In what has come to be known as the "new quest for the historical Jesus" they have used the tools of historical criticism to demonstrate that there is a continuity and historical correspondence between "Jesus as proclaimer" and "Jesus as proclaimed"; they have clearly asserted that such a correspondence is necessary to prevent faith from degenerating into a mere mysticism or moralism. Even Bultmann had admitted rather reluctantly that one could speak of an "implicit Christology" in the sayings and actions of Jesus which is made explicit in the kērugma, and this concept has been developed by the scholars of the "new quest." Biblical faith cannot be grounded on myth alone.

Norman Perrin, who is closely identified with the post-Bultmannian developments, has even raised anew the question how we may distinguish "the true from the false" faith images of Christ. His statement is worth quoting at more length:

> In this situation [many different forms of proclamation] we introduce the second aspect of our position: We believe we have the right to appeal to our limited, but real, historical knowledge of Jesus. The true kerygmatic Christ, the justifiable faith-image, is that consistent with the historical Jesus. The significance of the historical Jesus for Christian faith is that knowledge of this Jesus may be used as a means of testing the claims of the Christs presented in the competing kerygmata to be Jesus Christ. To this limited extent our historical knowledge of Jesus validates the Christian kerygma; it does not validate it as kērugma, but it validates it as Christian (1976:244).

Perrin notes further that in the New Testament itself there is an "absolute identification of the earthly Jesus of Nazareth with the risen Lord of Christian experience," and he continues, "this early Christian equation justifies us in using that historical knowledge to test the validity of claims made in the name of *Jesus* Christ and the authenticity of a kerygma claiming to present Jesus *Christ:* to be valid and authentic these must be consistent with such knowledge as we have of the historical Jesus" (1976:245). Perrin himself, of course, is not a systematic theologian, but Wolfhart Pannenberg has done a full Christology from this perspective which he entitled *Jesus—God and Man* (1964, 1st ed.). He grounds his theological statements in the historical words and deeds of Jesus as these have been discerned by the biblical critics. He justifies his theological interpretation of Jesus' person and work, which, we may note in passing, is remarkably orthodox in history itself as the revelatory medium.[8]

We might also note here that all of these systems were developed in a polemic and apologetic context. All of them, including post-Reformation orthodoxy, were developed in the state universities of Europe, and they attempt to justify biblical studies and theology as valid empirical disciplines. This has imposed what we might call a contextual or methodological norm on them. They are all apologetic in method and content.

Of course apologetic theology has a valid and important work to do, but we should not expect too much from it. The apologist seeks to establish a position on the presuppositions of the opponent or to show why these presuppositions are wrong. Such an approach naturally leads to minimal rather than maximal statements. These minimal statements have value in defense of the Christian belief system, but they are hardly adequate to nurture and guide the full life of the church.

Part of Karl Barth's significance lies in the fact that he broke with this apologetic tradition and did theology as *church* theology. He attempted to speak for a confessing church. To be sure, he spoke as a modern man, but he bracketed the modern empirical and rationalistic presuppositions in order to make a logically coherent statement of the way faith understands the world vis-à-vis unfaith. Thus he offers a theological confession of the contemporary modern church as an alternative to the worldview of scientism.

Liberal theologies written in and for the church have attempted to work within the parameters of the liberal apologetical minimums. In their concern for balance and rationality they have all too often failed to do justice to the passion and daring of faith, and they have ended up justifying the cultural status quo. Orthodoxy, on the other hand, in its passion for traditional definitions and speculative logic, has failed to challenge faith to dare new missionary theological approaches and has ended up justifying its system.

Perhaps both of these *rationalistic* systems have failed for the same reason: they have tried to substitute theoretical justification of logical statements for an authentic practical response of the church to Jesus Christ as *Lord.* A theology for the church calling it to discipleship and mission should

---

7. The "new quest" actually took its name from a book by James Robinson by the same title (1959), but there was a broad spectrum of critics from both left and right who thought Bultmann had been too radical in his denial of the possibility of historical knowledge of Jesus.

8. Frank Tupper's work (1973) on the theology of Pannenberg is an excellent review and analysis. He points out that Pannenberg broke with both Barth, with whom he had studied, and Bultmann and reestablished a historical and biblical base for theology.

not attempt to commend itself primarily by rational argument of either the orthodox or liberal varieties. Rather, such a theology should be a historically based, logically coherent witness to the meaning and challenge of Jesus Christ for discipleship in our present-day world. Certainly it is the return to an emphasis on praxis that has made liberation theology an exciting alternative to more rationalistic systems. In the final analysis, theological statements can be justified only in the response of the church to those understandings. Jesus' final commission to his church was to "teach them to *do what I have taught*" (Matt. 28:20), and he promised to be with us in the accomplishment of that task.

Our Present Approach and Norms

The purpose and approach of the present essay is somewhat different from that of the theologians and historical critics who attempt to define the distinction between "faith-knowledge" and "historical-knowledge" and to justify biblical studies and theology as worthy of modern people's attention even on modern presuppositions. Our assumed context is the church in its missionary vocation, and our aim is to help the church understand the implications of its message both for its life of discipleship and for its proclamation of the gospel. We shall begin, therefore, with the acceptance of the New Testament as the reliable witness to the continuity and historical concurrance between the earthly Jesus and the church's experience of the risen Christ.[9] We do not assume, of course, that it was written according to the norms and intention of modern scientific history writing; rather, it is a Spirit-inspired, authentic *witness* to Jesus. Further, we assume that its purpose and contextual norm was missionary proclamation, i.e., to communicate the original events across different cultural and language boundaries and thus to establish and nurture the church of Christ.

As the faith perception of God's disclosure in Jesus Christ we accept it also as part of that historical revelation. Perhaps we can use a comment by Reginald Fuller as a foil to accentuate our meaning. He wrote, "Christology is not itself part of the original revelation or action of God in Christ. Jesus does not hand out a ready made Christology on a plate" (1965:15). The comment is certainly well-taken as a caution against reading too much explicit Christology from the historical Jesus himself. Undoubtedly many of the sayings reported in the Gospels are not verbatim sayings of the pre-resurrection Jesus in their original context. As they come to us in the Greek they are already a translation of a spoken original in Aramaic, and they have been edited in light of their new cultural setting and to include the further revelation which had come through the resurrection and gift of the Holy Spirit. This, of course, is precisely the promise recorded in John 16:12-13, namely, that the Spirit "will guide you into all the truth."

But, and this is our present point, *by definition the New Testament documents with their inchoate Christologies do i.. ,...: participate in the "original event" of revelation.* Revelation is a concrete historical process of disclosure and response so that the apostles' faith response which grasped the intended, true meaning became part of the revelatory event. This, as I understand it, is what the orthodox doctrine of inspiration has always intended to affirm. And this is the basis of the biblical documents' theological significance for us. Thus we begin with the New Testament witness to "Christ as the truth is in Jesus" as the basic data for a contemporary theological description of "Jesus Christ God's Son Savior" (*ICHTHUS*).

This inclusion of the New Testament witness in the original event does not resolve the problem of differences in the interpretation of Jesus as the Christ which appear in its pages. Indeed, it is precisely these differences and the partial character of many of the metaphors used that creates the ongoing necessity for theological discussion. But I would maintain that there is a *Gestalt*, a consensus of conviction, a faith impression that emerges in the New Testament witness, and this *Gestalt* becomes the norm for evaluating the variations in the terminology and images of the individual writers.

Perhaps it can be compared to that total personal impression left by any strong individual who in the process of development may well have displayed several different personalities in a lifetime. It is an impression that emerges indirectly rather than as a scientific description. It is a composite image formed both from the reports of Jesus' words and actions and the response of those who met him and from the reflective response of the early church. Granted that it is impressionistic, but is not that the mode of *self-revelation*?

As one might expect, the New Testament documents witness to this person of sacred memory using the various cultural vocabularies and religious thought forms current and available to them. Thus one finds a wide variety of literary forms, styles, and terminology. The *kerygmatic* or evan-

---

9. I do not mean by this to dismiss lightly the necessity for historical analysis and evaluation. We should not use the texts of the Gospels indiscriminately as though all accounts lay equal claim to literal interpretation. This is not the place to go into the intricate problems of a historical hermeneutic, but we should point out that there are many indications in the text itself that the stories from Jesus' life are not all intended as simply literal reporting of a newspaper variety. Even so, on any except the most skeptical assumptions we do have a considerable body of historical material with which to draw a portrait of Jesus. And for those of us who accept the authenticity of the apostolic witness to Jesus as the Christ, the picture emerges credible and clear. However, as Stephen Neill has noted in his *Jesus Through Many Eyes*, "it is always prudent to start with a minimum rather than a maximum claim" (1976:170). (We might note in passing that this is an excellent summation of the New Testament data by one whose career included many years of mission in Asia.)

gelistic proclamation tells the story of Jesus highlighting its demand for repentance. The *didactic* exhortation builds upon and expands Jesus' own teaching and example in the context of church life. The *prophetic* preaching interpreted what was implied in Jesus' life and work relating its meaning to the whole of salvation history. *Apocalyptic* symbolism was used to interpret Jesus in the patterns of messianic eschatology already current in Palestinian Judaism. Furthermore, the vocabulary and thought forms reflect the influence of the historical and cultural contexts in which the message was being proclaimed. These early evangelists and apostles were marvelous cross-cultural communicators.

This characteristic of the New Testament witness itself makes it inherently impossible to read a standard, universal Christology from its pages which can then be transmitted from culture to culture. The apostles, inspired by the Holy Spirit, drew upon their living memory of Jesus and their experience of the living Christ to proclaim a gospel that would be understandable and relevant to their various audiences. In the preaching of the church today we are left with essentially the same task except that we are still dependent upon their composite memory and authentic reflection of the self-understanding of Jesus for our normative impression of the original Christ event.

Much has been written recently about beginning our Christology "from below," that is, with the account of a concrete historical person rather than an ontological picture such as was developed in the third- and fourth-century creeds. We will say more about this in a later chapter, but here we should note approval of such an approach in the sense that we take as our point of departure and norm the original situation—the "Christ event" as we know it from the composite witness of the New Testament.

We might attempt to delineate and defend further the theoretical and methodological implications of our present approach, but in actuality the approach must finally be justified by its discernment of and faithfulness to the New Testament image of Jesus as the Christ and by its effectiveness in communicating that message in the great variety of contemporary situations.

Postscript on Theology and Experience

We have said that Christology is theology and have noted the need for a coherent theological portrait of Jesus. Does that mean that we are going to speculate, theorize, and dogmatize about Jesus? Should we not be more concerned to *experience* Jesus as Christ, proclaim him as Savior, and follow him as Lord? Would it not be more useful to share the personal stories of our experience with Christ? Is not the experience itself theological, thus giving the stories the character of theology? After all, life is more than logic; indeed, logic is often too narrow for life's realities. What does a theoretical analysis of Jesus' identity have to do with practical Christianity? I am convinced that it is vitally related to each of the above-mentioned practical areas. In a word, it is *theory in the service of practice.*

First, there is a reciprocal relation between theology and experience. Theology conditions and enriches our individual experience and in turn is much influenced by it. Theology's importance lies in the fact that it not only is molded by and reflects our experience, but it also helps to mold that experience. It is a kind of lens that brings experience into focus; and when the dimensions of an experience are more clearly seen and understood, the experience itself is in turn enriched. For example, knowledge and understanding that come through study of a great work of art can enhance our experience of it.

Our theological perception of Jesus definitely influences our experience of him as the Christ of God. Reflective analysis upon an event can and often does modify the experience itself because experience is more than immediate sensual impression of an event. It is *impression* of an empirical happening plus perceived dimensions of its meaning. The latter may be intuitively grasped in the initial event, but often it comes as the result of reflection and analysis. One can see this process of reflective perception molding the experience and witness of the first disciples already in the pages of the New Testament. For example, the Christ witnessed to in Colossians and Ephesians clearly shows a depth of reflective understanding beyond that of the early sermons in Acts 2 and 3.[10]

Second, the proclamation of Jesus as Christ is largely communication with language, and the language of the church is the primary concern of theology. As a discipline of the church its main concern is to clarify the verbal message of the church, i.e., what it teaches to its members and what it preaches to the world. So the witness of the church to the lordship of Jesus as the Christ is one of theology's primary concerns. However, we must not confuse its task with evangelistic proclamation as such. It has the specialized function of examining critically the language which the church uses in its confessions and preaching. And I would add that this critical examination

10. The original Christ event inevitably already included intuited interpretative elements. We may call this experienced happening the original event or "event #1." As one reflects upon and analyzes event #1, the experience of that happening changes, creating event #2. This process is unavoidable; in fact, most of the New Testament witness already represents at least stage number 2. The intuited understanding of the disciples before the resurrection (event #1) was inadequate and in some cases wrong (e.g., Peter's perception of Jesus as the Christ at Caesarea Philippi). Further events and theological reflection changed their experience (event #2). The responsibility of theological analysis is to maintain authentic continuity in the church's experience of the original Christ event.

must be self-consciously done within the specific cultural context in which
the theologian is working. Theology is concerned with communication of
the message of Christ in the great variety of cultures and languages of the
world.

Third, theology is concerned precisely with the mission of the church
in the world under the lordship of Christ because the mission of the church
is theological. It is concerned with both the goal and strategies of the
church. For example, whether the church should engage in social service,
and if so, how it should be engaged is a theological question. Methods of
evangelism are obviously related to our understanding of salvation.
Strategies for peace witness and for advocacy of justice are determined by
our concepts of eschatology and Christ's authority. Is Jesus the spiritual
"head of the church" only, or is he also king of the universe? Such a
theological question is concerned with practical affairs.

However, we must insist again on the more specialized function and
purpose of theology. Its immediate purpose is clarification of meaning, and
its primary method is reflective analysis. It is a descriptive and analytical
process aiming at the clarification of our language about God. As Saint
Anselm of the eleventh century put it, "Theology is faith seeking understanding." *Faith* is a conviction and trust based upon hearing the word
about Jesus as the Christ and experiencing it as "the power of God for salvation" (Rom. 1:16-17). And *theology* is our attempt to express the meaning
and implications of this experience for our life in the world.

We speak of theology as a rational discipline in the broad sense, but
this does not mean that humanistic rationalism is its final norm or that it is
abstract, speculative, and theoretical. Theology must and does recognize
the various dimensions of meaning in our lives—the esthetic, psychological,
and spiritual as well as the empirical and logical. And, as we have seen, it
must take intuition and experience seriously. Rational in this case means
that it is not merely impressionistic. It is analytical reflection examining distinctions, similarities, and implications of language. Thus it calls for careful
and sometimes technical use of words. As a rational discipline it attempts to
make a coherent and logically consistent statement about our experience of
God.

Perhaps we can understand this better by contrasting theology to
preaching and personal testimony which are also verbal activities of the
church. Preaching is essentially proclamation and exhortation to inform,
inspire, and encourage. It should be informed and guided by theological
analysis, but its immediate goal and style are different from theology.
Testimony is a form of sharing one's experience with others, and we have
already talked about the relation of theology and experience. One primary

form of testimony in the church is the confession of faith. Again, theology is not simply a confession of faith; rather it is an attempt to give a reasonable account of the church's confession, relating it to the various aspects and dimensions of our life in the world.

Chapter 2

The Language of Christology

Christological statements through the ages have inevitably used the philosophical terminology of their era and therefore reflect various philosophical definitions. The orthodox statements of the early ecumenical councils like Nicea and Chalcedon used the terminology of Platonic philosophy. Indeed, more than most Christians realize, the theological debate between modern orthodoxy and liberalism is a matter of philosophical assumptions and definitions rather than the interpretation of a given text.

This present work also makes certain assumptions of a philosophical nature about the meaning and use of language and the nature of experience and reality. This chapter deals with some of these more technical matters which are important especially in transcultural communication. The reader who is not particularly inclined to philosophical analysis and wants to get on with theological and biblical interpretation may wish to go immediately to the section in this chapter on "The Nature of the New Testament Witness to Christ" (pp. 58-59). Then if questions of meaning and use of terms arise, he or she may wish to return to this discussion.

Descriptive Models from Various Cultures

Christianity makes a unique claim for Jesus when it calls him "the Christ, the Son of the living God" (Matt. 16:16). The technical theological word for this is incarnation, i.e., the embodiment of God. Of course Christianity is not the only religion to claim that its founder-leader had a special relationship to God or was a special manifestation of God. Indeed, Hinduism speaks of incarnations of gods in human or other animal life. However, even if we assume that all these claims relate to the same basic kind of human experience of the divine, we can by no means assume that they have the same meaning. They represent different cultural systems with their different conceptions of life and its meaning, and they use a variety of linguistic modes to describe these concepts. To understand the unique claims for Jesus it is helpful to see them against the backdrop of these other claims. We will not attempt a detailed comparison and contrast of the claims but will note briefly several patterns which represent options that also have been used to interpret Jesus' significance.

The concept of incarnation was quite common in the ancient world where the dominant patterns of thought were polytheistic or pantheistic. In polytheistic mythology there are many examples of *divine heroes* born to human mothers and sired by one of the gods in a sexual union. Such polytheistic promiscuity in which a divine spirit impregnated a human female was relatively common in the mythological legends of ancient Egypt and Greece.

The *avatara* of Hindu tradition are also widely known and have often been compared favorably to the Christian concept of incarnation. Indeed, the word *incarnation* is used to translate *avatar*. The *avatar* is a mythical descent of the god Vishnu in order to save the world from some great evil. There were at least ten such major interventions identified. Vishnu temporarily came into the world in disguise as a king (Ram), a *rishi* (Buddha), or even as animal (turtle and boar), and he used his disguise to rescue humankind from demons, ignorance, and other evils.

This concept is based upon a monistic, mystical view of the universe which equates divine being with the spirit or life force that is immanent in all things. Thus every individual is to some degree an incarnation. The *avatara* are only special instances of Vishnu's intervention to save the world from chaos. In such a system it is quite easy to conceptualize mythically some special human savior or even a coincidental natural intervention like a rainstorm as an incarnation.

In the biblical tradition the theophany or appearance of God may be compared to the *avatar*. But the definition of theophany differs in its dualistic presupposition. In the theophanous phenomenon of the Bible the divine being is not and does not become human. God merely becomes temporarily visible in angelic or human guise for the immediate purpose at hand. When Jesus' relation to God is described in theophanic terms, we tend to get a *docetic* picture of him.

In many cultures the king or emperor has been considered a divine incarnation. In the Hindu system such status is based upon the monistic assumptions noted above. For example, in Nepal, which is a Hindu state, the king is installed as the incarnation of Vishnu for his people at the coronation. In Japanese tradition, however, the emperor's divine status as representative of the nation was his by ancestral inheritance. The Sungoddess, *Amaterazu Omikami*, sent her grandson from the heavenly sphere to be the first emperor of Japan, and the royal family is descended from him.

The Buddha represents yet another pattern of deification. Guatama made no claims of divinity for himself. Indeed, he was agnostic concerning the existence of gods. However, his followers, especially those of the Mahayana tradition, have deified him. One might say that Buddha demythologized the Hindu system, and his followers remythologized it by making him the object of the new myth. And the Hindus themselves helped this process by recognizing him as an *avatar*. In this same fashion some have claimed that Jesus was divinized by his followers despite his own disclaimers.

Finally, there is the pattern of divine-human relationship which may be called *inspirational* in contrast to incarnational.[1] The experience of being seized, inspired, or possessed by the divine spirit so that the person becomes the *oracle* or divine mouthpiece is well-known in many religions. In Japan a number of new religious movements have been begun by an *ikigami sama* or living god. For example, the foundress of Tenrikyo was said to be so indwelt by the god as though she were a living shrine.

The Nature of the Problem

Although various individual theologians throughout history have used one or another of these models to explain who Jesus was, the Christian faith in its normative statements has always maintained that the experience of Jesus as the Christ transcends all of them. It was not his followers who divinized Jesus. He was more than a temporary theophanous appearance of God. He was not merely a mythological manifestation of the mystical reality of which we are all evanescent particles. Rather, he was experienced as the self-disclosing presence of God among humankind in a fully human life with all its creaturely limitations; and for this the language of incarnation or embodiment has been used. Whether this can more adequately be expressed in ontological rather than inspirational terms is open to debate, but at any rate the church has always maintained that Jesus was far more than a prophetic witness to God.

Christology is in fact a God-statement. Stated briefly, the doctrine of incarnation holds that in Jesus Christ the eternal Creator-God came to us in an earthly, human existence. This was not merely a temporary descent or change and return to a former mode of existence, leaving history as it was prior to his coming. Rather, God's presence among us in Jesus actually introduced a change into the human situation that continues in history. Through the life, death, and resurrection of Jesus the earthly pattern of death's domination has been effectively challenged, and the possibility for eternal life has been opened through the resurrection. Furthermore, God is continuing an incarnational relation to the human family which was initiated in Jesus Christ through the Spirit.

This is a statement about an unanticipated, unique event *in history*, but more, it is a statement about God. Such an unanticipated and unique (i.e., nothing like it has happened before or since) event which is understood in Christian faith and experience as a disclosure of God presents us with real problems of communication. Since it is unanticipated and unique, to what can we compare it? For example, the resurrection of Jesus is like nothing before or after it in history. Only Jesus himself experienced it, and there is no clear description of it by any observer. To what can we compare it in our experience?

Further, since we are speaking of God who is not accessible to empirical investigation, what analogies shall we use? What in the Christ event can provide the analogy of God's presence? His miraculous acts? His servanthood? His death on the cross? His resurrection? Or what linguistic modes shall we use? Since we are not describing the kinds of facts that we speak of as scientific, i.e., facts that can be repeated and experimented with in the laboratory, then we cannot, strictly speaking, use the empirical linguistic mode of speaking. Shall we then resort to mythical images? But can myth satisfactorily describe Jesus as the *historical* presence of God among us? Myth is primarily the mode of monistic conceptualization and fits the mystical worldview much better than biblical concepts.[2]

Rudolph Bultmann, who has had tremendous influence on modern theological discussion, interpreted many of the New Testament images as mythological and concluded that they must be demythologized because

---

1. The Spirit's "indwelling" is also recognized in the Bible, but the distinction between God and humans is so profound that there is no tendency to divinize prophets. However, there have been some attempts to define Jesus' relation to God in inspirational rather than incarnational terms. Schleiermacher's definition of Jesus' divinity as "God-consciousness" is one example. On the contemporary scene G. W. H. Lampe has attempted such a definition. See his "The Holy Spirit and the Person of Christ" (1972:111-130) and his Bampton Lectures for 1976 entitled, *God as Spirit* (Oxford, 1977: esp. chap. 3). C. F. D. Moule offers a criticism of such Christology in *The Origins of Christology* (1977).

2. In *The Marriage of East and West* (1982) Bede Griffiths compares the Hindu, Jewish, and Christian views as mythological visions of the universe with their various symbols, and he pleads with Christian theology for a return from the dualism of Aristotle to a more holistic Vedic concept of existence which he thinks is also reflected in St. Paul. Griffiths is a Benedictine monk who has given his life to dialogue with the Hindu scholars of India. He is deeply concerned to convey the truth of Christianity and in turn to understand the truth of Hinduism. However, when for the purposes of dialogue he assumes that the biblical mode is mythological, one must at least question whether he has not already obscured a significant difference in the two systems.

myth no longer effectively communicates the meaning of the gospel in the modern, secular world. Since we cannot use empirical language to speak of God, he held that myths are best translated into existentialist language of self-understanding. Thus, for example, the myth of the resurrection is to be an expression of the apostles' belief in the lordship of Christ. *If*, for example, the resurrection is a myth, this is one viable way of dealing with it in the modern context. Our question is whether it is properly understood as myth.

The problem has two major facets which we must explore, namely, the ontological and the linguistic. Each culture has its worldview—its concept of being (ontology) and modes of analogy.[3] Thus similar statements in two different cultures may have different meanings and call for quite different responses. By the same token, statements which sound the same may be in different linguistic modes and thus convey different meanings. If what is spoken in a mythical/mystical mode in one culture is understood in an empirical mode in another, meanings may become confused. For example, if the statement that the Buddhist lamas of Tibet levitate (a mystical experience) is understood in empirical categories, we might expect to see them flying like airplanes! While this is especially troublesome in communicating across cultures, it often causes difficulties in what may seem to be familiar cultural settings, especially where cultural norms are in flux. Thus we need to consider our modes of analysis and discourse before we begin a theology of Jesus as "the Christ of God" (Luke 9:20).[4]

Modal Options for a Theological Analogy

We have observed that God is not an empirical datum. We cannot see, touch, or hear God like we do physical objects. Thus our common language of religious experience is not, strictly speaking, empirical. When I say, "God spoke to me" or "God is here," I intuitively recognize that my statements are not to be taken literally in a physical sense. I am using the figurative mode of language. In the same way when we say, "Jesus was God with us," we are not using a strictly empirical mode of expression. Theological language is, by and large, the language of analogy. That is, we are attempting to understand and describe a spiritual reality which we perceive only indirectly as a kind of reflection by comparing it to the direct data of historical experience.

We cannot do a detailed philosophical analysis here, but we should take time to observe the major ontological and epistemological options that are available to us and to explain some of the implications of choosing one or the other set of assumptions. We have three basic patterns or modes from which to choose, namely, the mythological, the metaphysical, and the historical. All of them, of course, are analogical, but they presuppose different ways of experiencing and understanding the universe which environs us. Thus they provide us with different ways of experiencing and understanding God's presence in Jesus.

Mythological Mode

Our first option is the mythological. Myth as a mode of expression functions as a kind of analogy in monistic systems, or what might better be called systems of ontological mysticism.[5] This is the view that the whole of cosmic reality exists on an interdependent continuum of being from the spiritual to the material and that the spiritual penetrates the whole, giving it life. In primitivistic polytheistic cultures gods and humans are thought to inhabit the same cosmological sphere, e.g., in ancient Greece the abode of the gods was Mt. Olympus. In animistic cultures the gods are identified with nature and cosmic forces. When such concepts are formed into abstract philosophical systems, a mystical unity of being which connects the whole both ontologically and epistemologically is spoken of.

In mythical cultures there is neither a clear contrasting distinction between the empirical and nonempirical nor the assumption that the empirical is the *real* by which all else must be measured. And this is reflected in the language of myth in which the symbolic and literal are not sharply differentiated. Instead of a metaphysical approach which depends upon rational analysis, or an empirical approach which uses strictly literal descriptive statements, these cultures tend to use the nonrational (poetic) language of symbol and ecstatic union. Symbol and being merge in reality just as the individual soul merges with the divine universal reality, and the myth itself

---

3. An analogy is a comparison of the partially known and the known on the assumption that there is a corresponding likeness. For example, when the Bible says that humans were created "in the image of God," we might translate "after the analogy of God's being." This does not imply that God is simply a supernatural human or that humans are gods in the making as the Mormon formula suggests. ("As man is God once was. As God is so man may become.") "Image" suggests the comparable, corresponding likeness of analogy rather than equality or sameness; but it is the conviction that there is an analogical image or likeness of God in humans that provides the basis for Christian talk about God. This analogy also informs our christological language (Macquarrie, 1967: esp. 212ff.).

4. Since the discipline of linguistic analysis has become prominent in philosophical discussion, many books and articles on the nature of theological language have appeared. Two fine examples written for those who are not already expert in the field are William Hordern, *Speaking of God* (1964), and John Macquarrie, *God-Talk* (1967).

5. Inasmuch as the ontological mystics claim a direct experience of the ultimate, nonempirical reality, it might be supposed that they would not need an analogous mode of expression. However, even for the most convinced mystics language breaks down into paradox when they speak of total reality as "nothing" or of an "experience" which has no describable object. In this latter case the use of the word "experience" is analogical. Thus in India, for example, which is traditionally monistic in its religious conceptualizations, the myth and symbolic images flourish in profuse abundance.

is perceived as the truth, i.e., not a symbolic representation of the truth.

In such a worldview the individual is related to the whole as a temporarily separated particle which can find its fulfillment or salvation only in reunion with the totality of being. The figure of a drop of water temporarily separated from the ocean is often used as an analogy. Although it is separated from the ocean, nevertheless it is one with the ocean, and in poetic language it is said that all the ocean is in the drop of water. Thus in Hinduism, for example, the individual soul (*atman*) is said to be one with the totality of divinity (*Brahman*) even though it now exists temporarily as a separated particle.

In such a conceptual system the divine humanity of Jesus is not perceived as a problem. Jesus is simply the supreme manifestation of the mystical reality in which we all participate to some degree. In this sense he is recognized as a special *avatar* of the divine. As the *embodied myth* he provides us with an image of the cosmic soul force which is our true environment and destiny—the divinity in which "we live and move and have our being." His life can be viewed as a mythical representation of the total reality.

As we shall note later, in this mystical worldview it is difficult to assimilate the biblical and Western concept of the individual as a person who exists in confrontation with the divine personal Other. The language of personal communion rather easily is translated into the language of mystical union, and the incarnation of God in Christ becomes a mystical symbol of the cosmic reality.

Rational Metaphysical Mode

The rational mode which used the analogy of being to analyze the metaphysical (spiritual) realm provides a second option. Traditional orthodoxy has used this approach in its theological definitions. From the third and fourth centuries A.D. to the present it has relied on the metaphysical language of the ancient Greeks to express the nature of God's presence in Christ. Indeed, the concept of incarnation, i.e., *enfleshment*, was developed in this conceptual context.

The metaphysical philosophy of Socrates and his successors represents the rationalization of the myths of Greek polytheistic religion. Instead of mythical divinities the philosophers spoke of cause, principle, dynamic, potential, and wisdom. (Remember that Socrates was charged with atheism and corrupting the morals of the youth of Athens.) In the process of rational analysis the distinction between the spiritual and material realms was increasingly well defined. They distinguished between the physical and that which lay beyond it, i.e., the *meta*physical, and they equated rational and ontological reality with the metaphysical. In this manner also the spiritual was associated with the causal principle. Thus the spiritual reality was conceived as perfect reality which is reflected in the imperfect, physical world. It is the rationally perfect pattern of the imperfect material world (Plato). Therefore, although the spiritual cannot be empirically examined, it can be known and described by a *rational analogy of being*. For example, God can be thought of as perfect Reason after the analogy of human reason.

I have described the process of rationalizing the myths because this is the same way in which the Greek church fathers attempted to rationalize the New Testament witness to Jesus as Son of God. They used the language of Greek dualistic metaphysics to interpret New Testament concepts such as "Word of God" and "Son of God." They attempted to define the presence of God in Jesus in rational ontological terms of substance (or essence) and natures and of "eternal generation" and incarnation of the preexistent Son of God. The classical creeds of orthodoxy all use this linguistic mode in what Avery Dulles has referred to as the "dogmatic" approach to Christology (Cook, 1981:133).

Jesus, the God-man was said to be a combination of the spiritual and physical realms understood as the natural and supernatural. The natural (humanity) included the rational and fleshly *psuchē* and *sarx* which was joined to the supernatural spirit (*pneuma* or *nous*). It was sometimes explained that the *Logos* (deity) took the place of the human spirit in Jesus. The definitive statement of this doctrine at Chalcedon (A.D. 451) asserted that although the divine and human in Jesus are discrete and unmixed, they are also without division or contrast of function. In our modern terms it was held that Jesus had a single self-consciousness in which he knew himself to be the God-man.

This language of orthodoxy has not been free of serious problems in spite of its precision. For one thing it has been virtually impossible to formulate a logically consistent theological definition of the unity of Jesus' self-consciousness and activity. Some Protestant theologians actually spoke of Jesus acting now in his divine capacity and again in his human. For example, Brenz, a Heidelberg theologian (1561) stated that Christ exercised his divine attributes secretly while at the same time also living according to human limitations. He said that while Jesus as a human being was absent from Lazarus at the time of his death, he was present with him in his divinity (Seeberg, 1952:374). But the most serious difficulty has been that in such combination theories the divine almost inevitably overpowers and dominates the human. For example, Johannes Wollebius, an early seventeenth-century Reformed theologian, said that "the Logos uses the human nature as its agent" (Beardslee, 1965:93). Or, as Martin Chemnitz, a

Lutheran theologian, put it, the human will must and always does submit and conform to the will of the *Logos* (Seeberg, 1952:375).[6]

Still others held that Jesus' human nature was not that of an individual man, but the *Logos* assumed generic humanity. According to the nineteenth-century theologian Gottfried Thomasius, the "Son of God" became the ego of a spiritual-corporeal human individual. But the *Logos* did not assume "an individual human being." The "divine ego" has "human consciousness" because the *Logos* assumed generic human nature, and this ego "is not fully homogeneous with ours" but "remains essentially divine. It is divine-human." Jesus Christ is the "man who is God," the archetypal man who is different from the original Adam and every Adam since (Welch, 1965:62-63). Thomasius was in fact attempting to present Jesus as a fully human personality within the limits of what is known as the *anhypostasis* theory of the incarnation. But despite his valiant efforts, the ego of this human, "self-emptied" *Logos* "remains essentially divine."

This docetic tendency has been almost universally present in orthodox theologies, and one cannot but suspect that it is in some major part inherent in the metaphysical conceptualization itself.

Today the adequacy of this metaphysical conceptualization has been challenged on both biblical and scientific grounds. On the one hand, the Greek psychology of discrete human faculties joined to a divine spirit is by no means identical to that of the biblical writers. And from the scientific standpoint the concept of the human individual as a combination of distinct, discrete parts such as flesh, psyche, volition, and spirit seems highly problematic. The concept of a pneumatico-psychosomatic unit in which one cannot speak of parts but only of qualities or interrelated dimensions seems to be a more useful descriptive model of the human person.

Thus while we should take the definitions of the fourth-century church fathers seriously because they accurately identified the issues and give us many helpful insights, we need not feel bound to them as we attempt to translate the biblical message into all the various modern cultural contexts. They already are interpretative extensions of the biblical terminology framed in the first instance for people of Hellenistic background and assumptions.

Historical Mode

In the modern period the historical mode with its analogy of person has begun to be used to explain the meaning of Jesus as the Christ. This way of speaking about the Christ has only recently been explored by theologians who are seriously interested in a restatement of those biblical convictions which orthodoxy sought to communicate.[7]

The hesitation of conservative theologians to adopt this vocabulary is quite understandable because the origins of historical consciousness and analysis lie in the modern rationalistic revolt against the classical Greek metaphysics which provided orthodoxy its philosophical base. The scholars of the Enlightenment viewed the historical Jesus as the peak of all human virtue and represented him as simply an exemplary figure from the past.[8] To the Deists of the early eighteenth century Jesus' superiority consisted of his eminently rational and ethical approach to religion. And to the historical critics of the nineteenth century he remained a naturalistic historical figure whom his followers proclaimed as a mythical deity.[9] Ever more stringent empirical norms were applied to the quest for this "historical Jesus" as the methodology of historical criticism developed and liberal theologians talked of doing Christology "from below," i.e., based upon the picture of Jesus produced by historical research.[10]

6. This same Chemnitz held that Jesus' humanity possessed divine majesty and attributes from the womb. And Lutheran theologians in general held that the ascended body of Christ was ubiquitous, i.e., everywhere present. See Jill Raitt's excellent article on "The French Reformed Theological Response [to the Formula of Concord]" (1977:178ff.).

Menno Simons tended to side with the Lutherans in this debate, and his language is often docetic. Especially in his explanation of the conception and birth of Jesus he argued for a human body that was entirely the product of a divine seed so that in effect his body was the flesh of God. See especially Menno's "Incarnation of Our Lord" (Wenger, 1956:819-20), and "Reply to Martin Micron" (Wenger, 1956:854ff.).

7. One example of this new concern with the historical mode among conservative theologians is Helmut Thielicke who writes, ". . . he [Christ] is to be sought in his deeds and this is where his unity will be found. This unity lies in the history of Jesus Christ with us and consequently in what he does, in his work on us." And again, "Finally, the Christology of Acts also begins with deeds of Christ. . . . Nor does Acts merely begin here; it also shows that there is no other point of access" (1977:322). Thielicke quotes Luther, as have theologians before him, to substantiate this approach from the source of Protestantism.

8. Otto Weber has characterized this movement well: "The historical Jesus, as they construed him, was transformed into the peak of all human possibilities; he became the epitome of all virtue, the beloved friend of all men because he loved all, the model of all morals. He was the opposite of what the tradition had continually asserted. He was not the One in whom God reaches out to us and takes our part, but rather he is the highest perfection of a religion in which man reaches out to God and gets God in his grasp . . ." (1983:146).

9. D. F. Strauss (1808-84) is a good example of this trend. He held that most of the materials of the New Testament Gospels were mythical in character and expressed the faith convictions of the early church rather than any historical reality. As Claude Welch puts it, he "worked in detail through the Gospel, leaving no possible contradiction or inconsistency unexposed. The resultant picture was of a thoroughly historical and human figure about whom we have very little reliable information" (1972:149).

Ernest Renan (1823-92), a Roman Catholic scholar who lost his faith in the supernatural as the church taught it, wrote a *Life of Jesus* in which he denied his divinity and pictured him as a genial Galilean preacher.

10. Schleiermacher is the one major exception to this trend, and he has not received from most conservative theologians the credit he deserves on this point. For him the earthly Jesus is without question the manifestation of Divine Being by virtue of his unique God-consciousness. If Schleiermacher errs, it is on the side of docetism (see Niebuhr, 1964:210ff.).

Albrecht Ritschl (1822-1889) was one of the first theologians to use the term "from below" as a technical term. He was convinced that we cannot make rational metaphysical statements about Jesus' divinity on the basis of objective research and logical speculation. We must begin with the historical Jesus as a human being (from below) and describe his moral and spiritual divinity in terms of his character and achievement. In this way we come to realize that Jesus has the "moral value of God" for us.

One of the more winsome and persuasive presentations of this point of view is that of Wilhelm Hermann (1846-1922). In his *The Communion of the Christian with God* (1892, 2nd. German edition) Hermann said that the "ground of faith" must be found in the ethical personality of Jesus. This personality is a historical fact that is accessible to the unbeliever as well as the believer. Belief in the deity of Christ does not come through rational or dogmatic convincement from the creeds but through the power of his personality to affect us. The reality of the "inner life of Jesus, which rises up before us from the testimony of the disciples as a real power that is active in the world" must overwhelm us in our inmost life (Hermann 1971:82).

Or again Hermann wrote,

> The one question of absolute importance is whether Jesus [the Jesus of history] gains a power over us through His personal life (p. 129). . . . We come to understand Jesus to be the divine act of forgiveness, or, in other words, we see Him to be the message through which God comes into communion with us; and so we recognize in His human appearance God Himself drawing us to Himself. This thought, that when the historical Christ takes such hold of us, we have to do with God Himself—this thought is certainly the most important element in the confession of the Deity of Christ for any one whom He has redeemed (p. 143).

And finally,

> If the Deity of Christ does not simply mean that a divine substance underlies the human life of Jesus, but that the personal God Himself turns towards sinners and opens His heart to them in that human life, then belief in Christ's Deity can only arise out of that which the Man Jesus brings about within us (p. 164).[11]

Existentialist "History"

One reaction to the rationalistic and empiricistic view of history came in the form of an existentialist criticism of historicism. The existentialists identified the historical with *personal existence* in contrast to the timeless, universal "being" of metaphysics. And they substituted existential categories like decision, responsibility, subjectivity, self-understanding for the impersonal, detached, objective categories of rational analysis and understanding.

They lost interest in a Jesus of the past, who according to the historical critics, may or may not have claimed to be the Messiah. History has to do with our present personal existence. Jesus' deity cannot be discovered as a timeless, rational metaphysical truth. But, on the other hand, the historical Jesus is not and cannot be simply identified as the Christ of God through historical research. Jesus as the Christ *is historical in the sense that his identity is revealed in an existential (historical) decision* and not in rational speculation or empirical events. He can become Christ the Lord only by a historical decision made in the present, i.e., by *faith.*

The relation between history and the personal dimensions of life is an important insight of the existentialists, but their individualistic, subjective concept of the personal is highly problematic because it *privatized* the concept of history. History becomes the inner personal history of each individual. Thus the "Christ of faith," i.e., the existential picture of Jesus as the Christ for me, becomes a private Christ, and the connection is cut between Jesus, the Christ in history (a historical event), and world history. The Christ is "historical in the sense that his identity depends upon an ongoing historical decision which relates him to the believer as lord and exemplar, but not in the sense of an objective manifestation of God's presence in a historical event" (Weber, 1983:147-48).[12]

History as Revelation

The most recent attempt to approach the question of Jesus' identity from the historical perspective comes from the theologians associated with the "Pannenberg Circle."[13] Pannenberg insists that history is the mode of revelation. He builds upon but goes beyond Barth in defining history as the sphere of revelation, and he is unwilling to make a qualitative distinction between "salvation history" and world history as Cullmann had done

11. Hermann is sometimes viewed as a bridge between Ritschl and the existentialists. He certainly does go beyond Ritschl's categories of moral value and example, but he clearly implies rejection of any metaphysical or essential deity of Christ; and in the end he leaves us wondering whether Christ's "deity" is more than an effect in our lives today.

12. Weber makes something of the same point but turns it in a slightly different direction (see 1983:147-48).

13. One should also mention Otto Weber (d. 1966), a contemporary of Barth and professor of Reformed theology at Göttingen, who insisted that the historical event must be the starting point for Christology. "In contrast to classic Christology, everything depends on the event." And of this event he continues, "The 'event' is not a silent act but a word-event, a proclamatory event, and thus a salvation-event. And therefore it cannot be objectified, for objectification would mean that it is integrated into the world of objects. Undeniably this event enters our 'world of objects.' But we cannot integrate it into our world . . ." (1983:152).

(Cullmann, 1950, 1963). *World* history is the sphere of revelation, and Jesus, the Christ, was born and fulfilled his destiny as God's self-disclosure in world history.[14] Whereas earlier historical approaches often ended up rejecting a unique divine union between Jesus and God, Pannenberg strongly affirms the necessity of recognizing such a union.

This concern for a historical understanding, at least in part, grows out of the nature of the biblical witness to Jesus. The kerygmatic proclamation of the church concerning Jesus as the Christ of God was fundamentally a historical witness to what had been experienced. It was not in the form of ontological speculation based upon some postresurrection oracular revelation. The theological interpretations of the apostolic community were tied to and controlled by what they had "seen and heard, and their hands had handled" (1 John 1:1). In the reports of the church's first sermons, for example, Jesus was presented as "a man attested to . . . by God" through his works and by the resurrection (Acts 2:22-24). The earthly Jesus was proclaimed to have been "Christ, the Son of God" after the resurrection, not on the basis of apocalyptic theological speculation but in accordance with their memory of the one who lived among them, died on the cross, and was raised from the dead.

For those who claim to stand in a biblical tradition this methodology as well as the doctrinal content of the New Testament witnesses ought to have some weight in the theological process. While the rationalistic philosophical tendencies of the early church fathers are understandable in their context and their concerns were valid, there is no reason why their metaphysical categories should become the normative mode for communicating the gospel for all time or in all cultures. As I shall hope to demonstrate, the historical categories of personal analogy—self-identity, self-disclosure, and personal relationship—provide a more adequate mode for modern understanding as well as a more biblical stance.

The Nature of Historical Being and Knowing

We have criticized the existentialist view of the historical as subjective experience and implied a definition of history as world history that is more in agreement with Pannenberg's concept. We need now to look more closely at the meaning of history as a mode for christological analogy and analysis. What does it mean to speak of a *historical analogy*?

History as Multidimensional

The concept of historical time is used to mark off the movement of time as it is experienced by self-conscious, rational creatures in contrast to simple natural or chronological time. History is the sphere of self-conscious interaction which we designate with the word *personal*. It designates the sphere of subjective activity, experience, and meaning in time. That is, the data of history are the activities of rational subjects (people) whose actions reflect decision, intention, and purpose; thus historical activity has a subjective meaning which is itself part of the event.

Events are the data of historical knowledge. They are *public* data, and thus perception of them can rightly be called knowledge. But an event is more than a factual happening. It is experienced as a compound of factual (objective) actions and personal (subjective) consciousness of relationships. The subjective is not a purely private state of consciousness. In an event it is shared public experience—a part of the objective data of historical existence. In this sense, then, we speak of the "Christ event." The experience of Jesus as "the Christ, the Son of God," was not a merely private, subjective vision. His sonship was experienced as a public event to which historical witness could be given. Such an event is a multidimensional experience involving both empirical actions and nonempirical elements of consciousness and meaning. And these nonempirical dimensions are an essential part of historical being. They cannot be dismissed as private subjectivity and mere imagination.

As we said, historical being involves the interaction of subjects (people). Historical being is that experienced existence in which historical subjects, in contrast to empirical objects, are known through acts of intended response and verbal communication in a relation we call *personal*. Historical subjects cannot be fully known as persons by empirical observation only. There must be subjective interchange. Personal being is recognized in the quality of relationships that are experienced. Our point

---

14. A group of younger German theologians published a symposium of articles on revelation in 1961 under the title *Offenbarung Als Geschichte*. Pannenberg was editor and contributor. See the English translation, *Revelation as History* (1968). Also for an excellent presentation of Pannenberg's position see *The Theology of Wolfhart Pannenberg* (Tupper, 1973). For Pannenberg's own definitive work on Christology see *Jesus—God and Man* (1977), first published in German in 1964.

Approval at this point of Pannenberg's methodological approach does not necessarily imply full concurrance with all of his conclusions. It has been pointed out by critics such as Jon Sobrino, for example, that he "gives almost no role at all to Christ's cross within systematic Christology" (1978:26) and that his theological approach tends toward rational explanation rather than transformation through the power of the cross. Sobrino, perhaps with some exaggeration, concludes that he "ignores completely the possibly revelatory role of Jesus' cross" (1978:28). Frank Tupper, his American expositor and critic, tends to agree that this is a weakness in his theology (1973:299f.). Pannenberg himself in his section on the eschatological kingdom of God and its relation to the lordship of Christ identifies closely with a traditionally Lutheran position of Christ's "hidden" lordship. Incorporation into the kingdom of Christ is simply through preaching (1977:370ff.). Compare Moltmann's criticism and his relatively greater emphasis on "demonstration" of the new beginning through the resurrection (1974:173ff.).

here is that *Jesus came as such a historical subject*, and his identity was grasped in just such a public personal interchange.

History, then, is a form or quality of being, not just a chronological progression of actions which can be measured by the movement of a clock. Just as the material realm is experienced as physical being, so the historical sphere is experienced as personal being. Material being is known objectively through detached observation and described in the empirical measurements of scientific experimentation. Historical or personal being is known subjectively through involved social participation and is described in terms of quality of relationship. Note that subjective in this context does not mean private. Historical personal knowledge is public, i.e., a shared experience that can be verified through appeal to the perceptions of others.

We have been accustomed to using physical being as a metaphor to describe the spiritual as metaphysical, or rational being. By an analogy the Deity is described as *Ultimate Reason*. However, since our most intimate knowledge of God has come to us by way of a historical event, should we not expect that personal being would provide a more adequate analogical likeness than the physical? Should we not speak of a *metapersonal* reality of God in Christ?

Challenges to the Use of Historical Analogy

The use of historical analogy has been challenged by both the empiricists who equate history with "facticity" and the mystical systems that think of history as a kind of illusion. Under the pressures of modern empirical and existentialist analysis the multidimensional—personal, subject-object experience of historical reality—has been split apart and objective reality or "factuality" has been recognized only in the empirical and rational elements. This equation of reality with demonstrable facticity is called historicism or positivistic history. Such a scheme relegates the subjective realm and experience to the category of non-reality, e.g., opinion, feelings, mythical interpretations, and in so doing rules out its use as part of the analogy for God.

In reaction, as we have noted, existentialist thinkers asserted the "truth of subjectivity."[15] Existentialist thought identified the historical with a present subjective experience of the historical individual and cut it loose from historical factuality. The historical is that reality which engages me existentially in decision and action at the historical level. Thus the categories of meaning and significance take precedence over facticity.

One example of this existentialist approach will help make this language clear. The resurrection of Jesus is not to be understood in the categories of factual history but of personal or existential history, i.e., of a faith experience of Jesus as living Lord. The whole idea of the deity of Jesus Christ is dealt with in the same way. Thus the existentialists reduce the factual data of our experience to a role of secondary importance and rule them out completely as information about God's presence in history. In place of the analogy of being they make an appeal to the "analogy of faith," which in this case is only another way of saying "existential relation and decision."

Over against this unfortunate schism we insist upon the unity and objectivity of the subject-object experience in the real world of historical activity. Here there are no facts which are not subjectively perceived and affected by the process of personal assimilation. On the other hand, the most profoundly personal, subjective meanings which prompt existential decision often are experienced as public (factual) data and have quite objective repercussions. We must not allow the personal to be totally privatized and thus subjectivized out of reality.

The use of a historical analogy has also been denegrated in the older systems of rational dualism and mysticism which relegate history to the shades of unreality. Dualistic philosophy considers history to be the realm of imperfection and impermanence, of incoherence and irrationality. It is associated with the material/physical which is considered both ethically and ontologically inferior. In the systems of mystical monism it is referred to as *maya* or illusion of reality. Thus, its analogical use is ruled out in favor of abstract reason which is said to reflect the divine Reason in a way that gives certainty to our truly rational speculation about God. Or in mysticism, historical experience of God is discounted for the superior direct spiritual experience.

But from the biblical perspective and, we might add, also from a modern Western perspective, historical existence is experienced as part of the larger whole reality. History is the dynamic aspect of total reality or being which we speak of as *becoming*. It is understood as a creative movement toward the consummation, which is both *eschatos* (finish) and *telos* (fulfillment). Paul describes it as the militant reign of Christ over the rebellious forces of the cosmos until "every ... domination, authority, and power" including death have been subjugated to God's authority, and God has become "all in all" (1 Cor. 15:24-28, NEB). On the one hand, history is

---

15. The phrase comes from Kierkegaard (1835-70). While he did not rule out the necessity of the objective in its proper place, he emphasized subjectivity as the relation of the knowing individual to the truth that is known. "When the question of the truth is raised subjectively, reflection is directed subjectively to the nature of the individual's relationship if only the mode of this relationship is in the truth, the individual is in the truth even if he should happen to be thus related to what is not true [objectively]" (see *Concluding Unscientific Postscript*, first published 1846 (1944:178)).

not a dream or illusion of reality from which we need to escape into reality. Neither is it a mythical or symbolic representation of the eternal, unchanging, nonhistorical reality. It is the process of being. It is a becoming that issues in being.

Historical Analogy as Metaphor

Understood in this way, history may be seen as the sphere of God's self-disclosure and used as an analogical referent to speak of God. In our multidimensional, experienced history Jesus was and is recognized as the Christ of God. The historical becomes the bearer of a *meta*-reality that transcends empirical facticity without depreciating its factuality. However, a word of caution is needed here. Inasmuch as we are speaking of the *self*-disclosure of being that transcends our historical existence, revelation cannot be simply equated with empirical actions (happenings) in history. Even within our historical experience of persons we do not simply equate the other self that is being disclosed to us with the actions and words of disclosure. How much more this must be true of God's self-revelation in Christ. Thus when we speak of God's acts or words, we must recognize that we are using historical metaphor.

From the biblical perspective, God, the Creator of history, transcends even that "being" of which history is the "becoming." He is not simply identical with total reality, not even in its eschatological consummation (pantheism). On the other hand he is not a totally different, detached spiritual being which has nothing in common with our historical being (ontological dualism). Rather, using a personal analogy, God is understood as that Being who gives reality (being) to creatures by sharing his own personal Being with them in the process of creation. History as the creative movement of God has its being in God, but God is not contained in history and cannot be directly identified with anything in history.

Therefore, even though we are not viewing history from a strictly empirical or positivistic perspective, still, strictly speaking, historical experience can function *only as a metaphor* of the divine self-giving. What we see in the creaturely sphere of history is not God. Only the eye of faith, that is, the perception of reality beyond the historical metaphor, can see God.

The Meaning and Function of Metaphor

Historical metaphor is a kind of analogy. The word "metaphor" itself derives from the Greek *metapherein*, which means "to carry across from one place to another." It is the same *meta* as in *meta*physical. Such metaphor is the mode of biblical revelation. Thus we speak of those historical people, actions, and words, i.e., events, that are so permeated by the power of God that they have the power to carry us beyond the empirical threshold and actually reveal God to us.

In this manner we say that the historical experience of personal interaction with Jesus Christ is the supreme historical metaphor of the divine personal reality which transcends history. Whereas in earlier revelation the *words* of the prophet, or the historical *happenings* had provided the metaphors, Jesus himself is the metaphor of God. He is the "Word of God" and the "Event" of salvation in which God is present to us in our historical existence. Thus when Philip said, "Show us the Father," Jesus replied, "Have I been with you for so long a time and you still say 'Show us the Father'?" (John 14:8-11). On the level of historical-personal experience God was truly present to us in Jesus' life, death, and resurrection so that, as Paul put it, we see "the glory of God in the face of Jesus Christ" (2 Cor. 4:6, NEB).

We must not try to explain such a metaphorical presence in the language of myth because the historical sphere is a real, constitutive part of the reality in God. But, on the other hand, it remains metaphorical because history is not the whole reality as positivism claims. In religious language we speak of this as a *sacramental* presence which is at once real on the historical level and yet points to a meta-historical reality beyond itself. This language of personal analogy has certain advantages as a theological mode of speaking about God's presence in Jesus. Nevertheless it cannot take us beyond the analogical description of the transcendent personal reality of God.

Beginning "From Below"

When we make a historical approach to Christology we are beginning "from below," that is, with the Jesus of history as the one in whom God was present and revealed. We begin with Jesus of Nazareth as experienced personal reality and ask who this Jesus is. We do not begin with later philosophical definitions and assumptions about the fact and nature of Jesus' divinity and humanity and then read the New Testament data in light of these assumptions.

On the other hand, we do not begin from below in the sense that we begin with empiricism's assumptions that only the empirically historical can be known. Christology is more than an exploration of the personality and psyche of Jesus—what might be called Jesusology. It is theological thought about our encounter with Jesus as the mediator of God's presence to us. Our conviction that he is the presence and grace of God to us provides the motivation for Christology. Thus it begins with Jesus as a human being, but the specifically christological question is his significance as the revelation of God to us.

The Nature of the New Testament Witness to Christ

Purpose not Theoretical

The New Testament accounts are essentially historical, not philosophical, and are written by participants in the drama of revelation. Generally speaking the purpose of the New Testament is not to give precise analytical descriptions of Jesus as a God-man, but rather to change people's relationship to God through a confrontation with Jesus. The Gospels give us an impressionistic portrait by presenting a collage of his works and teachings. This is clearly sermonic in character, and not the work of scientific historiography. The epistles presuppose knowledge of this historical picture and translate the message of God's self-disclosure into functionally equivalent terms for the contemporary Hellenistic world.

This is not a disadvantage. Indeed, it is an advantage. Experienced reality cannot be captured in the direct descriptive language of the laboratory or newspaper. Like experiences of love and beauty, it is given to us in acts of personal relationship which light up the inner meaning of our lives and give significance to them. Such was the experience with Jesus. To communicate this the New Testament church developed its own patterns of kerygmatic recital, prophetic utterance, and personal testimony.

Paul's epistles are a case in point. Paul's purpose was not theological criticism and clarification of Jesus' person and work, but rather the proclamation to pagans of God's true identity and plan for the salvation of humankind. He was first of all an apostolic missionary attempting to find dynamic equivalent terms in Graeco-Roman culture to convey the meaning of the originally Hebraic message of God's salvation in Christ. He begins with the reality of the historical, i.e., apostolic, experience of God in Christ, and not with the theological formulas that Jesus is the preexistent God. His concern even in the theological sections of his epistles is practical. Thus his statements about Christ relate directly to the expression of the new creation—death and resurrection with Christ—in the lives of the believers, or to the self-understanding and strategy of the church as the body of Christ.[16]

Immanuel Language

We can characterize the New Testament language about Jesus Christ in two ways. First, it was what we might call Immanuel language. Its emphasis is upon God present and working among us in and through Jesus. The question with which it deals is not whether Christ is God and how that might be possible, but whether God is present with us in the life of Christ, and if so, *how* he is present. This shifts our attention away from theoretical questions about how a divine and human nature are related to each other in Jesus and focuses it on how God is present and available to us through

Christ. The linguistic categories are those of revelation rather than ontology.

When Jesus is called "Immanuel, God with us," this is not an ontological statement that Jesus is of one substance with the Father, or more simply, that Jesus is God. The phrase "God with us"following the verb "is" functions as a verbal adjective. That means that in Jesus' presence we experience the presence of God. He is the expression or act of God's communication with us. He is God-reconciling-us-to-himself: God acting.

This is the language of experienced reality. On the one hand, it is not myth. On the other, it is not a strictly empirical or rational description of objective actions which can be put on display or analyzed into categories of essence. The language is that of historical event in the sense that it is experienced in a time and place. The apostles participated in this historical event of "God with us," and afterward they bore witness to that divine presence and power which they experienced in and with Jesus.[17]

Inclusive Language

The second characteristic is its inclusiveness. The focus on God's saving relationship to us in Christ has resulted in the free use of inclusive language to describe Jesus as God's Son. Although the titles and other descriptive language unquestionably assign priority and unique preeminence to Jesus as Son, parallel language describing the relation of believers to God is routinely found. The difference is qualitative but not exclusive.

While we do not want to make too much of this parallelism, it is evident that Christ's sonship is *for us*, and *inclusive of us*. His life in God is ours to share. His mission of suffering is ours to "fill up" (Col. 1:24). We should never interpret Jesus' person and work in categories which are exclusive of the disciples' participation in his life and mission. The point rather seems to be that it is only *through* him as "firstborn of creation," "firstborn from the dead," "pioneer," "only begotten," "head of the body" that our participation in God's family as true children is possible.[18]

---

16. For example, take the two famous passages of Philippians 2:6-11 and 2 Corinthians 3:17-18. The first is embedded in a moral exhortation to share Christ's attitudes. The second tells us that we are being changed into the likeness of Christ who is the image of God.

17. By contrast the creeds of Nicea and Chalcedon were drawn up in a highly politicized situation and sought for precise definitions that gave the philosophical essence of the matter and could provide the basis for ecclesiastical and political unity. The problem being resolved was heresy, i.e., deviation from the one, universal church, which generally had both cultural and political implications. This shifted the focus of theological meaning from its original New Testament intention. Chalcedon's mode is philosophical God-language, not "Immanuel" language.

18. Hendrikus Berkhof notes that "despite this clear line in the New Testament (and its background in the Old Testament), there has been a great reluctance in history of the church to honor this perspective [that believers are children of God], for fear that it might detract from the exclusiveness of Christ" (1979:286). We shall deal further with this concept when we speak of solidarity with Christ in Part II.

Attempting a Definition

Chapter 3

The Man, Christ Jesus · *Humanity*

Jesus, a Word About Humanity

In a theology for discipleship the importance of Jesus' full humanity can hardly be exaggerated. The Anabaptists of the sixteenth century who put great emphasis on following Christ in faithful obedience clearly understood this point. While they framed their doctrinal statements in the orthodox language of the era and insisted on Jesus' full deity, they nevertheless emphasized his sinless humanity as the exemplar and prototype for a new humanity.

Marpeck, for example, speaks of "His holy Manhood" (Klassen and Klaassen, 1978:535). His concern for the proper recognition of Jesus' humanity was related to the ethical reality of redemption rather than metaphysical explanations. He explains that salvation is precisely through the humiliation of Christ, even to the cross, death, and descent into Hades. It does not come by power but by his submission to death. Thus in the essential nature of his humanity (weakness) he is honored as the true Son of God. "The Man Jesus Christ (who alone accomplishes in the believers the good pleasure of the Father) . . . is Lord, Ruler, Leader, and Director of His saints" (1978:509-10). This "Son of man" is the "hominized" word of God to us (Klaassen, 1981:34).[1]

---

1. In his "A Clear and Useful Instruction" (Klassen and Klaassen, 1978:69ff.), Marpeck countered the "spiritualists'" docetic view of Christ as follows: "The Scriptures are also a witness to the true teaching of the humanity of Christ and the teaching of the apostles; through Christ's humanity, the inward must be revealed and recognized . . . . The flesh cannot with assurance be set free and redeemed in anyone without the external key (which is the humanity of Christ)" (1978:76). Again in "Concerning the Humanity of Christ" he wrote, "No man can call the Son of Man 'Lord' without the Holy Spirit. Even the unclean spirits can call Him a Son of God, indeed, even a Lord. However, to ascribe honor to the Son of Man as a true

Implicit in the insistence on his full humanity are two basic convictions: (1) that God is a self-giving Creator who fully identifies with us in our need, and (2) that our humanity finds its true fulfillment in this one who is the prototypical "image of God."

This was the original import of the words *became flesh*, that is, was embodied in an earthly existence (John 1:14). The "becoming flesh" was not merely a highly effective communicative technique by which God could tell us who he is in our own language.

The Word in flesh is also a demonstration of the meaning and destiny of human existence. It also defines his very nature as *agapē*. We come to know the true nature of love in the fact that God fully shared our human existence.

At the heart of the Christian message, then, is the conviction that Jesus is the fulfillment and thus the revelation of God's intention for human life. The Johannine prologue asserts this in two ways. First, it speaks of the *Logos* (Word) as the one through whom all life has been created. Humanity finds its form and destiny in him. Nothing has come into existence apart from his life. The implications of this kind of statement are even more explicit in Colossians where it says that the universe was made "in . . . through . . . and for" the Christ (1:15-17).

The English word *inform* expresses this double function of *Logos* as both creative and expressive of human meaning and destiny.[2] That is, the *Logos* of God informs the world in the sense that it both gives form to and imparts self-understanding to creation. In Christ we see who God is; at the same time we see what God intends for us to be as creatures formed in his image.

Second, John says that the *Logos* embodied in Jesus is the "true light" throwing light on the meaning of human existence from the beginning (John 1:4-5). The world of nature and history is open to many possible interpretations and raises many questions. Is there a pattern and purpose in nature and history? What does it mean to be human? The word spoken in Jesus comes as an answer to these questions. He is the "true light" on the enigma of human existence. In him we see God's intention for the world, and through him humankind can reach its true destiny as the children of God. Again a word from Paul suggests this way of thinking. Jesus came, he wrote, in order that he might be the first among many children who would follow (Rom. 8:9).

All docetic[3] attempts to attenuate Jesus' humanity detract from these central tenets of the gospel, and they were vigorously opposed by the apostolic witness. Writing at the end of the first century, the author of 1 John equates docetism with the spirit of antichrist (2:22-23; 4:1-3).

Jesus as Prototype of Humanity

The New Creation

Jesus was the prototpye of authentic humanity. As we have just seen, in John's Gospel the word spoken in Jesus comes as an answer to the question of what it means to be fully human. His life not only reveals the inner being of God to us but also opens to us our own self-identity as children of God. Or as Paul puts it, he is the archetype and the beginning of a new humanity (1 Cor. 15:49; Eph. 2:15). In his relation to God as a human being we see what is the proper relation of all humans to God, and we come to understand that humanity can find its ultimate fulfillment only in the theonomous relationship.[4]

Remember that Paul's radical conversion and strenuous missionary labors among the Gentiles grew out of his conviction that Christ is the beginning of a new humanity. "In Christ" there was a new definition of what it meant to be human. The old "Jew-Gentile" definition was no longer valid because Jesus, a Jewish man, demonstrated what it meant to be a child of God apart from the old lines of distinction (Eph. 2:14-15). To be "in Christ" meant to be in a "new order of human existence" (2 Cor. 5:17)—in an order where old status symbols were abolished (Gal. 3:26-28; Col. 3:10-11). The resurrected Jesus appeared to Paul on the road to Damascus as the prototype of the new humanity. According to Paul, he is God's true image (Col. 1:15), thus the true Son of God declared to be such by the Spirit of power in the resurrection (Rom. 1:4).

The New Testament refers to this prototypical role of Jesus in several different ways. Most directly the idea is conveyed in the concept of Jesus as the image or form of God (Col. 1:15; Phil. 2:6) and as the "man of heaven" (1 Cor. 15:48-49). Jesus as the "second Adam" fulfills the image which the

---

man of the race of men and to confess Him as their Lord and God, this no unclean spirit can do.... For the very reason that He is the *Son of Man* [italics mine] He will be a Judge and not for the reason that He is also the Son of God, one essence with the Father" (1978:509).

It is true that Menno Simons and Dirk Philips mistakenly put undue stress on the special creation of Christ's human body in order to assure his sinlessness. Nevertheless they insisted that Jesus was truly and fully human and became our pioneer and example. It was precisely the full humanity and its nature that was at issue between Menno and the Zwinglian theologians. See "The Incarnation of Our Lord" (Wenger, 1956:785ff.). They were mistaken in the physical aspects of true humanity, but their understanding of Jesus' full identity with us in our human situation was fully in accord with Scripture and experience.

2. We might add that this double meaning is also implicit in the word *logos*. *Logos* is not only a communication but also a rational form.

3. The word "docetic" comes from the Greek *dokeō* which means "to seem" or "to think." It is the technical term used to describe all those theories of Christ's nature which detract from his humanity, i.e., only make him *seem to be* human.

4. Theonomous is contrasted to autonomous and means that the concept of human can be defined only in terms of a relationship to God. To be human means to have the capacity to recognize our dependence upon and responsibility to God.

first Adam failed to attain, and we are to be made into his likeness (2 Cor. 3:18; cf. 1 John 3:2). The Ephesians symbol of "creating *in himself* one new humanity" also suggests the idea, and the numerous passages which present him as exemplar indicate a prototypical role.

The Philippians 2:6-11 passage speaks most clearly to the prototypical element in Jesus' humanity.[5] Here he is contrasted to Adam, the first human—"man of dust"—in whom the image did not reach completion. Adam grasped at autonomous self-fulfillment and failed in his achievement. By contrast Jesus "emptied himself," and in full subjection and obedience to God he fulfilled the image promised in creation. The characteristics of the image, then, are meekness, obedience, forgiveness, and servanthood—"true righteousness and holiness" (Eph. 4:23-24).

Contrasted to Other Models

If talk about Jesus as prototype sounds theoretical and abstract, its significance will be quickly evident when we compare it to other prototypes that have been and are still being used to define what it means to be human. The Greek "heroes," some of them "divine men," and Aristotle's "philosopher" were such representations of ideal humanity. In this tradition are also the Japanese samurai, the Jewish "just man," and of more recent American vintage, Superman and most recently Rambo.

Perhaps the oldest and most common source for the definition of humanness has been the tribal prototype. The tribal self-image and values become the standard for defining what it means to be human, and only those people who belong to *our tribe* qualify. Those outside the tribe or nation are automatically inferior.

This view is characteristic not only of so-called primitive tribes, but it lies behind the first-century distinctions between Jew and Gentile reflected in the New Testament. It is also the view implicit in modern nationalistic imperialism which assumes an inherent superiority of the conqueror over the conquered. It is clearly reflected in the history of America and South Africa in the attitudes of whites toward blacks and "coloreds." It is blatant in the Japanese war records that refer to human beings of other nations who were being used for medical experimentation as "logs." And it is even reflected in the history of the church's missionary activity in its tendency to make derogatory cultural distinctions between "Christian" and "heathen."

This prototype is not only the oldest; it is the most deeply rooted and pervasive. It underlies the concept of human that allows for cannibalism. Those outside the tribe are on the level of other animals. It is the basis for distinctions between killing the *dehumanized* enemy in war as a heroic act and murder of a fellow citizen. Thus it is most significant that already in the

first generation of the church men and women who had been thoroughly
conditioned to this way of thinking saw that Jesus' self-disclosure called for
a radical break with this tribal definition.

The Jesus prototype also challenged the class or caste definitions in
which social status is the measure for human worth (1 Cor. 1:26-27; Gal.
3:26-28). It eliminates the autonomous standard of rational superiority
which was epitomized in Aristotle's self-sufficient, male philosopher as the
ultimate model of human excellence. It also offers an option to the modern
secular evolutionary classifications of anthropologists and philosophers
which depend upon phenomenological characteristics such as size of the
cranium, manual dexterity, sexual characteristics, capacity for abstract
thought, and self-awareness. In contrast to all of these, Jesus as prototype
suggests a theonomous model in which self-fulfillment is achieved through
recognition of our ultimate dependence and responsibility to God.

The Nature of Jesus' Humanity

Clear recognition of Jesus' humanity is found in the New Testament
from the earliest to the latest writings. He is represented as fully human—
physically, psychologically, morally, and spiritually.[6]

New Testament Presuppositions

The New Testament contains little or no evidence of a legendary
divinization of the human Jesus. John's Gospel (ca. A.D. 90-100 or later)
does take a theological perspective that emphasizes Jesus' unity with the
Father in authority and purpose, but this does not lead him to detract from
the fully human characteristics of this "Word become flesh." And the first
Epistle of John, which is also late, underscores Jesus' humanity against an
inchoate docetism. The fact that such docetic ideas developed later makes
the fixing of the canon with "eye-witnesses" important. What is perhaps the
earliest written statement by Paul that Jesus was "born of a woman born
under the law" (Gal. 4:4) is never challenged. Even the virgin-birth accounts of Matthew and Luke, seen in their contexts, underscore Jesus' humanity by their very lack of mythological characteristics. The one born of
Mary is flesh of our flesh.

Paul's statement in Philippians 2:7-8, "born . . . into the *schēma* of
human existence, and humbled himself . . . unto death . . . on a cross," is
quite historically precise. He was the "son of David" with a genealogy, that

5. Cullmann and more recently Dunn, in contrast to the Bultmann school, have
understood this passage to be an example of "Adam christology" (see Dunn, 1980:115).

6. See, for example, Galatians 4:4; Romans 1:3-4 (written ca. A.D. 50); Hebrews 2:14;
4:15; 5:7-9 (ca. A.D. 70-80); synoptic Gospels and John (ca. A.D. 65-100).

is, a historical lineage. Whale's comment that Jesus came into history and not out of it is only partially correct (1941:109). Jesus is the continuation and fulfillment of a historical, cultural tradition attached to an ancestoral lineage. He had an individual historical existence. He came to be in the sequence of events at a particular time and place. His contemporaries knew his family (John 6:42).

Defining Jesus' Humanity

Classical statements of the humanity of Jesus have been formed in the ancient Greek categories of flesh and spirit. Especially in the Neoplatonic tradition the physical and spiritual were thought of as ontologically contrasting substances (see pp. 46-48). The spiritual belonged to the divine, eternal realm while the flesh belonged to the earthly realm which was corruptible and mortal. Human beings were described as a combination of flesh and spirit. The physical body with its rational mind was indwelt by a spark of the divine spirit. Indeed, the dynamics of history depended on this fateful combination, and the triumph of human culture represented a triumph of the spirit over flesh.

The classical definitions of Christology were formed in this milieu. In the case of the divine-human being, Jesus, the physical and rational elements identified as human were said to have been joined with the very substance of God. In such a context it is quite understandable that the church fathers were concerned that (1) the spirit which joined with flesh to create the God-Man be clearly identified with God himself, and (2) that the influence of the flesh be minimized. Flesh represented a lower, imperfect mode of being, and there was concern lest theories of enfleshment might involve God in the compromise of his perfect being. The argument in the fourth century was whether in the strictest sense God simply assumed "flesh" (Alexandrian)—a position that would involve deity in the least essentially human involvement, or whether in a broader sense the deity assumed a human nature or "manhood" (Antiochian).[7] In the following centuries Alexandrian terminology generally prevailed so that a minimal concept of humanity was usually associated with orthodoxy.

The arguments about the nature of Jesus' humanity were complicated still further by Augustine's concept of "original sin." That sin, which is both penalty and offense, is a corruption of the physical body and mind through sensual desire or concupiscence. It is a defect inherent in the flesh. In fact, flesh practically became synonymous with concupiscence or the selfish sensual desires of the body epitomized in the sexual desire. Since this original sin is inherited through the process of procreation, the questions of Jesus' humanity (flesh) and his sinlessness were inevitably related. On the one hand, theologians insisted that Jesus was God *in the flesh*; on the other hand, they insisted that his flesh was free from original sin through a virgin birth.[8]

From the biblical point of view as well as that of more modern concepts of "humanity" this preoccupation with flesh seems to be somewhat beside the point. Furthermore, it has caused unnecessary difficulties in the theological dialogue with religious traditions such as Islam. However, the traditional language of incarnation continues to condition much of Protestant and Catholic theological vocabulary.

In biblical thought flesh in contrast to spirit indicated weakness, dependence, and vulnerability to death. The full phrase, "flesh and blood," of which flesh is often the shortened form, pointed to the sphere of human existence (Heb. 2:14). It is true that in Paul's writings flesh sometimes indicated the existential selfish concern, desires, and passions that characterize human life, but it does not yet have the Augustinian meaning of concupiscence, and he does not hesitate to say that the Christ was made in the "likeness of sinful flesh."

When we insist on Jesus' full humanity we are not primarily concerned with one or the other of the components that make up human existence. While the physical is a fundamental aspect of our humanity, we are concerned with far more than that. Our concern is for a personal-social *Gestalt* which distinguishes the human from the *non*human and the *in*human. We are concerned to define the humane as well as the human. We want to know that God can truly understand and empathize with us because he has shared our human struggle. As one writer put it, a God who has not suffered with us might be "merciful," but strictly speaking he cannot be "compassionate" (Samuel and Sugden, 1983:209). What we insist on is a full personal identification with us in our human historical existence—an identification which involves Jesus in the existential frustration and dilemmas which we face as we attempt to obey the voice of God. This is implied in the Apostles' Creed's use of the word "suffered" as a descriptive term for Jesus' life and ministry.

---

7. This is an extremely complicated debate which made use of many fine linguistic and philosophical distinctions. Was Jesus "God incarnate" or a God conjoined to a man? Did he have two natures or one? J. N. D. Kelly, *Early Christian Doctrines* (1958:280ff.), has a good discussion of the century-long debate. See also Alan Richardson, *Creeds in the Making* (1941), for a brief lucid treatment.

8. "Only there was no nuptial cohabitation; [between Joseph and Mary] because He who has to be without sin, and was sent not in sinful flesh, but in *the likeness* of sinful flesh, could not possibly have been made in sinful flesh itself without that shameful lust of the flesh which comes from sin, and without which He willed to be born, in order that He might teach us, that everyone who is born of sexual intercourse is in fact sinful flesh, since that alone which was not born of such intercourse was not sinful flesh" (Augustine, 1902:269.)

It is not enough to say that Jesus was "generic man," i.e., that he was "impersonal generic human nature" in whom "the divine nature was dominant and controlling" (Boettner, 1947:197). His self-consciousness was that of a human male, a Jew, a self-educated "rabbi" and prophet from Galilee. He had a human self-will that needed to be submitted to the will of God. This was the point at which he was vulnerable to temptation. As the writer to the Hebrews put it, "He was tempted in all points like we are" (4:15).

We must conclude that Jesus, because he was limited in all these ways, did not have unlimited knowledge. He himself said that he did not know the time of the end—only the Father knows that (Mark 13:32). He showed surprise at the unexpected (11:12-13). Luke's language about him growing or advancing in "wisdom" as well as age and physical stature certainly suggests a development from less to more knowledge and understanding. But even more startling is the statement in Hebrews 5:8 that he "*learned* to obey" through suffering and in this process was "made perfect." All this certainly infers that he was vulnerable to making mistakes, which, of course, are not the same as sins.

Some will react to such a picture for fear of denegrating the purity of Christ, but such is not the fear of the New Testament writers. They are uncompromisingly clear about his purity and sinlessness, but they insist on his full existential identity with us—and for a good reason, as we shall see. Jesus' perfection as the Son of God lay not in some divine infallibility underneath his humanity but in his perfect dependence as a fallible being upon the Father's infallibility. Rather than reject his human fallibility in identifying with us, we must reexamine the New Testament conception of sinfulness. "Fallible human" does not equal "sinner."

Sinlessness of Jesus

The doctrine of Christ's sinlessness has been an integral part of the creedal statements about Christ from the beginning. Indeed, the doctrine is already clearly expressed in the New Testament. John speaks clearly of Jesus' relation to the Father as unmarred by sin. In 2 Corinthians 5:21 Paul says that this one whom God "made to be sin for us *knew no sin.*" And the writer to the Hebrews, who presses the temptations and suffering of Jesus as a human son of Abraham to the limit (5:7-10), qualifies his statements with "yet without sin" (4:15; cf. 1 Pet. 2:22).

Two passages in Paul's writings might be interpreted to suggest that Jesus shared our sinful human nature. In the passage from 2 Corinthians quoted above, Paul says that God made Jesus "to be sin for us." However, the meaning here seems clearly to be "made him to suffer the consequences of our sinfulness" because it is the "innocent one" who is thus the instrument of God's purpose. The second passage in Romans 8:3 is of a different nature. Here Paul says that Jesus was made "in the likeness of sinful flesh." The nature of Paul's argument about the victory of Christ over the law in our behalf leads him to stress that Jesus had the handicap of a "sinful nature" that we have. But this does not necessarily suggest a conscious sinfulness on Jesus' part. Here one may compare Galatians 4:4 where the handicap is stated as "born under the law."[9]

We must be clear about our concept of sin as we seek to understand the sinlessness of Christ. In the Augustinian tradition it has been given an ontic as well as a moral definition, and this has had unfortunate theological implications for understanding the nature of Jesus' humanity. According to Augustine, sin is biologically inherited from Adam, and it involves all human beings in a condition of both corruptness and guiltiness. All humans are born with a sinful corrupt nature and are thereby guilty before God because of Adam's sin. Thus in order to preserve the innocence of Christ's humanity, Christ must be freed from "original sin." He must be born without sinful corruption and guilt as well as demonstrate a continuing moral strength to resist temptation. But let Augustine speak for himself:

> But it was a nature entirely free from the bonds of all sin. It was not a nature born of both sexes with fleshly desires, with the burden of sin, the guilt of which is washed away in regeneration. Instead, it was the kind of nature that would be fittingly born of a virgin, conceived by His mother's faith and not her fleshly desires. Now if in his being born, her virginity had been destroyed, he would not then have been born of a virgin . . . (Outler, 1955:360).

This concept of sin as ontic corruption and inherited guilt of the individual raises serious moral questions about the righteousness of God in creation. And the idea that it is transmitted through the sexual act itself, which is viewed as sinful lust, goes far beyond anything in Scripture.[10] We do not need to accept this explanation in order to take seriously the devastation and universality of sin which both Scripture and human experience affirm.

Our point here, however, is that where such a definition is accepted it

---

9. Fuller (1965:209) and Dunn (1980:115), along with others, interpret "form of a *doulos*" in Philippians 2:7 to mean submitted to slavery or bondage to the power of sin and death in full likeness to human existence. If this interpretation is followed, this passage also should be included here.

10. The Psalmist's anguished confession, "In sin did my mother conceive me" (Ps. 51:5), may certainly be taken as a poetic hyperbole confessing David's profound sense of guilt. The text is never used in the New Testament to point out the nature or extent of human sin, and it should not be used as a technical theological definition. Indeed, it is nothing short of scandalous that it has been made to carry so much theological freight.

has had serious implications for the definition of Christ's humanity. If Jesus must somehow be freed from moral corruption and guilt which inescapably define *human* existence by virtue of birth itself, then Jesus' humanity must be defined as essentially different from ours. And this is the Augustinian answer. Jesus, by virtue of a miraculous birth, has assumed a physical body and a rational soul like other humans, but he has escaped our existential humanity—a full personal identification with us in our historical human existence. Indeed, this consequence in itself raises questions about the legitimacy of Augustine's theological definition of sin.

The other way to approach the problem is to reexamine the validity of Augustine's concept of original sin. If we think in terms of social and personal solidarity in sin (which is the biblical perspective) rather than a corruption of individual substance (flesh), then there is no inherited moral stigma attached to being born in such a historical sinful situation. Jesus could be made in "the likeness of sinful humanity" without being himself guilty of sin. If to be made in the likeness of sinful flesh means being subjected to death (and "the wages of sin is death"), struggling with temptation and resisting sin "to the point of shedding [his] blood" (Heb. 12:4), and learning "obedience through what he suffered," then we can confidently say that he suffered our handicap, yet without sin.

Sinlessness does not mean that Jesus was not subject to normal psychological and spiritual as well as physical development, or that he had no human self-will to be submitted to God, or was immune to real temptation. *Sin is asserting one's self-will in opposition to God's will*. Sin is putting oneself in God's place and refusing to come under his authority. Thus by sinlessness we mean that Jesus never set himself in conscious opposition to the will and authority of God—not even when it meant his own agonizing, humiliating death. He always did the will of the Father. In this respect he was the true image and Son of God. And, of course, from the biblical perspective, to be in God's image is what it means to be fully human!

Reasons for Emphasis on Jesus' Humanity

Humanity in the Arguments of Paul and Hebrews

Both Paul and the writer to the Hebrews are explicit about the necessity of the Christ's humanity in order that he might be our Savior. The reasons can all be summed up in the phrase, "for our sake." We have suggested that the phrase "made him to be sin" does not mean "made him sinful," but it does emphasize that in solidarity with us he shared our sinful condition in order that "in union with him we might share the righteousness of God" (2 Cor. 5:21 TEV).[11] This solidarity of Christ with us so that we can be identified with him is the constant theme of Paul's letters.

The concept of solidarity, which we shall examine further in Part Two, is most obvious in Paul's designation of Christ as the "second Adam" (Rom. 5:14-19). It was necessary for there to be a new beginning point for the race—one who, like Adam, would be the origin of a new humanity. Note how explicitly the references are to "the one *man*, Jesus Christ." Only one who is himself in solidarity with the human race can actually be the new beginning and source. Or according to Romans 6 it is Christ's death (his radical humanity) that becomes the nexus of solidarity and the possibility for new existence. Only as we participate with Christ in death can we also share the resurrection (cf. Phil. 3:10-11).

In addition to such passages Paul speaks of Christ's reconciling mission of freeing us from the "curse of the law" which required him to live "under the law." Not only has Christ reconciled us *to God* as "mediator" (1 Tim. 2:5), but in his human body on the cross he has suffered the curse of the law and thus reconciled warring human factions (Gal. 3:13; Col. 1:21; cf. Eph. 3:11-19). Or again he cites Jesus as our *exemplar*, which means more than following his moral example to the best of our ability. We are to have his "mind" and to be conformed to his image (Phil. 2:2,5; 2 Cor. 3:18; Eph. 2:11-19). This does not mean that we are to be superhuman; rather, we are to emulate his humanity.

Perhaps the single most striking passage which argues for a full humanity, however, is the Romans 8:3-5 reference already cited. Here, as we noted, the whole argument requires an emphasis upon Jesus' "likeness to our sinful nature." Following his analysis of the relation of law and sin in Romans 7, Paul says that God sent his own Son "in the likeness of sinful flesh" to deal with sin's tyranny over us. In a nature like sinful human nature God brought judgment against sin.

Paul's argument runs as follows: The law shows us what is right and wrong, but because of sin's power over us we claim that we cannot keep God's law. That is, we justify our sinning because of our "sinful nature." Thus we excuse ourselves and justify sin's power. And thus we are caught in the vicious cycle of sin and death. But Jesus came in a sinful nature like ours and challenged sin's power. He did what we claim could not be done. He destroyed our excuse and condemned, i.e., brought a sentence against the tyrant, sin. He freed us by demonstrating that one in our condition can keep the true intention of God's law.

The writer to the Hebrews echoes most of these themes in his own

---

11. The New English Bible translates: "... one with the sinfulness of men" and offers the alternate reading, "sin-offering for us." The TEV reading, "God made him share our sin ..." is open to misunderstanding.

way. Christ is the compassionate priest-mediator, and the priest needs to understand fully and share his people's condition (Heb. 2:17-18; 4:15-16; 5:7-10). As one of us he met and overcame the powers of death "for us." Quite in contrast to the fictional Superman who overwhelms his enemies by superior force and thus escapes suffering, Jesus faced and endured the worst that the powers of death could do. His victory by God's power is a human victory—a victory for us (2:14-15). And last, in order to be the "pioneer and perfector of our faith" (12:2), he learned the way of obedience through suffering so that we may find salvation through following him.

Jesus' Humanity and Our Understanding of **Agapē**

This review of New Testament material has been necessary because it is constantly overlooked in approaches which are predisposed to see in Jesus only the divine Savior from the guilt of sin. A truly evangelical doctrine of the person of Christ requires emphasis upon the full humanity of Jesus. It is not simply a bias of those who see Jesus as an example of social action and morality. But we need to press the theological explanation beyond the review of biblical passages. The major reason why we are concerned to emphasize the full humanity of Jesus as the expression of God's self-revelation is that the nature of God as *agapē* is at stake.

The essence of *agapē* in God is seen in his willingness to share fully our human existence, thus endowing it with full personal potential.[12] God's coming to meet us in our human frame of reference, fully participating in our historical situation, identifying with us in our suffering even though we had brought it upon ourselves, and taking upon himself the burden of our resentment and hostility in order to restore a fully personal relationship with himself is the essence of *agapē*. Only thus could God bring us to full personhood which is the corresponding image of his own personal existence as *agapē*. Thus any depreciation from his complete identification with us in Jesus, whether implicit or explicitly intended, detracts from the fullness of God's grace.

Excursus on the Virgin Birth

In spite of the fact that the virgin birth has held center stage in orthodox theology for many centuries, we must admit that it is not central to the theology of the New Testament writers. In contrast, for example, to the resurrection, it plays virtually no theological role. It is for this reason alone that I have chosen to treat it as an excursus. Further, I have attached it here at the end of the chapter on the humanity of God's Son because, as I understand its use in Scripture, the account does not teach a metaphysical preexistence of "God the Son," such as was defined in the fourth- and fifth-century creeds, but rather points to the *true origin* of Jesus as God's Son in history. As Otto Weber has so aptly put it, this passage "is a kerygmatic statement about the origin but not the roots of Jesus" (1983:102).

The problem in interpreting the virgin birth account involves its empirical status. As with any other miraculous event whose actual happening may not be in question, we still cannot refer to God as an empirical explanation. As we saw in chapter 2 we cannot make empirical statments about God and his activities among us because God is not an empirical datum. Miracles remain faith data. The problem arises when the virgin birth is considered a rational or empirical explanation for the deity of Jesus.

This is what Weber means when he says that the virgin birth account does not describe the "roots" of Jesus. For example, in the family tree of Jesus we cannot supply the "Holy Spirit" as father of Jesus—a point the genealogies of Matthew and Luke discretely illustrate. Only the negative statement, "not of Joseph who is his legal father," describes the empirical situation as the wording of both accounts suggests (Lk. 3:23; Mt. 1:16). Again, the question here is not the *truth* of the virgin birth accounts, but only their empirical status. The true source of Jesus' being is God through the quickening power of his Holy Spirit.

Only Luke is absolutely explicit in his mention of the virgin birth at the beginning of his Gospel, but he makes nothing further of it. Matthew, more by implication than explicit reporting, refers to it as fulfillment of the Isaiah prophecy (7:14) but, again, is silent about it afterward. Mark seems to assume Jesus had a normal birth and family life (6:1-6).[13] There is reference neither to scandal nor to any suggestion of a miraculous birth that might account for Jesus' special calling. John, whose theological standpoint might have led him to begin with a miraculous birth, emphasizes rather his lowly origins. The fact that God is Jesus' "Father" or that Jesus is the "Word become flesh" is never argued on the basis of his birth, but rather on his character and works. Paul seems to have been utterly unaware of the virgin birth tradition or else ignored it.

This silence cannot but raise the question why the virgin birth has

---

12. *Agapē* is the essential characteristic of personal being as we know it in human beings. The most complete expression of personhood is the recognition of and the loving respect for others as persons. In a real sense our personhood is a gift from other people with whom we interact. At the human level our parents and families give us our personal being as surely as they give us our physical being. This endowing of others with personhood and responding to them in loving respect is what Martin Buber called the "I-Thou" relationship and what the New Testament calls *agapē*.

13. Some have called attention to the designation of Jesus as "son of Mary" (Mark 6:3) in this passage as an indication that Mark also knows of a virgin birth. If he did, it is fair to ask why he so studiously avoids reference to it. It seems more likely that the tradition of Joseph's early death is substantiated here. Mary is listed as head of the house.

been considered so fundamental for Christology in the orthodox tradition. There are several reasons. First, it was argued that a virgin birth is necessary to protect Jesus from the defilement of original sin.[14] This was developed further into the more precise concept of *immaculate conception,* and finally in 1854 Pius IX made not only Jesus' but Mary's immaculate conception a dogma of the Roman Catholic Church. Second, it was argued that the virgin birth is the way in which God the preexistent Son came into human existence without a change of divine substance. In this way virgin birth and preexistence of Jesus as Son of God are related.

A third, more modern argument is that the verbal inerrancy of Scripture requires us to acknowledge the historicity of the virgin birth. Such an argument implicitly assumes also a literalistic hermeneutic. Modern literalists have been strongly, if subconsciously, influenced by the pervasive empiricistic assumption that only the empirical is real. Thus a virgin birth or conception must be interpreted as the Spirit's physical impregnation of Mary without any male instrumentality or it is not "true."[15] All of these reasons for insisting on a literal interpretation of the accounts are peripheral to the central issues of Christology and, as we have already noted in the case of the first argument, have dubious support in the New Testament.

It is highly unlikely that the original writers intended a literalistic interpretation such as that upon which modern science insists. On the other hand, the account cannot simply be written off as first-century myth.[16] Perhaps we should understand it more in the genre of poetry and allegory.[17] On the human side Jesus emerges from the virgin Israel, i.e., faithful Israel in contrast to adulterous Israel (Jer. 3). In a real sense the whole history of the faithful remnant is the conception and prenatal development of Jesus as the Son of God. Note how Luke pays special attention to the faithful remnant in the story—Anna, Simeon, Zechariah, and Elizabeth.[18] On the divine side Jesus comes from the Father. He is the climax of creation ("the son of . . . Adam, the son of God," Luke 3:38), and he comes as a new creation through the power of the Spirit (1:35).

Our clues for the intended meaning of the Holy Spirit conception must be taken from its use in the passages themselves. Matthew uses the angel's announcement to assure Joseph (and Jewish believers) that the unusual circumstances of Mary's pregnancy, which are not explained, were according to prophecy and truly of God's Spirit. It comes as a dream linking the unusual circumstances to the sign of Isaiah 7:14, which was a sign that God's promise of special salvation for Israel would certainly come to pass. Emphasis falls on Joseph's faith and submission to the word of the Lord given in the dream.

In Luke's account Mary receives the angelic announcement of a messianic savior, the "Son of God." She accepts the word that in a miraculous way God's plan for the salvation of the world will come to fruition through her. And this will be, not by her own machinations but by the work of the Holy Spirit. Luke's emphasis is upon God's initiative and human

---

14. Apparently Ambrose (340-97), bishop of Milan, who was Augustine's mentor, was the first to relate his virgin birth to Jesus' sinlessness. As Hans von Campenhausen puts it, Mary "becomes the means of guarding Christ himself from all defilement by original sin" (1964:79).

15. One of the best examples of a discussion of the virgin birth which begins explicitly from the presupposition of verbal inerrancy has been written by John Gresham Machen. His *The Virgin Birth of Christ* (1932) is a scholarly defense of the position that a literal virgin birth is taught in the Bible. His argument is many-faceted, but its whole methodology is predicated on the concept of verbal inerrancy.

16. Early Christians, living in a more mythically inclined culture, tended to understand the story in mythical categories like they understood the concept of sacrament mythically. And, we might add, they did so quite unselfconsciously. For example, "holy water" was actually thought of as water infused with the Spirit of God. Spirit was understood as a highly refined, potent substance which could actually mix with water or indwell human flesh. Bultmann has insisted that the account is just another example of Hellenistic mythology which moderns can accept and use only if it is demythologized. Of course mythical legends about heroes conceived by one of the gods can be cited from Egypt and Greece, but the differences in setting and presentation between these legends and the biblical accounts raise serious questions about understanding the Gospel story as myth. Furthermore, myth certainly does not fit well with the Judaic-biblical modes of thought.

17. Modern Western culture is so dominated by scientific presuppositions that it is not readily apparent to the average reader that there are options other than myth or literal statement for interpreting language. This raises the problem of finding proper terms to describe various genre of biblical language. But in fact there are many different uses of language found in the Bible. For example, J. C. Wenger (1954:74) describes the language of creation in Genesis 1 and 2 as follows: "Since the whole account is theocentric as to emphasis, geocentric as to standpoint, written in non-scientific language, and *highly poetic in character* [italics mine], it is evident that scientists will be disappointed if they seek information concerning God's creative process from the record in Genesis 1."

The miracle of incarnation is of the same order as that of creation, and the accounts of Jesus' conception have the same "highly poetic character." Interestingly enough Wenger does not recognize this point, although he says in connection with the virgin birth accounts that "the fact of incarnation itself is a tremendous miracle and a profound mystery" (1954:195). We agree and merely point out that as in the case of creation the accounts of its "creative process" are not the stuff of which scientific investigation is made. Compare the account of Israel's escape from Egypt as related in Psalm 77:11-20.

As for the word "allegory," I would only point out that the use of an account as allegory does not speak definitively to its original status as event. Paul certainly is not throwing doubt on the Abraham account when he speaks of it as an allegory in Galations 4:24. My point in using the word "allegory" is not to deny the Spirit's special influence in the miracle of Jesus' conception. Rather, it is to point out that the accounts of miracles cannot be used to certify scientific information. Avery Dulles, in his insightful article, "Symbol, Myth, and the Biblical Revelation," says that the Bible is full of symbolism—both symbolical words and events. Then he notes that "one cannot lay it down as a general principle that symbolism in a narrative is evidence against its historical realism. On the contrary, the central mysteries of the Christian faith derive much of their symbolic value from their historical reality." (First published in *Theological Studies*, March 1966, and reprinted in *New Theology No. 4*, edited by Martin E. Marty and Dean G. Peerman, New York: Macmillan, 1967, p. 46).

18. The church has for centuries dealt with much of this material as symbol and sign. In

submission. Mary is clearly the figurative representative of the church as we see when the promise of the angel to Mary (1:35) is repeated in Acts 1:8 to the disciple band who will receive power when the Holy Spirit comes upon them. Through them the Holy Spirit will form the new "body of Christ" to continue the saving mission of Jesus.

Theologically, then, the virgin conception makes the same two points that John's Gospel makes again and again in the face of Jewish opposition. First, Jesus' true origin and identity was not "according to the flesh" but from the Spirit of God. His is the original birth "from above" (*anōthen*, John 3:3), and all who believe in him are given the right or authority to be children of God, i.e., "born ... of God" (1:12-13). The Jewish leaders stumbled because they recognized only Jesus' lowly earthly origins. Thus their conclusion was that he was "a child of fornication" (8:41), a "Samaritan" (8:48), and "demon possessed" (8:52). But Jesus resolutely claimed that "God [was] the source of [his] being" (8:42a NEB) and that he had not come on his own initiative (v. 42b).

This second point, namely, that Jesus was sent into the world by God from the beginning, stands in clear contrast to the inference of *adoptionism*, i.e., that Jesus was chosen by God to be the Christ on the basis of his achievement. This kind of interpretation might be read from Mark's Gospel inasmuch as he introduces Jesus as God's Son only at the baptism (1:11; cf. the language of Acts 2:22-24, 36; 3:19-20). By contrast the Holy Spirit conception tells us that we should not think of Jesus as an autonomous human being who achieved moral and spiritual status and consequently was adopted by God for God's purposes. Rather, Jesus represents God's initiative and choice from the time of his conception.

In the earliest period of the church one further point was made from the birth accounts, namely, that Jesus was in fact born of an identifiable mother, Mary. This insistence on a historical beginning for the "only Son" was in opposition to docetism which in one form or another defined Jesus' deity as a spiritual existence independent of and only incidentally related to the earthly Jesus. Thus the Apostles' Creed combines the two phrases, "*conceived* of the Holy Spirit" (antiadoptionism) and "*born* of the virgin Mary" (antidocetism), into one statement.[19] For us then, the virgin birth accounts can continue to give a theological witness to the true origin and identity of Jesus as the Christ of God without being pressed for information of a scientific nature.

Roman Catholic tradition, for example, Mary as virgin mother represents the church. Barth speaks of the virgin birth as a sign pointing to the incarnation of the preexistent Jesus as the Son of God (1956:172-202); many modern theologians who do not hold to inerrancy treat the account as theological symbol. My own concern is to be faithful to the intention of Scripture in our modern context. After some years of experience in Asian cultures, I have become much more aware of the multidimensional possibilities for meaning in such a passage and of the significance of symbolism for meaning. In this regard we must remember that the Bible is an ancient Eastern and not a modern Western book.

Luke's first chapter, somewhat in contrast to the rest of the book, is a collage of narrative, allusion to Old Testament prophecy, and poetry. The source of the tradition which he followed is probably an early Aramaic tradition in the church. Taking into account this literary setting, the historical context, and the association of ideas in the passage itself, it seems unlikely that Luke intended an empirical physical meaning to be read from his account.

19. This meaning of the Apostles' Creed has been noted by many theologians, but Pannenberg's comments and discussion of the virgin birth in light of contemporary theology are most helpful (1977:141-150).

Chapter 4

Divinity

Jesus, Son of the Father: The New Testament Witness

We have noted that what happened in Jesus was unanticipated and unique. The presence of God was manifested in Jesus in such a way that it could not have been anticipated from nature, general human experience and reasoning, or even from Israel's experience or the word of the prophets.

The prophets had presented God in highly personal terms and spoken of humans being "in the image of God," but such an image was only reflected in the mirror of the law. Only as humans stood under obedience to *Torah* could the blurred outlines of the covenant image be seen. But Jesus demonstrated a relation to God that was not mediated by law. Indeed, he dared place himself above the law. The prophet Jeremiah had prophesied the coming of a more intimate relationship patterned on the prophetic experience itself (31:31-34). But the idea of a relationship of obedience and trust, of a knowledge born out of personal intimacy, and an authority of shared purpose and power such as was seen in Jesus was not imaginable. Indeed, it could be understood only as blasphemy when it was manifested in the life of Jesus of Nazareth.

The Language of Witness

New Testament Language (Kerygmatic)

Now we must explore further how the New Testament presents this unique event as the salvation of God. But first we must call attention to two hermeneutical consequences of this surprising and unique Christ event. The first is that the apostles had to develop their own linguistic mode which we refer to as gospel or *kērugma* (proclamation) to communicate it. And second, Jesus himself unavoidably becomes the normative referent for all theological descriptions of the Christ event.

The Gospels were written as a kind of theological narrative of Jesus' acts interspersed with his teaching and the writer-editors' own editorial comments.[1] They are not biographies in the modern sense of that word, and they are not a chronological history of the events of Jesus' career. They are a witness to the "visitation of God" (Luke 7:16) by those who had participated in the experience. They were written as a continuation of the history of salvation. Jesus is portrayed as the fulfillment of God's promised salvation. Thus the Gospels concentrate on illustrative events and teachings with almost half of the material focusing on the last few weeks of Jesus' life.

The Gospels tell about the wonderful acts of God done through Jesus (Acts 2:22) in a way that leaves no doubt about the writers' own convictions. There is nothing neutral about their accounts! But the writers simply do not theorize about the person of Christ. They make it abundantly clear that they believe Jesus to be a special revelation of God—one that went beyond Moses and the prophets, and in fact fulfilled the Law and the Prophets. They attribute to him the authority of God, the character ("glory") of God, the power and salvation of God, the works of God, and the truth of God. They use traditional Hebrew terms, which had come from the prophets, to indicate his superior status. They speak of him as Messiah, Son of David, Savior, Son of Man, Son of God, Lamb of God, Servant of the Lord, and the Lord's Anointed. But even the language of passages such as John 17:5, 21, 24b and Matthew 11:27 stops short of theological analysis and suggests the language of intimate communion rather than substantial union.

Therefore answers to our more analytical theological questions about how God was related to Jesus are given quite indirectly and must be found in the implications of the events themselves. The manner in which they are given is indicated in Jesus' answer to John the Baptist when he sent from prison to know whether Jesus was indeed the Messiah: "Go and tell John what you hear and see. . . . And blessed is he who takes no offense at me" (Matt. 11:4-5). In the same manner the Gospel of John presents the works of Jesus as signs to the disciples in order that they "may believe that Jesus is the Christ, the Son of God" (20:30-31).

What we have said about the character of the Gospels is essentially true also of the Epistles. They maintain a kerygmatic stance and adapt their witness to the various cultural situations to which they are directed. They do not offer a theological analysis of the person of Christ. They identify Jesus with the risen "Lord," and they ascribe cosmic authority and eschatological

---

1. It is necessary to refer to the Gospel writers this way in light of the fact that they were clearly working with materials from the oral tradition of the church (Luke 1:1-4). One might even use the term "compilers," although they freely added their own touch to the finished product.

salvation to him. They add exalted designations such as "head of the church," "fullness of God," "firstborn of creation," "Alpha and Omega," and "heavenly high priest." Some of these are extensions of the more traditional Hebrew thought patterns, and some reflect Hellenistic influences. However, although all of this functionally equates Jesus with God's salvation, there is no unequivocal statement that Jesus is "our God" such as one finds only a few decades later in the writings of Ignatius of Antioch.[2]

Implications for Christological Interpretation

Since these kerygmatic, or witness, accounts are the basic materials that we draw on for theological analysis and description in Christology, we must more explicitly note the implications of their literary character for our use. To speak of the New Testament as witness does not mean that it is a neutral reporting of facts. It is not a detached reporting of what happened at a distance but a sharing of what happened to those who are giving witness. It is the reporting of an experience that changed the whole direction of the writers' lives! It is, therefore, the kind of truth that Kierkegaard called subjective or what is today often called existential truth.

Further, the purpose of the witness is to persuade those who hear it. The writers are not simply persuading their listeners that the facts reported are accurate; rather the listeners should also participate in the experience of Jesus as the Savior from God. The event to which the the writers testify is a "salvation event," one that is continuing in the experience of the church as the body of Christ. They give testimony as participants in the continuing mission of the Christ.

This does not mean that accuracy of reporting and interpretation of their original experience was unimportant. But the accuracy, or better, *authenticity* of the report had to be checked by reference to the experience itself and not by its logical consistency as a theological formula. Thus one does not find a standardized *orthodox* language system in the New Testament, but an appeal to *apostolic witness.*[3] For us the "original experience" as historical event is mediated through this apostolic gospel of God's salvation in and through Jesus as the Christ. And because this gospel does not give us a standardized christological formula, we test our descriptive statements, not by their conformity to some rational formula either in the New Testament or the creeds, *but by their adequacy to describe Jesus as God's saving presence with us—Jesus as he is known in apostolic experience.*

Jesus as the Norm for Hermeneutics

The second consequence for Christian theology is that Jesus of apostolic experience—the historically concrete "Jesus of faith"[4]—becomes the final criterion for all statements about the salvation of God in Christ.

It is generally recognized that Jesus did not fulfill messianic prophecies in the manner that anyone expected, and that only in light of what actually happened could the New Testament writers make prophetic connections and point out fulfillments. This is clearly the implication of Luke 24 where the risen Christ astounds the disciples with the insight that it had all been predicted in the Law and the Prophets. Their surprise involved a reinterpretation of the prophetic tradition and indicates that they recognized the normative authority of the new thing that had happened in Jesus. The apostolic experience of Jesus was genuinely *kainē* (new in kind), and the *Kainē Diathēkē* (New Testament) is the product of this reinterpretation of the history of salvation in the light of Jesus.

Norm for Hebrew Bible (Old Testament)

The general implications of this for understanding the Hebrew Bible as the Christians' *Old* Testament are also generally recognized. In the

2. Ignatius was writing about A.D. 112. In his epistle to the Romans he speaks of "our God Jesus Christ, being in the Father." In Smyrneans 2 he attributes the power of the resurrection to Jesus himself. And in Ephesians 1:1 he calls the blood of Jesus "God's blood." These might be compared to 2 Clement (ca. A.D. 120) which begins by saying, "Brethren, we ought to think of Jesus Christ as God, as the judge of the quick and dead."

The passage in Titus 2:13, which is the nearest to this in form, differs in that it identifies Jesus with God, the eschatological Savior. Ignatius speaks of the ascended Christ as now our God, who is presently being made visible in the suffering of Christians.

A second passage which deserves comment in this context is John 20:28. It might be noted that both this and the Titus passage are late in origin, probably not too far from the date of Ignatius' epistles. But without pressing the implications of this for theological development, we note again a certain difference of perspective in this and the Ignatian texts. John makes the words a surprised expression of worship. Further, as Fuller (1965) points out, the phrase "Lord and God" was commonly used in the Roman imperial cultus to refer to the emperor. His paragraph is worth quoting. "The early Christians were very restrained in calling Jesus God, and it is not frequent until Ignatius. But in John 20:28, in one of the latest strata of the gospel material, the risen Jesus is addressed in a formula which, as Deissmann notes, could have been lifted straight from the imperial cultus: 'My Lord and my God.' That the emperor could be called a god would undoubtedly facilitate the ascription of this appellation to Jesus. In a world which was used to the imperial cultus the kind of scruples which the Jewish mind would have against it would be less operative. What the emperor falsely claimed to be is true of Christ!" (1965:88).

3. It was not long, perhaps a century, in the life of the church until these two concepts—orthodoxy and apostolicity—were treated as synonyms, and as the theological controversies continued, the true meaning of apostolicity was largely lost sight of. I have dealt at greater length with the nature of the New Testament witness in *The Authentic Witness* (Kraus, 1978:esp. 55f.).

4. This is the title of Michael L. Cook's recent book on Christology, *The Jesus of Faith: A Study in Christology* (1981). Fr. Cook is intentionally reversing the old "Christ of faith" formula which was contrasted to "Jesus of history." Along with Moltmann, Pannenberg, and a growing number of theologians, he is convinced that we must make the concrete, historical Jesus of Nazareth as he was experienced and confessed by the disciples the beginning point for Christology.

Reformation, for example, Luther was quite explicit on this point, making Christ the hermeneutical center of biblical witness. His way of doing this was to give typological interpretations to many of the figures and events of the Old Testament, making them spiritual representations of Christ.[5] But the more radical implications of this hermeneutical principle to which the Anabaptists called attention were overlooked by Luther and have often been overlooked or forgotten since his time. It is not a matter of merely adding the new to the old as a kind of climax and fulfillment but of fundamentally reinterpreting the prophetic tradition in light of its unexpected "fulfillment." Indeed, if Jesus was to be considered the fulfillment, the first-century Jewish—and indeed, the present century also—interpretation had to be revised, as Paul came to realize (Phil. 3:7-8).

To say that Jesus of Nazareth is the fulfillment of the Hebrew history and Bible already means that Christians are reading it as preface to Christ. They are interpreting it as a preliminary statement which is now understood in the light of Jesus' coming. Thus for Christians the Hebrew Bible has become the *Old* Testament—a historical record of types and shadows that must be understood in the light of their archetype. Its definitions and regulations, while pointing in the right direction, must be corrected and interpreted in light of the new reality revealed in Jesus.[6]

An understanding of this relation between the new and the old is important because it affects our theological methodology and thus our interpretation of Jesus and his mission. While we continue to recognize the Old Testament's importance as the historical hermeneutical context for Jesus, we do not begin with its view of God and creation as the definitive criterion for interpreting the meaning of incarnation. For example, while we say that Jesus is the fulfillment of the Law, this does not mean that we recognize him as the Christ because he met all the expectations of the prophets or perfectly fulfilled the stipulations of the Mosaic Law.

Rather, when we recognize that Jesus is indeed the Messiah, the perfect image of God, we begin to understand how he is the fulfillment of the Hebrew Bible, and it is then that it becomes for us a vital, if only preparatory, part of God's revelation in Christ. Jesus is the fulfillment of the Hebrew Bible only when it is understood in the light of his coming and as a preface to it. Thus methodologically the "types and shadows" must not be allowed to provide the hermeneutical framework and definitions for understanding the reality in Christ.

The interpretation of the atonement is a case in point. The Old Testament sacrificial system does not supply the normative parameters for interpreting the death of Christ. Rather, what happened in the cross and resurrection shows us what that system was pointing forward to. Its inspired witness has been superseded by the coming of the Messiah to which it points. Now he becomes the normative criterion for understanding its mode and content. It is his coming that makes it "old."

However, the Old Testament gives us the historical context for understanding the thought patterns and metaphors used in the Palestinian setting and thus for understanding much of the New Testament witness. In this respect it has great religious value as a guide and corrective to cross-cultural interpretations of the New Testament materials. But our point here is that it does not have final theological authority for interpreting the Christ event and its resultant eschatological outlook as that was revealed in Jesus. Indeed, it must itself be reinterpreted in the light of Jesus if it is to be used as a Christian source.[7]

Perhaps one further example of a christological approach to the Old Testament material will help to make the point clearer. If we begin with a concept of the *Logos of God* as it is revealed in Jesus, then a passage like John 1:1-5, rather than Genesis 1-2, becomes our norm for understanding the word of God in creation. We do not discard Genesis, but inasmuch as Jesus is the "Word of God" and the true "image of God," we interpret the Genesis story in light of the revelation which has come in him. Thus understood, creation becomes part of the theological background and framework for understanding who Jesus is. Or, to put it another way, while we could not infer a human embodiment of God from the creation story itself, once

---

5. Luther's test, "*ob sie Christum treiben*" ("whether they present Christ") was used by him to evaluate the "chief books" of the New Testament. But he also made Christ the central figure of the Old Testament, which prepares the way for him. In his preface to the Old Testament he wrote, "Here you will find the swaddling clothes and the manger in which Christ lies, and to which the angel points the shepherds [Luke 2:12]. Simple and lowly are these swaddling clothes, but dear is the treasure, Christ, who lies in them" (Luther, 1960:236).

However, in his free use of typology as a connecting device Luther oversimplified the relation between the two testaments and freely used the Old Testament as an authority for theology and ethics. See Kooiman's *Luther and the Bible* (1961) for a good exposition of Luther's position.

6. This principle is already clearly recognized in the New Testament itself, and we are merely taking our clue from its use of the previous Scriptures. For example, the writer to the Hebrews contrasts the old as "mediated by angels" while the new comes directly through the "Son" (2:2; 3:4-6; 8:5; 10:1). Paul speaks in the same vein of the old as the "letter" (2 Cor. 3:6ff.). And Matthew explicitly contrasts the teaching of Jesus with the old tradition (Matt. 5:22, 28, 32, 34, 39, 44).

7. Our point here is the theological use of the Old Testament relative to the New, and not its inspiration. This was a major difference between the biblical Anabaptists—Sattler, Marpeck, and Menno Simons—and the Protestant Reformers. They took Jesus' words, "I have come not to abolish them [law and prophets] but to fulfil them" (Matt. 5:17) and " . . . but I say to you" (5:22, 28, etc.), very seriously (cf. Heb. 1:1-2, 2 Cor. 3:7-11).

This is the serious hermeneutical mistake of dispensational premillennialism. It takes its normative clues from the Jewish apocalyptic and the Old Testament prophets. Of course, the New Testament writers used these current thought forms, but they proved to be like "old wine skins" when filled with the gospel message!

we experience such a divine self-giving in human form we can see that it fulfills the concept already present in creation. Thus the climax of creation may properly be interpreted as pointing to the "image of God" in Christ.

Norm for New Testament

But we must press this hermeneutical principle beyond the reinterpretation of the Hebrew Bible. The normative character of the original apostolic experience of Jesus as the Christ also applies to the individual texts of the New Testament and to our own experience of Jesus as Son of God. Several implications follow.

To begin with, it means that the apostolic *Gestalt* of Jesus as the Christ of God becomes the final test for christological statements (see chapter 1, p. 35). This New Testament *Gestalt* takes precedence over individual New Testament statements. The individual texts are to be used as *witness to* the original revelational experience and not as normative theological pronouncements. In this sense, then, we must say that Jesus himself—and not statements of rational inference about him—is our touchstone for what it means to be "Son of God."

For us "who have not seen" (John 20:29), this can only mean an appeal to the original apostolic experience. We stand in the "apostolic tradition" when our experience confirms their witness and the truth of Jesus as the Son of God becomes our own subjective truth. Our experience, however, can never displace the apostolic witness as the norm for understanding who Jesus is. Neither can a scientific reconstruction of the "historical Jesus" replace the apostolic witness. The historical Jesus is a probable picture created on the basis of modern empirical historical assumptions and methodology, and while it has its value in the hermeneutical process, it remains a subjective, modern reconstruction.

God's Approved Servant ("Signs")

As we have said, the New Testament does not give us analytical descriptions of Jesus' relation to God. Instead it presents him as the one who did the works of God. Then it adds commentary, as it were, by using fitting titles and metaphors to speak of his identity and status. Our task here is to examine this material for its theological significance. What do the signs and titles tell us about Jesus' special relation to God whom he called Father?[8]

Signs in the Gospels

Jesus' works are presented in the Gospels as signs of his messianic identity. Our concern is to establish what the signs indicate about Jesus' special calling and relationship to God. Do his works point to the popular image of him as a supernatural being incognito who now and then exercises his innate divine power? Is he the preexistent Son of God now indwelling a human body, and do his miracles, as it were, betray that identity? Or is he a prophet like Moses at Pharaoh's court, whose superior powers are intended to impress a skeptical audience with the superiority of the God of Israel (Exod. 7:10-13)? Or, again, do his signs demonstrate and authenticate his authority as the one who has come from the Father and does his will? What do the signs indicate about this Christ which the Gospels are presenting to us?

According to Mark, Jesus came as the *servant of God* to announce and usher in the new age of God's salvation. He came announcing the beginning of God's rule (Mark 1:15), and this raised the question of his credentials. Who is this servant-son (*pais*) who claims to speak for his Father? Thus Mark immediately introduces him as the one who has the authority and power to do the saving works of God. Jesus first demonstrated his authority as God's servant over the forces of evil (1:23-27). Then he exercised the power of God to heal (29-34). And third, he forgave sins (2:5-12), which is clearly the prerogative of God. Thus Mark dramatically ushers this messianic servant of God onto the scene. His works are the attestation of the authenticity of his servanthood (10:45), and they establish his authority as directly from God, unmediated by the Law of Moses (2:28).

In John's Gospel Jesus is God's Son sent by him to do his work and glorify him on earth (13:4; 17:3b-4, 17). John offers eight signs, including the resurrection, which demonstrated to Jesus' disciples that he was truly the Son of God doing his Father's will. His mission is to reveal the Father, and he asked to receive glory for himself only in fulfilling that mission (13:31-32).

The nature of the signs and what they establish concerning Jesus' identity is especially critical for the argument of John's Gospel. Since the works are crucial indicators of Jesus' identity, the question is whether they are the works of God. Do they glorify God whom Jesus claims to represent? If so, they authenticate his claims as Son (10:25, 37). However, if they are *his own* works issuing from some innate supernatural power, as the Pharisees assumed, then they are the works of a "law breaker" and "sinner" (9:16, 24b), not the works of God. Thus on the assumption that the signs are wonders, the Pharisees could argue with some plausibility that such works are magic and have their source in the prince of demons (10:20). If Jesus' works are viewed as wonders, i.e., spectacular displays of his own

---

8. Many excellent New Testament studies are available to trace the formation of New Testament Christology: See Cullmann (1963), Fuller (1965), Moule (1977), Stephen Neill (1976), Dunn (1980).

supernatural power as a deity in disguise, they do not authenticate his relation to God as his Son. He can claim sonship only as he can demonstrate complete obedience to the Father's authority and does only *his* works (5:19-20). This is clearly the argument of John.

This is a penetrating psychological as well as spiritual insight and marks the difference between magic with its origins in the mysteries of nature and the miracles of Jesus as works of God. "Signs" are not wonders. They do not convince by their spectacular quality but by their character as acts of salvation which lead to belief in God. Only those who by the insight of faith understand the nature of God's salvation can recognize Jesus' works as signs of his intimate relation to the Father. The persuasiveness of his works lies in their intrinsic moral and spiritual character as the works of God's Holy Spirit (Matt. 12:28-32).

What, therefore, do these signs establish concerning Jesus' identity as God's Servant-Son? First, as we have already noted, they do not glorify Jesus as a supernatural being; rather they glorify God as his Father. They establish the character of the one whom Jesus claimed to be his Father, and thus in a reciprocal manner they establish the genuineness of his relationship to that one. Second, they indicate that Jesus' sonship is to be understood as a relation of complete reliance on and obedience to the Father. If we may change the figure, it is only as he fulfills the role of human son in the covenant image of God that he is recognized as the Son of God.

Resurrection as Sign

The resurrection of Jesus is the ultimate sign confirming his identity. According to Romans 1:3-4 the claim for Jesus' messianic status rests on two kinds of evidence. From the human, Jewish perspective he qualifies by way of Davidic descent. But the resurrection is the powerful sign that convinces us that he is the holy Son of God. His spririt of love and power was indeed the Holy Spirit, and not, as his opponents claimed, a demonic spirit.

Again, our major concern is to know what this sign tells us about Jesus' special relation to God, but the nature of the resurrection as a sign is also involved in its meaning.

We note first that the resurrection is, like the other miracles, a sign to believers and not a wonder to the world. Witnesses of the risen Christ were "chosen by God" (Acts 10:41). He did not appear to the skeptical, hostile world. Thus it is an appeal to faith in Jesus as the living Lord and messianic Savior. Just as his miraculous works were given different interpretations and explanations during his lifetime, so the resurrection remains a challenge to faith and not an empirical or rational proof of his deity.

Second, in contrast to the signs which were done *through* the mediation of the earthly Jesus, the resurrection was in no sense accomplished through him. It was the work of God done *to* him independently of his own instrumentality. Thus it is entirely God's ratification of Jesus as the Christ. He was, as Paul said, powerfully designated messianic Son of God through the resurrection (cf. Acts 17:31).

Since the resurrection is a sign, one entirely independent of human agency, we should be alerted to the fact that we are dealing here with what Thielicke has called "non-objectifiable" history and not with what scientific historians call public history.[9] This does not mean, however, that we are dealing in the sphere of private subjectivity (see chapter 2). While there is no final empirical historical *proof* of exactly what happened, there is solid historical evidence that something of great significance did happen in the historical sequence of events—something that can be properly labeled "event." This event which involved Jesus himself was such that it convinced his disappointed and skeptical followers that he was alive again after his death and burial. As it has well been said, it was the risen Lord who created faith in the disciples, and not the faith of the disciples that created a risen Lord!

The nature of the resurrection is theologically important insofar as it is an essential element of the salvation offered in Christ. Our concern is not so much to know the physiological details of Jesus' resurrection but to understand the relation of cross and resurrection and to be assured that what happened in Jesus' case is a genuine victory over death in all its dimensions (Rom. 6:9). Salvation in the kingdom of God as Jesus proclaimed it means salvation from death, and if Christ was not resurrected, then we have no assurance that he was right; and we are still under the dominion of sin and death (1 Cor. 15:12-19). In this sense Christ's resurrection is an anticipation of the eschatological salvation, that is, an event *before its time*, and we cannot expect to know its full nature until we participate in the eschatological experience. Thus we do not expect to understand fully its empirical aspects as an "objectifiable" event.[10]

9. Both Helmut Thielicke and Otto Weber hold that the resurrection as historical event is "non-objectifiable" (see Thielicke, 1977:432; Weber, 1983:75). Weber says of it, "When one then speaks of the 'historicity' of the Easter-event, this is another kind of 'historicity' than that of the 'history of death' " (70). George Ladd, another evangelical scholar, also seems to hold this view without explicitly using the word. He quotes Neville Clark with approval: " . . . the empty tomb stands as the massive sign that the eschatological deed of God is not outside this world of time and space or in despair of it, but has laid hold on it, penetrated deep into it, shattered it and begun its transformation" (1975:101). What Ladd says following this quotation seems clearly to indicate that he sees the resurrection as a non-objectifiable event in time.

10. Gordon Kaufman has argued that the modern category of "hallucination" is the most adequate term to describe the appearances of the risen Christ (1968:422-25, see footnotes 24, 29). As he himself recognizes, the term is "repugnant" to most Christians because it implies that the experiences were illusion and thus deception. Whatever the technical merits of the

The most adequate—and virtually the only—attempt to describe the resurrection at all is found in 1 Corinthians 15. Here Paul uses a number of metaphors, but in short his point is that it is a *transformation* from the "fleshly" mortal body (*sōma*) to a "spiritual" body (*sōma*) beyond the power of death.[11] The fleshly body dies and is buried like a grain of wheat, and what emerges is a new life from and in continuity with the old, transformed into a new plant (vv. 36-38; cf. Phil. 3:21).

Paul does not speak of the resurrection of the flesh but of the body (*sōma*). *Sōma* includes what we would call the personal *Gestalt*—self-identity with power for activity, love, and personal relationships. So, to use his language, we might say that Jesus' *sōma* was transformed from its earthly (which includes both the physical and psychic), mortal existence into the dynamic freedom and power of a spiritual existence. Beyond this we should not speculate. But it is enough to be assured that Jesus' death on the cross was not defeat and did not mean the failure of God's salvation.

Of more immediate theological interest is the meaning of this sign of Jesus' sonship to the Father. What does it tell us about the relation between him and God?

First, a historical resurrection is the ratification of a historical Jesus of Nazareth as the servant of Yahweh. It marks him out from all others as the Son of God. It is an endorsement of his understanding of the messianic role as one of servanthood (Mark 10:45). We might even speak of it as the justification of Jesus' faith and understanding of God's true nature and will. It is a clear voice from heaven saying, "*This one* is my beloved Son."

Second, we have said that Jesus as Messiah is the norm for all christological statements. Now we can point out that *it is precisely his resurrection that indicates this normativeness*. The cross and resurrection have a reciprocal significance. The cross is the disclosure of God's saving love because it is *the cross of the resurrected one*. And the resurrection is the act of God's justifying power because it is *the resurrection of the crucified one*. The resurrection did not exalt Jesus to the position of victorious Lord, thus making him Son of God; but it identified the crucified servant-son as the true Son of God. Or, again, the resurrection is not simply the reexaltation of the divine Son who temporarily assumed a human role which was not essential to his sonship. Rather, it is the exaltation precisely of the crucified one. John underscores this point by making the cross itself the exaltation (John 8:28-29; 12:32, 34).[12] But Paul in the same vein tells the Corinthians that he preaches only a *crucified* Christ (1 Cor. 2:2).

This points us again to Jesus' complete trust and obedience as the essence of his sonship (cf. Phil. 2:7). How this is to be described ontologically is not entirely clear. But the explicit and consistent assertion of the

New Testament that God raised Jesus (the man) from the dead throws suspicion on any theological definition of his sonship as a kind of divinity hidden under the guise of his humanity.[13] It is the human Jesus of Nazareth who was "crucified, dead and buried," who is designated by God to be his Son by the resurrection (Acts 2:23-24), and not a crypto-god who proves his divine identity by raising himself.

Titles Attributed to Jesus

The titles given to Jesus, mostly after the resurrection, give us some indication of the apostolic assessment of his role and status, but they cannot, of course, be used for logical analysis of his ontological nature. They do not, for example, prove his essential deity as "of one substance with the Father" or establish his divine-human nature. They simply point us toward the divine mystery.

Messianic Titles

The most common title given to Jesus was simply the Christ (Messiah). It is difficult to extract one interpretation and expectation of the Messiah and his mission from the language which lies back of the New Testament in the apocryphal and pseudepigraphal writings.[14] However, while the

_____

term may be, Kaufman does not allay our suspicions that the "Other" in the experiences was indeed an illusion. His explanation that such "hallucinations"/illusions(?) often accompany "*extremely significant experiences*" does not seem sufficient. Perhaps the best we can do in an age dominated by scientific definition is to affirm the validity and authenticity of their experience as historical event without pressing for empirical terms to describe the *somatic* transformation of the entombed Jesus.

11. To us spirit and body seem antithetical, but not so in Paul's meaning of spiritual. The Hebrews did not think of escape from a body into a formless spiritual existence as freedom from death! Paul had no desire to be freed from a bodily existence into an amorphous spiritual existence. For him that would have meant a lack of individual, personal identity and power to act. He describes it in 2 Corinthians 5:1-5 as a kind of nakedness.

To say spiritual is essentially to say life in a dimension beyond the power of death, and Paul understood that Jesus' *sōma* was translated from its earthly *psuchikon* (mortal) existence into such a heavenly *pneumatikon* (immortal) existence (1 Cor. 15:42-50; cf. Phil 3:21).

12. Especially in John 8:28-29 Jesus says that it will be precisely in his crucifixion—when they have "lifted him up"—that they will perceive his relation to "the Father" as one who always does what is pleasing to the Father. In Paul's words, the word which was embodied in Jesus is "the word of the cross" (1 Cor. 1:18).

13. This view appears rather crassly in some of the early atonement theories in which the humanity of Jesus is merely a disguise or bait to lure the devil into overstepping his bounds by trying to kill him. But it is covertly present in most definitions of Jesus as preexistent God substance now hidden from view in human flesh.

14. There were different interpretations of the messianic promise at the time of Jesus' coming. Some interpreted the Messiah as a collective concept. Israel, as God's anointed (messianic) nation, would be God's servant. Others held that the Messiah was to be a prophet-king like David, who would deliver Israel from oppression and bondage to other nations. Ernst Jenni has done an extensive article—and a bibliography—on the Jewish "Messiah" (1962; see also Ringgren, 1956).

Messiah was a highly exalted figure, he was not thought of as God himself. He may be called the "Son of David," or "the Son of Man"—the heavenly figure of Daniel's vision.[15] And there is evidence from the Dead Sea Scrolls that "son of God" was also used as a messianic title in pre-Christian Judaism (Fuller, 1965:32). He was expected to bring God's judgment and salvation to Israel, and he was to rule as God's representative on earth. Thus he was closely associated with the reign of God, but the Messiah was not equated with God either in the rabbinic or apocalyptic literature of the Jews which lies back of the Gospels. Thus we cannot assume from any historical precedent that the title Christ, either before or after the resurrection, implies divinity in the Chalcedonian sense.

But what of the titles *Son of God* and *Savior* which are immediately associated with the messianic title in the New Testament? Do these not point to his deity? It seems clear that in the first instance these are simply further designations of the messianic status and mission. The mission of the Messiah was to be Israel's savior, and his exalted status as God's anointed king is designated in the title *Son of God* (cf. Ps. 2:7). However, the titles take on a meaning of their own in the apostolic vocabulary.

The title *Savior* does not appear to have been used for Jesus prior to his resurrection, and in the post-resurrection period new dimensions were added to its Jewish meaning. The Jewish messiah was expected to save Israel, but the church soon recognized Jesus as *savior of the world.* Further, he was preeminently known as savior in his death and resurrection, and these events are interpreted to be God's work on our behalf. "*God* was in Christ reconciling the world to himself," wrote Paul (2 Cor. 5:19; cf. John 3:16; 4:42; 1 John 4:14). Thus Jesus is equated with God's salvation promised in the Old Testament (Acts 5:31; 13:23), and he may be called "our savior" in a way parallel to the Isaianic designation of Yahweh as Israel's savior (43:3; 49:26; 63:16; cf. Titus 2:13-14).

In the first Palestinian churches Jesus' role as universal savior seems to have been interpreted as an eschatological role. Jesus would return as Christ, the Savior. However, while this hope for an eschatological salvation was not abandoned, his cross and resurrection came to be understood as even now the beginning of salvation for all humankind.[16] He is even now the savior of all those who will come under his lordship (Rom. 10:9), and all those who are "baptized into his death" even now are raised to newness of life (Rom. 6:3-4). Or in Ephesians 2 it is said that his cross has made peace between Jew and Gentile (vv. 14-15), and ultimately the whole universe will find its unity and fulfillment in him (1:10). This extension of his saving activity exceeds the limits of the older messianic metaphor and enhances the divine status of the title, Savior.

In somewhat the same manner the title *Son of God* takes on a new dimension of meaning following the resurrection. To signify this, adjectival phrases such as "beloved," "only (begotten)," and "firstborn" are added to his designation as son. "Son of God" emphasizes his divine character and authority. As the Son he is the one who knows and reveals the Father in a way that only one in the family could do. He displays the divine glory, the "grace and truth," which is the personal character of the Father. He exercises the full authority of the Father (John 14:10). He shares his purpose and power—all this to the degree that it can be said that anyone who has seen the Son has seen the Father (14:9).[17]

15. The "Son of Man" title has a number of meanings. It may simply mean "a man" (Mark 2:10 and parallels). As such, of course, it speaks of his humanity rather than divinity. It may also refer to the Messiah as the exalted Lord, especially as the eschatological Lord. When it is so used it is associated with—if not synonymous with—the title "Son of God" (Mark 14:62 and parallels). Thus the title itself has an air of ambiguity about it so far as Jesus' divine identity is concerned, and to my knowledge it has never played a major role in the theological definition of Christ's person.

16. Martin Hengel traces the historical roots of the conviction that Jesus' cross was a vicarious sacrifice (*Atonement*: 1981). Second Peter, whose composition all acknowledge as late, has five references to Christ as the eschatological savior (see 1:11, et al.). The apocalyptic vision continued and was adapted to the new situation in the church at the end of the first century as we shall note further in Part II (cf. Rom. 3:24; Phil. 3:20).

17. Bultmann and virtually all the historical critics who follow the form critical method interpret the Son of God title as a Hellenistic divinity title, and they give Hellenistic meanings to passages such as Philippians 2:6-11 and 2 Corinthians 8:9. Thus they agree that these texts teach a pre- and post-existence of Jesus as the Son of God.

Such agreement may on first reading seem to confirm the traditional interpretation of orthodoxy. This kind of interpretation of the passages becomes evident already in the early second century as the Hellenistic categories used to contextualize the message in the first generation began to be the orthodoxy of the third- and fourth-generation Gentile Christians. But a moment's reflection gives one pause.

If Bultmann, et al., are right about the meaning of these passages, then they are indeed mythological in nature, and they must be treated as myth, as, indeed, the Hellenistic Christians did. Third- and fourth-century Graeco-Roman culture was certainly mythologically oriented. Undoubtedly most, if not all, Christians of this period understood christological dogmas mythologically, and a way of dealing with them as such lay readily at hand. They could and did interpret them as *mysteries* of the cult (sacraments), and they could rationalize them into speculative metaphysical theological formulae following the precedent of the Greek philosophers. Developments in the early centuries clearly demonstrate both of these trends in the church.

In the modern period when mythology began to be recognized as such and sharply distinguished from the empirical descriptions, orthodox theologians simply read the Greek metaphysical definitions of the fourth century into the texts of the New Testament. By such an anachronistic hermeneutic modern orthodoxy avoided the question of the New Testament's linguistic categories. Unless we are prepared to continue such an anachronistic tour de force, we must look for more adequate alternatives.

There are good reasons to doubt the adequacy of myth as an interpretative category for the material of the New Testament, as we have seen in chapter 2. And it is extremely unlikely that the original writers intended metaphysical speculation. Therefore it seems best to rely on the Hebraic categories of history, metaphor, allegory, personification, parable, and poetry to understand the titles for Jesus as the Christ. That is, we recognize the Hellenistic terminology

Thus the metaphors which first derived from kingship become independent symbols whose content now derive neither from the original idea of kingship nor from the messianic referent itself but from the reality experienced in Jesus Christ. Jesus, the crucified and risen Savior is the Son of God.[18]

Lord (Kurios)

Of all the designations for Jesus the title Lord most clearly implies his divine status and gives him the most exalted dignity. It was the title most widely used in the apostolic churches of the first century. To understand its significance one must see it in its ancient Graeco-Roman setting.

In the Hellenistic world *kurios* was used to indicate the divine status of the Roman emperor. The first-century Christians were quite aware of this comparison when they confessed that "Jesus is Lord" (Rom. 10:9; 1 Cor. 8:6; 12:3; 2 Cor. 4:5; Phil. 2:11). In the Hellenistic Jewish setting *kurios* was used in place of the sacred name, Yahweh, which out of reverence they would not pronounce.[19] Thus when the New Testament writers say that Jesus is Lord, they intended to identify him with the name of Israel's covenant God[20] and to assert his lordship in contrast to Caesar.

The church gave the title Lord to Jesus as the exalted King. They spoke of him as seated at "God's right hand," the place of supreme authority, and his title Lord indicated the universalization of this authority. He is first of all Lord of the church, but more he is King of the world. As Lord he reigns over all earthly authorities, and finally he will be manifested to the whole world as "Lord of lords and King of kings" (Rev. 17:14).

By the use of such titles, then, Jesus is identified with God's purpose, power, authority, and personal character. In a word, we might say that he is identified with the *name* of God. Indeed, for the church "Jesus" is the new name of "God our Savior." But none of these titles simply equated Jesus with God. As we will note further in the next chapter, there is a built-in ambivalence or paradox even in the use of the most exalted title, Lord, which both identifies and differentiates him from God.

Theological Analogies

Alongside the titles which attribute divine status to Jesus are also designations which have the character of theological analogies. Two of these, namely, *Word of God*, and *image of God* have special importance.

Image of God

The analogy of Jesus Christ as God's image is used in a number of ways in the New Testament. It points to the incarnation, in which the true image of God is finally formed in Christ, as the climax of creation. We will develop this further in the next chapter. It points to Jesus as the locus of God's presence, as the one who reveals God's true nature, and thus as the

---

as an attempt to contextualize the message for the third and fourth centuries, but we must interpret this new language as being in continuity with and consistent with the apostolic experience and not vice versa.

18. While theology is not limited to historical analysis of such theological terms, we must give a reasonable account of how we establish a theological meaning that is consonant with the historical setting. We cannot, nor do we wish to, avoid the historical meaning. Indeed if, as we have said, we begin with the Jesus Christ of the historical event, and if we make the New Testament, itself a historical document, the norm for meaning, we must take historical meaning seriously. But we must also add that historical development, meaning, and methodology are also part of the hermeneutical debate.

Bultmann followed Bousset (1865-1920) in tracing the historical process by which the title Son of God was first associated with the messianic status and then in Hellenistic Christian circles began to denote the deity of Christ. He assumes that the term derives from the Hellenistic conception of the "divine man" *(theos anēr)* and that this deity included a mythical pre- and *post*-existence as Son of God. This derivation is highly questionable, as has been pointed out by others (Fuller, 1965:69; Dunn, 1980:16f.), and certainly Bultmann has gone too far in simply assuming that Paul's usage of the Son of God title "takes this understanding for granted" (Bultmann, 1951:131). Compare his explanation of how Paul answers the question how Christ's death can actually affect us: "It finds an answer in the statements in which *Paul describes Christ's death in analogy with the death of a divinity of the mystery religions*" (Bultmann, 1951:298; his italics).

As Fuller well says, "The Gentile mission did not take its Christology from the thought of its converts" (1965:232). We must make a clear distinction between the cultural and language context as *the occasion* for using certain ways of speaking and as *the source* of its content. Anyone who has been closely involved in cross-cultural communication, especially where cultural assumptions and definitions differ widely, will recognize how acute and complex this problem is. One cannot say that the new terminology which is used has no significance for the meaning that is transferred. Obviously it does. But the speaker's/author's own cultural tradition, especially where reporting experiences and concepts from within one's own tradition, must be given predominant weight in discerning the meaning.

Since our witnesses stand in close relation and continuity with the Hebrew Bible and the original Palestinian experience of Jesus as Messiah, we must give weight to their *intended meaning* as well as the cultural setting that occasioned the language used. The work of men such as W. D. Davies (1958), Oscar Cullmann (1950), Reginald Fuller (1965), and more recently James D. G. Dunn (1980) in tracing the meaning back to pre-Christian Palestinian and Hellenistic Jewish sources is far more convincing.

19. The word *kurios* was supplied for the Aramaic *mar* or *mari* (lord) used in the Palestinian churches. But it had more significance for Hellenistic Jews who used the LXX, where *kurios* was used for the sacred name, YHWH. Among these Jews *Kurios* had fully established itself as the title of Yahweh in the post-LXX period," writes Fuller. "To begin with, *kurios* lay to hand as the translation of *mar*. . . . This would lead to the application of Psalm 110:1 to Jesus. Again, once *kurios* was firmly established as a title for Jesus, this would pave the way for the transference to Jesus of certain LXX passages where the original [was] *kurios* Heb. YHWH . . ." (1965:68). Thus the identification of Jesus with the lordship of Yahweh in explicit contradiction to the claims made for Caesar seems clearly intended.

20. Note how in Acts 2:21, 38 Peter first identifies Jesus with "the Lord" in Joel's prophecy, and then in verse 38 substitutes "be baptized . . . *in the name of Jesus*" for Joel's "*all who call upon the name of the Lord* shall be saved" (Joel 2:32).

one who becomes the prototype for our own formation as God's children.

In the first instance the image metaphor is most likely an allusion to Adam who was created in God's image. But when it is so used (e.g., 1 Cor. 15:45-49), it contrasts Jesus with the first Adam rather than simply identifying him with humanity. The rabbis of the first century had greatly exaggerated Adam's perfection and glory before the fall. In some cases they even ranked him above the angels. Paul, who uses the metaphor most often, seems deliberately to replace this rabbinic idea that Adam, "the first man," is the prototype with Jesus as the "second Adam" and the heavenly prototype.[21] He is the true image and son who "reflects the glory of God and bears the very stamp of his nature" (Heb. 1:3; cf. 2 Cor. 4:6).

Fundamentally, the image analogy speaks of Jesus as the "glory" and presence of God among us. In Colossians Paul speaks of him as the "image of the *invisible* God" and associates him with the creation as both its dynamic and form (1:15-20; cf. Heb. 1:3-4). Jesus is both "beloved Son" (v. 13) and the "first-born of all creation" (v. 15b). But the implicit emphasis here in Colossians is on the visible presence of God. In the same way Jesus is spoken of as the glory of God (2 Cor. 3:18). The image is the glory, i.e., the character of God manifest in Christ (cf. John 1:14b). And this character of God dwells fully in him (Col. 2:9).

The use of the image (*eikōn*) analogy in this cultural context calls for elaboration of two further implications. First, there is an allusion to the contrast between Jesus as God's true image and the many idolatrous images (*eidōlon*). An idolatrous image is a human representation of God. Its power is given to it by its human creator. Further, it is used to control and manipulate God for its creator's purposes. By contrast Jesus is God's self-representation, the "firstborn of creation," and "Son of God"—the one through whom creation came to be. As the true image of God he exercises God's authority and power.

Second, in the ancient pagan world and in cultures like India today the image is considered to be the sacred presence of the one it represents. It is functionally equal to the divinity and provides a visible, focused reality for the worshiper. This is certainly part of the idea lying back of the reference to Jesus as the true *eikōn* in contrast to the "shadows" (*skia*) of things to come in the old covenant (Heb. 10:1). It may also lie back of Paul's reference to the "fulness" of God dwelling in Christ (Col. 2:9), i.e., God is fully present to us in Christ. And Jesus' words to Philip, "He who has seen me has seen the Father" (John 14:9), have the same connotation. Jesus is the true and living image of God and actually participates in the divine reality which he represents.

Finally, Christ as the Son who is the true image of the Father is the prototypal image into which we are being formed. Norman Porteous points out that in the New Testament there is a distinct shift in the use of the "image of God" concept (Porteous, 1962:684).[22] In the Old Testament Adam or humankind was said to be formed in the image of God, but in the New Testament only Christ is unreservedly said to be in God's image, and humankind in general can achieve the image only as they are conformed to the image of Christ (Col. 3:10; Rom. 8:29). Even now those who recognize Jesus as the true image are in the process of transformation into his likeness (2 Cor. 3:18), and in the eschaton his image will be perfected in us when we are in his presence (1 John 3:2). We will develop this concept further in Part Two.

Word of God

The Word of God analogy is used only once or twice. In John 1:14 Jesus is said to be the "embodiment of the Word." In Revelation 19:13 the victorious Christ of the eschaton is given the name "The Word of God." The only other passage which might possibly refer to Christ as word is 1 John 1:1, but this most likely means the gospel about Jesus. However, because the John 1:1-14 passage provided the biblical nexus for the development of the Nicean-Chalcedonian definition of Christology, we must offer a more careful interpretative analysis of its theological significance.[23] By equating the preexistent *Logos* with the Son they could speak of Jesus as the earthly manifestation of "God, the eternally begotten Son."

We need first to understand why and how the Nicean Fathers interpreted this passage as they did. Their primary reason for giving the passage a highly technical philosophical interpretation is quite clear. They were concerned to maintain the reality of Jesus' essential union with God. And according to the Greek philosophical modes of thought the only way to

---

21. W. D. Davies pointed out years ago that this rabbinic setting offers the most probable context for understanding 1 Corinthians 15:45-49. Paul, in contrast to the rabbis, makes the "first Adam" a "man of dust" and makes the "second Adam" the "heavenly man."

22. See also Porteous (1971) for a further discussion.

23. James Dunn offers a careful and penetrating analysis of John's prologue in exploration of the origin of the New Testament concept of incarnation. In his concluding paragraph he writes:

"John it is then who sets the terms and provides the norm for the subsequent discussion on the Christian understanding of God and of Christ. For if Christ is the Logos, *theos* and not *ho theos*, the Son and not the Father, then the modalist option is ruled out (one God who manifested himself as the Son). And if the Logos *is* Christ, or became Christ, and not merely spoke through him, then the option of seeing Christ simply as an inspired prophet is also inadequate. But how can one speak finally of the Christ who is both one with the Father (10:20) and less than the Father (14:28), both Word become flesh (1:14) and 'only begotten god' (1:18)? That is the question which racked the church throughout the patristic period and continues to tease and test the minds of Christians still..."(1980:250).

do that was to assert his eternal unchangeable and unchanging *substantial* identity with God. John's categories of God as the Word which became incarnate in Jesus provided their point of departure.

Their interpretation began with the assumption that the Word is a hypostatic personification within the being of God. That means that the Word shared the essential substance of deity but also could be individuated. The Word was both "God" and "with God." Then they equated this Word with the Son of God (vv. 1, 14b) who is eternally begotten by the Father and who eternally shares his essential deity. Finally, they held that this eternally begotten Son, the Word, without any change in his essence was united with a rational soul and flesh of a human being through conception by the Holy Spirit in the womb of Mary. This one was then born of the *Virgin* Mary, "Mother of God," insofar as his humanity is concerned. In this way the unchanging nature of deity was preserved, and at the same time the dynamic becoming in history was recognized.

The major question, however, is whether John's categories were intended to be interpreted in this philosophical way. If we begin with assumptions and definitions from the Hebrew worldview, we get quite a different picture. In Hebrew thought God's unchanging nature is not thought of in static substantial terms but in dynamic moral and relational terms. Indeed in the Bible God is conceptualized as dynamic, creative, and acting with power on the historical scene. In him being and becoming are united.[24] He is the God who comprehends both beginning and end—the Alpha and Omega points. He is the eternal God who enters into and acts in the temporal development, working out his purposes in the process. His immutability is his steadfastness of character, that unchanging nature of his goodness and faithfulness which makes him consistent and trustworthy.

Within such a conception of God and his relation to the world the reality of Jesus' essential union with God can and must be stated in quite different terms. If this Hebraic setting is the proper context for interpreting John's concept of the *Logos*, and I am convinced that it is, then we must question the adequacy of the Nicea-Chalcedon definition as "a perfect synthesis of biblical data" and a standard for all succeeding theological interpretations.[25] With this in mind we must look more closely at the passage.

John's Prologue

In the first fourteen verses of his Gospel John makes four fundamental statements. (1) The Word *was with* God in the beginning. (2) The Word *was* God. (3) This Word *has been present* from the beginning of time giving life and light. (4) And now this Word has been *fully expressed* through its embodiment in Jesus, who is called the only Son.

As Cullmann points out, the meaning of these statements will be much influenced by one's interpretation of *Logos* (Cullmann, 1963:251). We can probably completely rule out the ancient Stoic concept of *logos* as "cosmic law which rules the universe" and the more Gnostic conception of Philo which views it as a "personified intermediary being" who was creator, revealer, and redeemer (Cullman, 1963:251-52). John's reference is rather to the creation account of Genesis 1:1-2 and to the *dabar Yahweh* (word of Yahweh). In the Old Testament literature this word of Yahweh is God speaking in revelatory and creative action. It is a dynamic act and not a divine being, although it is sometimes poetically personified like God's wisdom or name.

John's prologue bears strong resemblance to some Old Testament and later Jewish passages that personify Wisdom and *Torah* (Law), but with some apparent, calculated differences. Wisdom, which was identified with *Torah*, was said to be a preexistent hypostasis. In some rabbinic writings it was called the "daughter of God" and considered to be the mediatrix of creation (Cullmann, 1963:257).[26]

---

24. Apparently the concept of God the Father eternally generating the Son is an attempt to recognize this dynamic element, but of course, unless this is conceptualized as an emanation (proceeding) from God, it leaves the Neoplatonic concept quite in shambles. On the other hand, it does not fit biblical categories either.

25. The quotation, "a perfect synthesis of biblical data," comes from B. B. Warfield (1851-1921), the great champion of orthodox Calvinism; and I have taken it from John R. W. Stott's recent book, *The Authentic Jesus* (1985:34). Stott's complete paragraph continues with full approval to quote Warfield. He continues, "At Chalcedon 'all the biblical data are brought together in a harmonious statement, in which each receives full recognition.' Indeed, the statement of the two natures in the one person is more than a New Testament synthesis; it is the foundation of the New Testament documents. 'All teaching of the apostolic age rests on it as its universal presupposition.' And this presupposition is derived from Jesus' own self-consciousness and self-testimony...."

For those in the Anabaptist tradition this raises a highly significant hermeneutical question. The Anabaptists self-consciously appealed beyond Augustine and Chalcedon to the New Testament Scriptures as the final authority for faith and life. Under the pressures of persecution they were unable to make a thorough revision on every point of doctrine, but their intended methodology is clear. It is no coincidence that the Christology language of men such as Hans Denck, Pilgram Marpeck, and to some extent even Menno Simons is different from the standard theological formulas. These men simply were not convinced that the metaphysical theology of the ecumenical creeds was a "perfect synthesis of biblical data."

26. Baruch 3:37-4:4 equates preexistent personified *Wisdom* with the Law given through Moses. According to Ecclesiasticus 24, *Wisdom* is with God among the hosts of heaven (v. 1), is "the word which was spoken by the Most High" (v. 3, NEB), comes to dwell in Israel (v. 8), and is identified with the covenant book of God, and the Law of Moses (v. 23). In a similar fashion the Wisdom of Solomon personifies *Wisdom* as the "image of God's goodness" (7:26) who lives with the Lord (8:3) and kept watch over Adam (10:1). Thus we have good precedent in the postexilic Judaic literature for the kind of expression that we find in John's prologue.

James Dunn has made an exhaustive review of this Wisdom language and concludes that this is the actual historical source for the New Testament language of preexistence and incarnation (1980:163-95).

If we take our clues for understanding verses 1-14 from John's Gospel itself, the contrast to *Logos* is clearly *Torah*. In 1:16-18 John as editor announces that "grace and truth" have come in Jesus Christ, the one who comes from the bosom of the Father, in contrast to "law" which was given through Moses. And throughout the Gospel this conflict of authorities—Jesus, the Son, versus the Mosaic Law as interpreted by the scribes—continues. Thus the postexilic Judaic setting seems to be the proper hermeneutical context for understanding the prologue.

If we follow this clue, a passage like Proverbs 8:22-31 makes an excellent backdrop against which to interpret John's meaning. Read in this way the passage asserts that God's true nature is revealed by the *Logos* as embodied in Jesus rather than by *Wisdom* as expressed in *Torah*. First, note that John chose "Word" instead of "Wisdom" to designate the inner being and nature of God. He says that "the Word [rather than Wisdom] was in the beginning with God" (cf. Prov. 8:22-26). Second, this Word not only existed alongside of God as a created being or personification like Wisdom, but it was truly the expression of God himself. (This same kind of contrast is stated elsewhere as a contrast between the "Son" as author of the new covenant and "angels" who mediated the old (cf. Heb. 1:3b-4; 2:2). Third, this Word can be spoken of as preexistent, both in the sense of existing in God at the beginning of the world's creation and as existing in the world as its true life and light even prior to Jesus' birth. And last, this Word is not a written law as the rabbis asserted of Wisdom, but it is embodied in a person in whom the glory of God is seen as "grace and truth."[27]

In Jesus Christ, then, we see the glory of God's only Son. No other person or principle can be put on a par with him as the revelation of the essential nature of God. In our passage this is expressed as the embodiment of the preexistent Word in the earthly Jesus. He is identified with the Word of God spoken "in the beginning."[28] In a later section we shall deal at more length with the concept of preexistence, but here we should note that the phrase "in the beginning" properly limits our speculation about how God existed *before* the beginning, i.e., what God is "in himself."

For us *the beginning* is God's expression of himself in creative, salvific action. This is his word which was in the beginning and is now fully expressed in Jesus. Thus to speak precisely, "God's self-expression (Word) in the beginning" is the primal revelation beyond which we can only speculate. To speak about an "eternal generation of the Son" by the Father, which is the technical meaning of preexistence, is at best a speculative extension of revelation which seeks to take us *to a point before the beginning*. Such language, which may have been appropriate in a given missionary situation, must nevertheless be brought under the authority of Scripture.

Our text tells us, then, that the self-expression of God which we see in Jesus already existed in the creation. It is the same creative, salvific word spoken at the beginning. It did not come into existence when Jesus was born. It was not first spoken from Sinai, nor was it perfectly embodied in the Law of Moses. Rather, the same Word first spoken in creation was spoken in its clarifying fullness in Jesus Christ so that his total being in the world is the expression of that Word.

Thus concerning Jesus as "Son of God" we must conclude that this language of embodiment speaks of his identity with God's self-revelation rather than ontological essence. When we think of the Word in these terms, then we are brought directly to the historical word spoken in Jesus and not to some prior word. Our eyes are focused upon him as the true Son and Word of God to us. Cullmann points out that "the Hebrew term *dabarim* (words) can also mean 'history,' and when one thinks primarily in terms of the life or 'history' of Jesus, it becomes natural to identify Jesus with the Word" (1963:261). He is the "word of truth" (John 17:17) and the word that gives eternal life (John 5:24). He himself is the good news of salvation.

---

27. The expression "glory of God" is probably the nearest parallel in the Hebrew language to the Greek "essence of God." However, it is not a substantial concept. In the Gospel of John Jesus' glory, which is the glory of God, is seen at its climax when he is crucified. His exaltation or "lifting up" is his crucifixion. Thus glory is viewed as the display of his essential character. We should not move from glory to ontological categories that are not immediately and necessarily tied to Jesus' concrete historical revelation of God in his ministry, cross, and resurrection.

28. That there is a concept of "preexistence" in John is obvious, although preexistence is not a biblical term. But how he understands the nature of this existence "in the beginning" is not entirely clear, and it obviously has more in common with Hellenistic Jewish precedents than with the philosophy of the third and fourth century A.D. Without elaborating, Dunn suggests that in this passage we have a subtle transition from Hebraic language of the *personification* of Wisdom to the *identification* of Wisdom-*Logos* with a particular person, Jesus (1980:243). This is a helpful conceptualization, but it still does not help us much with the ontological picture.

Chapter 5

Jesus,
the Self-Disclosure of God

Reasons for Inquiry into Christ's "Deity"

In chapter 3 we said that the christological question is the question about the meaning of our human existence and destiny in God. We saw how Jesus is the Word of God about the meaning of human existence. In chapter 4 we examined the way in which the New Testament itself bears witness to Jesus of Nazareth as the Son of God. And now we will look more directly at the theological language of the church as it has attempted to understand the relation of God to us in Christ.

Ultimately the crucial question about Jesus is explicitly *theo*logical, i.e., it is a question about God. How is God related to the universe and especially to the human race? How does God make himself known? What is God's will for us? How does God manifest his life and authority among us?

Our inquiry into the nature of God's presence in Jesus Christ is not simply a religious one in the narrow sense of that word. That is, it is not restricted to the agenda usually thought of as religious—the cult, personal morals, or speculative opinions about God. It is in a special way related to the nature and meaning of our human life together and the destiny of historical existence. We are concerned about the source and authenticity of Jesus' life and teaching because if what his life implies about God and his relation to the world is true, then the nature and destiny of human existence is profoundly affected.

Further, not only does the scope of our theological concern extend beyond the religious sphere, it focuses on God rather than the earthly Jesus. Our questions are not primarily about Jesus' supernatural qualities—

whether he did miracles, had supernatural knowledge, or was born of a virgin. Rather, our concern is with his relationship to God as his Son and image, and with God's relationship to us through him. Of course, the immediate object of our inquiry remains Jesus of Nazareth, but the nature of our concern and the focus of our questions is changed. Is Jesus Christ the authentic representation of God's authority and power? Did he come from God? Is he the "Way" to God? In short, is he truly the self-disclosure of God?

Incarnation—A Word About God

Our provisional definition of incarnation in chapter 2 spoke of the Creator-God who came to us in Jesus. This might have left us with the impression that a Creator-God who was already known as such now uses Jesus to make another facet of himself known to us. Now we must point out that when we speak of Jesus' deity we are saying something far more radical than that. It is not that the God of Moses—the Creator, Law-giver and Judge (i.e., God, the Omnipotent and Transcendent One)—who is already well-known humbles himself temporarily to become our servant and savior in Jesus who is his Son. Rather, we are saying that the God who at best was dimly and inadequately known through creation and law reveals the fuller dimensions of his character to us in Jesus.

Thus when we speak of Christ as deity we are not saying that Jesus is a god or divine man like the Creator and Judge who has revealed himself in nature and the Law. Rather, we are saying that God is the kind of God who relates to the universe, human beings, and history like he related to us in Christ. His Law is the law of love. His power, authority, and judgment are exercised among us like Jesus' power, authority, and judgment were expressed. God, our Savior takes the form of a servant. He comes as one of the disinherited and oppressed. His kingly crown is made of thorns. He dies as a criminal executed on a cross because the political and religious powers judge that that is the only way the nation can be saved. But because he is the God of life he rises from his grave in order to continue his work as Savior-Servant of the universe. And this is not one small link in the chain of history. It *is* the chain. This *is* the pattern, the *Gestalt* or form, that God takes in relation to us.[1]

---

1. Bonhoeffer first spoke of God as the God who lets himself be pushed out of his own universe: "God lets himself be pushed out of the world on to the cross. He is weak and powerless in the world, and that is precisely the way, the only way, in which he is with us and helps us. Matt. 8:17 makes it quite clear that Christ helps us, not by virtue of his omnipotence, but by virtue of his weakness and sufferings" (1967:188). More recently Moltmann has picked up something of the same concept when he speaks of Jesus as "the crucified God" (see esp. chap. 2, 1974:32ff.).

Incarnation and Preexistence

The language of preexistence is one way of talking about Jesus as the revelation of the *eternal* God. On the human side Jesus represents historical development, but on the divine side he discloses eternal reality. The God disclosed in and by Jesus is not a morally evolving deity which is now for the first time brought to life and light in Jesus. God is the "pre-" and "post-" existent one—the "Alpha and Omega." The love and power of God which finds full human expression in Jesus Christ is an eternal reality in the world. The Word spoken in Jesus is the word from "the beginning" (John 1:1).[2]

In order to underscore Jesus' identity with this eternal reality the language of eternal existence is applied to him. Jesus also is called the "Alpha and Omega" of history (Rev. 1:8; 22:13). He did not become the "Son of God" through a historical sequence of events—not at creation, at birth, at baptism, or even in resurrection—but he shared God's eternal glory and he was sent from the bosom of the Father. John's language is the most explicit. Already at the beginning he was in and with God as the Word of creation. And as God's continuing life he was in the dark world as light which could not be extinguished. It seems clear that this is not intended as an ontological statement about the existence of the human Jesus before his birth, but rather an emphatic identification of the Word spoken in Jesus with the eternal Word.

1   Theologically three major points are being made here. First, Jesus has the preeminence or primacy as the revelation of God's nature and will. Here we must make our point by referring again to the implicit contrast being made to Wisdom-Torah which were given a personified preexistence in Jewish teaching. Logos-Son, not Wisdom-Torah, are the preexistent reality in God.

2   Second, incarnation was not merely God's corrective response to sin. It was his eternal plan and promise. The Christ was already in the intention and plan of God before creation (Eph. 3:11). This idea is extended in Paul's thought that Christ is "first-born of all creation . . . before all things," and that he is the principle and goal of creation, and that all things find their unity in him (Col. 1:15-17; Eph. 1:10).

Third, the salvation which has been offered in Jesus did not become a historical possibility for the first time in him. He predates himself, as it were. He was the rock from which the water of salvation flowed to save Israel in the wilderness (1 Cor. 10:4). He was before Abraham, and Abraham saw him (John 8:56-58). Indeed, this "Light of the world" (8:12) had been shining from the beginning. It is the light that has enlightened every person coming into the world (John 1:5, 9-10).

The incarnation in Jesus was not simply a brief event in human history, but rather the climax of a long historical process in which God in many and varied ways disclosed himself to the human family. In Jesus the light that previously had been caught only in fragmented reflections or was known only by the shadows it cast is focused on a perfectly formed convex mirror which lights up the world both past and future with the glory of God. Or to change the figure, here in Jesus we recognize the one "who is and who was and who is to come, the Almighty" (Rev. 1:8). This "Jesus Christ is the same yesterday, today, and for ever" (Heb. 13:8).

A Self-communicating God

The incarnation, then, is first of all a word about the nature of God and creation. It tells us that God is self-communicating, for precisely in Jesus revelation becomes fully a *self*-communication. When we speak of Jesus as the embodiment of God we are saying that his revelation of God is not primarily a teaching about God (*guru*), nor primarily the reporting of God's oracle (prophet). In Jesus God is *presenting*[3] himself as our Savior. God is acting in our behalf, showing himself as the gracious Creator-Sustainer.

This is the way we should first understand John 1:1-5, which is a statement about God before it is a statement about Jesus.[4] The Word expressed in Jesus is the self-expression of God. Thus John tells us that from the begin-

2. The word "preexistence" itself does not occur in the Bible or in the major creeds, and we need to be careful to understand what it does and does not mean. It does not mean that Jesus existed before his birth. In the ancient Greek world and later Judaism there was the belief that souls existed prior to their entering into earthly, fleshly existence (see John 9:2; Wisdom 8:20 for allusions to this belief). However, there seems to be no allusion to this in the biblical references that suggest preexistence.

The concern of the creeds is to assert that Jesus as the Son of God is of one essence with the Father. This is stated as an eternal begetting in the Chalcedon formula: "Before time began he was begotten of the Father, in respect of his deity, and now in these 'last days' . . . this selfsame one was born of Mary the virgin, who is God-bearer in respect of his humanness." If one uses these categories of divine substance, then, of course, to say that Jesus is "God-substance" can only mean that as God he existed from eternity.

For those of us who are concerned first with the definitions of the New Testament and only after that the creeds, we must ask whether this is the intended meaning of the Bible itself. As I have explained elsewhere, I have serious doubts that it is. We are on much firmer ground if we find the context for preexistence language in the Hebraic personification of Wisdom rather than in the hypostatization of a Platonic ideal or in the mythology of Hellenism.

One of the most recent New Testament studies to deal thoroughly with this issue is James Dunn's *Christology in the Making* (1980). I find myself largely in agreement with his conclusions.

3. The English word "present" has a double meaning. As a verb it means to give or show something. As a noun it means to be in the presence of. Precisely this double meaning is indicated in the designation of Jesus as *God with us*. God *presents*, i.e., introduces, himself to us in Jesus; as a self-introduction we can say that Jesus is "God-with-us."

4. It is doubtful that John intends to hypostatize the Word like Philo, the Jewish platonic philosopher, did. J. B. Phillips catches this idea beautifully in his paraphrase: "At the beginning *God expressed himself*." And the *Living Bible* totally misses the point when it uses "Christ" for "*Logos*," suggesting not only hypostatization but complete individuation.

ning God is the self-expressive God, not transcendent and aloof as in the Greek Neoplatonic philosophical thought which greatly influenced the orthodoxy of the fourth and fifth centuries. God is not hidden, revealing his will only in written form as in Islam's *Koran*. Neither is he the silent reality which can be discovered only in the discipline of meditation beyond all human rationality as in the practice of *zazen*. How different the whole meaning of John's Gospel would be if the first verse read, "In the beginning was *satori* (enlightenment).[5]

On the other hand, God is not simply mysterious vitality in nature as the Japanese word *kami* might suggest. Through the Word which expresses God to and in creation, we understand that God confronts nature as subject confronts object. God creates and communicates with that which he created, not as procreative force or emanating source, but as personal Creator.[6]

Thus, on the one hand, the creative Word of John 1:2 distinguishes God from creation as the rational personal being who speaks to it. On the other, in distinction from Greek and Asiatic modes, God is not simply abstract being or rational principle but the self-expressive, the compassionate one, that is, the one who feels and experiences with us.

A word is a personal expression, not simply a subjective thought. It is not a word until it is spoken in an act of communication. The word expresses creative power and enlightening truth. It is the dynamic of both creation and revelation. According to John, then, in and from the beginning God existed as this self-expressive Word; incarnation, first mentioned in verse 14, is the climax of this self-communication.

Incarnation—Mode and Climax of Creation

When John says that all things were made by the Word which was embodied in Jesus, we can paraphrase: "God's self-expression as it was in Jesus Christ is the genesis of all that exists." The manner in which God's creative power is manifest in Christ, then, is the clue to understanding the creation process.[7] Or, to put it slightly differently, incarnation as it was realized in Jesus is the recreative process by which the original intention of God in creation is being achieved. This is clearly implied in Ephesians 1:10 where we read that in Christ, the incarnate one, all things in heaven and on earth will find their ultimate unity and fulfillment.

When the incarnate Word is identified with the word of creation, we learn that creation is also an act of grace. Thus the word of creation should be understood as an invitation of grace rather than a command of law.[8] As we have seen, the Jewish scholars of the postexilic period identified the personified Wisdom of God with the Law and spoke of Wisdom-Torah as the agent of creation. They said that God created the world so that the wisdom of the Law, which expresses his very nature (glory), could find expression. Thus God's inner character and mode of operation is understood in a legal metaphor. The order of creation is the product of legal commandments and obedience. Law is the *modus operandus*, the highest principle operating in the universe, and human history will find its consummation in perfect obedience to the law.

But for New Testament writers the essence of God's being (glory) finds only fragmented expression in nature and the Law, and it is fulfilled in Christ who is called the expression of "grace and truth." Thus the identity of Jesus as the self-expression of God is fundamental for understanding the *mode of God's being in the world*. What does this *incarnational* mode of being in the world imply about the ongoing process of creation and human destiny? What does it tell us, not only about God's intention and goal, but about the way in which he is working to accomplish that goal? These are the broader issues implied in the questions about incarnation. Our questions about Jesus are questions about God and human destiny.

Jesus and God: Identity and Differentiation

Methodological Limitations

Our statement speaks of God coming to us in Jesus Christ. This is at the heart of the Christian conviction, but to describe this theologically in-

---

5. The Buddha assumed for practical purposes that there is no God other than the interior reality of the self. In any case, there is no communication from God—no word. Enlightenment (*satori*) is not a revelation from another being. It is a human achievement or intuition. Usually it is said to come through disciplined meditation. Further, it is basically an adjustment to what is. It is a means of coping, not creating. It is the realization that the attainment of spiritual harmony and calm depends upon the erasure of desire for change. It does not speak of creative dynamic to change the evil situation, but of a change of the individual through resignation.

In Islam Allah is completely inscrutable. He does not reveal himself. Only his will is revealed in an infallible written form which is preserved in heaven. A copy of this original was dictated by the angel, Gabriel, to Muhammad.

6. The titles and theological analogies which we examined in the last chapter each point to the revelation in Jesus as a self-revelation of God. For example, Son is one who is in the image of his father and bears his character. The Word is a direct expression of the self. Glory and grace are not attributes but personal characteristics.

7. While the concept of creation *de novo* and *ex nihilo* is emphasized to make the philosophical point that there is no ultimate reality outside of God, it is quite clear that the creation described in Genesis 1-2 is a *re-creation* of the chaos. It is a reconstitution of life and order out of the darkness and formless chaos by an act of self-communication. Here, then, already is the implicit concept of redemption by a self-incarnation which is fulfilled in Christ as well as the basis for understanding salvation through Christ as a "new creation" (see chapter 11).

8. In his chapter on "Creation and Creaturely Beings" Macquarrie says that the "Being" of God manifests its creativity in his "letting-be." He writes: "But what is most typical of God (Being) is, in the language we have used, his 'letting-be,' his conferring of being, his self-giving to the beings. This letting-be is both his creativity and his love. In St. Thomas' language, 'It is out of his goodness that God bestows being on others' " (Macquarrie, 1966:208).

volves us in a real problem of understanding and expression, as we saw in chapter 2. Christ's deity was not immediately observable or self-evident. It could not be directly perceived like his humanity. We cannot point to any empirical characteristics which unquestionably demonstrate his deity. Others have done miracles and spoken the effective word of forgiveness. And even the resurrection accounts consistently say that *God* raised him from the dead, not that Jesus by his own divine power arose. Nor is the resurrection presented as scientific proof to a skeptical world. Rather, God was manifested to those who had known and believed in the earthly Jesus. Even here in the climax of his earthly manifestation God confronts us in such a way that we must make a decision. God does not overwhelm us with wonders which compel belief but beckons us with signs which, if followed, lead us into his presence.

Thus we must begin our investigation of Jesus' unique relation to God with the awareness that we are methodologically limited and cannot expect to remove the mystery as scientific investigation intends to do. Our purpose in seeking to understand more fully who Jesus was and how God was present to us in him is not to satisfy our rational curiosity or to develop creedal statements which give us control of the way to God. Rather, we seek to understand in order to offer more adequate spiritual service and reasonable worship.

Biblical Language of Identity and Differentiation

When we examine the New Testament language about Jesus we soon realize that its descriptions of God's relation to him are not standardized or logically precise. A variety of metaphors and indirect references to his identity present different conceptions of Jesus' relationship to God, and some of these actually contain conflicting ideas. One suggestion is that he was adopted by God as his Son in light of his obedience (Acts 2:22-24, 36). Mark's Gospel by itself might lead us to conclude that this "Son of God" first became aware of his unique relationship and role at his baptism (Mark 1:1, 9-11). On the other hand, there is the suggestion that Jesus was Son of God from birth by virtue of a special conception by the Holy Spirit (Luke 1:35). But in Romans 1:3-4 Paul says that Jesus was designated Son of God according to the Spirit of holiness by his resurrection from the dead. Other texts suggest that in some sense he existed with God before his birth as a human being (John 1:1-14; Col. 1:15-16).

In addition to these variations there is a difference in the way Jesus' actual relation to God is described. Some language associates him with God in the most intimate union, and other passages clearly differentiate him as an individual being in the service of God. Further, the same writer may use a variety of metaphors and terms in different contexts. In short, there is no systematized or standardized Christology in the New Testament, and we must resist the temptation simply to read later orthodox systems back into the Scripture. If we work historically we must begin with the record as it is.

The first theologically significant characteristic of our New Testament data for interpreting the nature of God's presence in Jesus is a certain duality in the use of language. It is as if our writers want to say both that Jesus is one with God yet distinct from him. This is what we are calling the language of identity and differentiation.

On the one hand, many statements speak clearly of Jesus as a man approved by God and raised by him from the dead. These are of different literary genre and located in different contexts.[9] For example, in the Gospels Jesus himself is portrayed as having a clear individual self-consciousness over against the Father whom he must obey. Or in more theologically oriented statements Paul may speak of him as "Lord, to the glory of God the Father," thus clearly distinguishing the two. The 1 Corinthians 15:24 passage actually pictures the *heavenly* Christ as handing the kingly rule back to God when he finally has overcome the last enemy, death.

On the other hand, in other passages Jesus is practically equated with God. For example, Thomas calls the risen Christ, "my Lord and my God" (John 20:28). And Paul can say that "in him the whole fulness of deity dwells bodily" (Col. 2:9). The celebrated texts in Titus 2:13 and 1 John 5:20 can quite naturally be interpreted simply to equate Jesus with the "true God," and "our great God and Savior," although we must also note that their grammatical construction allows for a differentiation between God and Christ.

Perhaps 1 Corinthians 8:5-6 is the most typical example of the ambiguity in Paul's writings. Here Christ is spoken of as the "one Lord" along with the "one God, the Father." Thus there are two, but they represent the one reality and authority of God over against the "lords many and gods many." Paul has no consciousness of serving two gods—two powers, authorities, or purposes. He is serving *the Lord, God.* Yet he freely speaks of them as two.

Correlating Biblical Variations

Our task is not to examine these various texts in detail. That is the work of New Testament scholars, and many excellent studies are available (Cullmann, 1963; Fuller, 1965; Moule, 1977; Neill, 1976; Turner, 1953). Rather, we must ask whether there is any way to correlate these two kinds

---

9. See, for example, passages such as John 14:28b; Acts 2:22-24; 3:13-20; Romans 8:11, 29; 9:5a; 1 Timothy 2:5.

of statements so that they correspond to our experience and give us a useful understanding of how Jesus can be called "Immanuel, God with us."

The biblical way of talking about God gives us a clue for understanding this duality in the use of language about Jesus. On the one hand God is viewed as the great Mystery, whose name the Jews of later centuries would not even pronounce. This one is the "I AM WHO I AM" of Exodus 3:14. His presence is like a consuming fire. He is the one whose face not even Moses dared to see on pain of death (Exod. 33:20). In our theological parlance this is "God-in-himself," the transcendent One—"the King of the ages, immortal, invisible, the only God, [to whom] be honor and glory for ever and ever" (1 Tim. 1:17).

But God is also spoken of as the Savior God who is named Yahweh and is active in history and nature. This Yahweh puts himself at the disposal of people through making a covenant with them. He agrees to restrict himself to a covenanted relation and act within the limits of that agreement. He makes himself available by revealing his *Name*, that is, his inner character and power.[10] He even spoke to Moses in the Tent of Meeting out of the pillar of cloud "as a man speaks to his friend" (Exod. 33:10-11). And he gave messages to the prophets so that the meaning of his actions could be known to people.

These are not two different Gods. Neither is God thought of as having several different faces.[11] In contrast to the imagery of Hinduism, the God of Israel has only one face which in its glory and mystery cannot be seen by mortals. But this heavenly Mystery makes himself available through the mediation of various natural and historical events.

Jesus and God

When God is thought of as the transcendent Mystery, Jesus is clearly differentiated from him. Indeed, Jesus himself called God his Father, and he taught us to approach this mysterious, invisible presence not simply in awe or fear but in trust as a wise, loving Parent. He showed us that the face which is too blindingly glorious to be seen is the face of holy love. And the mysterious presence which had been obscured by the smoke and thunder of Mt. Sinai is in fact a gracious presence which has seemed fearful only because of our misunderstanding and ignorance.

However, when God is thought of as the one who reveals himself in saving grace, Jesus is identified with him. Jesus is *God in his self-revealing action*. Immanuel is not the name of the transcendent, invisible God, but of God presenting himself to and with us.

The terminology expressing this is fairly regular and easy to classify. When Jesus is related to God as transcendent Spirit he is differentiated according to our designations for God. In relation to God as the Father-King he is the Son and Messiah. To the Spirit-Creator he is Agent and Mediator. To God, the eternal Judge, he is the eschatological Son of Man into whose hands judgment has been given. And he is the image of the invisible God. Each of these suggests a role directly under and in the service of God.

Jesus is identified with God as he is present with us in salvific action. Indeed, his name is Jesus (Savior). His salvation is God's salvation. Paul's characteristic designation of dynamic identity is Lord (kurios). This is the name of God as the covenant-making Sovereign. Jesus is not merely the human go-between like Moses who received the covenant for Israel. He is identified with the one who gives the covenant. For Paul, Jesus has all the authority of Israel's Yahweh.

In John's Gospel Jesus is identified with the self-revealing God as "the Word," "the Light of the world," and "glory of God." The identity motif is especially characteristic of John who presents Jesus as the one who completes the mysterious predicate of the "I AM WHO I AM" name given to Moses. In a series of "I am" pronouncements Jesus supplies the salvific metaphors which reveal the God of salvation: "I am the bread which came down from heaven." "I am the light of the world." "I am the door . . . the good shepherd . . . the resurrection . . . the way" (John 6:41; 8:12; 10:7, 11; 11:25; 14:6).

Perhaps the term "Son of God" is the best of all these designations to express both the identity (union with) and the distinction (individuality). As a son Jesus is distinct from the Father. He is sent by the Father, learns from . . . depends totally upon . . . is obedient to and glorifies the Father. But also as the Son he is the stamp of his nature and reflects the glory of his character. He is the confidant and beloved of the Father. As Son he can say, "I and the Father are one," and "he who has seen me has seen the Father" (John 10:30; 14:9). This seems to be summed up well in the words, "He who does not honor the Son does not honor the Father" (John 5:23).

Theological Language of Identity

Self-revelation

Although the above New Testament terminology is fairly clear, it still leaves us with the basic theological question of how to conceptualize this

10. "And he [God] said, 'I will make all my goodness pass before you, and will proclaim before you my name, 'The Lord'; . . . The Lord, a God merciful and gracious, slow to anger, and abounding in steadfast love and faithfulness, keeping steadfast love for thousands, forgiving iniquity and transgression and sin, but who will by no means clear the guilty . . .'" (Exod. 33:19b; 34:6-7a).

11. In the Elephanta cave temple dedicated to Siva the central image is the three faces of Siva, the "Trimurti," depicting him as creator, destroyer, and preserver. In most cases these differing aspects of divine power are symbolized by a plurality of gods and goddesses.

relation of Jesus and God. The differentiation is quite evident and simple to conceive, but how shall we conceptualize the identity? Shall we speak of a unity of essence as the early Greek church fathers did?

Cullmann is convinced that the biblical language will not support this extended meaning. He agrees that the New Testament teaches the "deity of Christ" but not in terms of "substance and natures" (Cullmann, 1963:323). He wrote: "But we shall see that these names too (Logos, Son) do not indicate unity in essence or nature between God and Christ, but rather a unity in the work of revelation, in the function of the pre-existent one" (1963:247). He insists that we must understand this language in the context of salvation history. We must understand the deity of Christ "strictly from the standpoint of *Heilsgeschichte*" (1963:306, 308-09). His point is well taken, but as a New Testament scholar he does not take us the next theological step. Shall we speak of Jesus' relation to God as a communion, or should we speak of a union or unity with God? And if we use the language of union, what kind of union is it?

Pannenberg has concluded that the concept of self-revelation requires us to speak of Jesus' "essential unity" with God. As I understand Pannenberg, he does not mean a substantial union in the Greek sense when he uses the word "essential," but he wishes to say more than a functional union. Jesus' relation to God is a "revelatory unity . . . that includes an identity of essence" between God and himself (Pannenberg, 1968:132; cf. Tupper, 1973:166ff.). But how shall we speak of this "revelatory unity" which leads Pannenberg to say that "he [Jesus] is one with God and thus is himself God" (Pannenberg, 1968:323)?

If we begin with the differentiation between Jesus and God, the language of communion provides an alternative conceptual metaphor of their "essential unity." Such a category suggests a union or unity of purpose, character, and will. Much of the New Testament language could be understood in this way. This was the approach of the Antiochean church fathers of the fourth century. They spoke of God (the *Logos*) united with the man (soul and body) Jesus, and they described the relation as an indwelling of God. Jesus' unity with God was one of the most intimate God-consciousness and communion of the *Logos* and the human soul (Kelly, 1958:301-309). According to such an interpretation the superiority of Jesus over the prophets lay in his more profound and sustained fellowship with God and his deeper understanding and shared character of God. In the language of John's Gospel, the Son is the one who is "in the bosom of the Father," i.e., is in the most intimate communion that is possible; therefore, he has the perfect knowledge of the Father (John 1:18; cf. Matt. 11:27).

The metaphor of communion is a helpful conceptualization, but is it enough? Does the reality experienced in God's revelation of himself through Jesus require us to say more than this? If we think of revelation as a communication of ideas or information, such an intimate sharing of fellowship might be sufficient. But when we speak of Jesus as the *self*-revelation of God, the language of communion alone does not seem adequate to describe the relationship.

When the revelation of God in Christ is understood as God's self-revelation or self-giving, then we must speak of an *identity of selfhood* between the revealed and the revealer (Pannenberg, 1968:129). Revelation in Jesus is not merely information about another who is different from himself. He himself in his life, death, and resurrection is the revelation. Jesus is more than an exalted prophet. He is a manifestation of God for our salvation. In him God makes himself present with us. Thus we are pressed to find categories of identity to express the relationship.

The Analogy of Person

Both Roman Catholic and Protestant orthodoxy have used the philosophical language of ontology to describe the unity of Jesus with the Father. They have spoken of Jesus as "equal with" but not "identical to" God. That is, he shares in or participates in the God-substance, but he is not the whole of God. God's fullness is Trinitarian in its form, and Jesus is one *persona* (not person in our modern sense of the word) in that Trinity. Each person is substantially God, but God is not identical to any one *persona* whether Father, Son, or Spirit.

The basic problem with this conceptualization is inherent in the analogy of being itself. God is conceptualized as an ultimate object rather than as ultimate subject. Of course such an object may be conceived as also personal, but the analogy itself does not indicate or require this. And, in fact, the theories of the third and fourth century spoke in terms of "mind" *nous*, rational *psuchē*, and flesh, not of personal presence. Such an analogy can only be conceptualized as a combination of parts, which, again, is the picture from the early centuries.

This conceptualization leads to a second, more serious problem in relating the doctrine of the Trinity to the incarnation. It is a problem more of ethics than ontology, namely, the problem of relating Jesus' disclosure of the personal-ethical nature of God to the eternal nature of the Trinity. Traditional Trinitarian hermeneutics has tended to interpret Jesus, the Son, in light of the totality of a Trinity understood through creation and Law, not vice versa. Thus the disclosure of God in Jesus does not change our understanding of God as Creator-Judge, Lawgiver, or Warrior for justice. It does not change our concept of the relation of justice and love. It merely adds a depth dimension as it were—the love dimension. The result is that the ethical character of God remains somehow different from and often even inconsistent with the picture of God the Son dying on the cross. Agapē as revealed in Jesus Christ is carefully circumscribed by the justice of the eternal Trinity.

In traditional terms we might say that in the interests of rejecting the heresy of *Patripassionism* the creeds fail to give adequate recognition to the radicality of the cross as an expression of the essential nature of God. In traditional orthodoxy the Christ of glory, not the Christ of the cross, reveals the eternal character of God. To be sure, this Christ of glory made the loving gesture of condescension before he was exalted to the throne where he will establish the justice of a *lex talionis* with the "rod of iron." Indeed, the rejection of his gesture of love gives the biting fury to his wrath.

This kind of Trinitarian concept is most graphically portrayed in the apocalyptic view of Jesus as the eschatological warrior-judge who ends history in a convulsion of violence and wrath. But it is also the hermeneutic that in subtler lines has furnished the justification for the use of violence in the "Christian" state as well as for violent revolution in the name of Jesus.[12]

If we use the analogy of person and speak of God as personal subject, then we can more accurately speak of Jesus' relation to God in terms of an essential *self-identity*.[13] We can say that Jesus' self-identity is his identity as Son of God, i.e., he shares God's identity for us. Such a statement is a theological assessment of what is implicit in Jesus' utterances and actions and not a statement about his psychological self-consciousness. I am suggesting that an analogy of personal identity and sense of selfhood describes the experience of God in Christ more adequately than the analogy of being. By analogy, just as we achieve our personal identity in the intimacy of family relationships, Jesus' self-identity was achieved in the family of God (Israel of prophetic understanding) as Son of the Father. And the experience of the original apostles as well as that of believers since then confirms the validity of this self-identity.[14]

Advantages of This Analogy

This is the language of social psychology rather than philosophy, and some may object that it opens us to the danger of subjectivity. However, if by subjectivity we mean having no empirically demonstrable object, the speculative philosophical language of spiritual being is no more empirical than the psychological language of personal being. And if it means that we have left the realm of the objective (i.e., logical, rational) categories and thus cannot give certitude to our concepts by logical demonstration,[15] our answer is that the analogy of person is based upon the certainty with which

12. Only recently have some Protestant theologians like Moltmann and Pannenberg seriously attempted to deal with this problem. Moltmann is especially sensitive to the difficulties and attempts what he calls a "Trinitarian theology of the cross" in which the cross itself becomes "the material principle of the doctrine of the Trinity" (1974:241). According to Moltmann the cross reveals both the tension and unity within God himself as he takes up his history into himself. It reveals God the Son "delivered up" and "abandoned" by his Father for the sake of all the godforsaken; and it reveals God, the Father who suffers the loss of his own fatherhood in delivering his only Son to death in order to be Father of all the godforsaken. Thus the cross of Christ is the cross of the "crucified God." And he concludes, "If the cross of Jesus is understood as a divine event, i.e., as an event between Jesus and his God and Father, it is necessary to speak in trinitarian terms of the Son and the Father and the Spirit" (p. 246). From a slightly different approach Pannenberg says, "If Jesus' history and his person now belong to the essence, to the divinity of God, then the distinction that Jesus maintained between himself and the Father also belongs to the divinity of God" (1968, 1977:159; see pp. 158ff. for his development of this theme).

In the Roman Catholic tradition, Karl Rahner, to whom Moltmann makes reference, and Jon Sobrino also deal sensitively with the question. Especially see Sobrino (1978:226). He has been much influenced by Moltmann.

Needless to say, this approach to the doctrine of the Trinity opens up new and far more biblical perspectives on the question. Understood in this way, Jesus and his cross are a full revelation of the eternal God.

13. The "self" is a social and psychological concept. We have referred to it earlier as "personal being" (see chapter 2). It is a social-psychological construct in contrast to spirit which in modern Western thought is a metaphysical construct and indicates a purely individual, even private existence. Self is an existence in relation to others. It is given to us in the self-giving relation of the other person and ultimately in the relation of God to us.

How we conceptualize the self's objective existence is more difficult than conceputalizing spirit because we cannot use physical metaphors to any advantage. Perhaps the new understandings of the relation of energy and physical being which are now being explored in physics will give us a more adequate basis for conceptualizing the self.

Of course, in empirical psychology the objective existence of a self apart from the body has been denied. But this is a philosophical problem with the empirical definition of "self" rather than with the term itself. Such empiricism also rejects as "nonsense" the metaphysical concept of spirit. Perhaps all that we are saying is that the ultimate metaphysical sphere is best understood in personal metaphors of self rather than the physical metaphor of spirit. But that is a significant difference! The concept of self and self-identity suggests a dualism of person and person (I and thou) and relates the immanent and transcendent in a way quite different from the traditional rational metaphysics. (For a perceptive although not conclusive treatment of the concept of self, see Reinhold Niebuhr, 1955).

14. The nature and content of Jesus' "self-consciousness" has been hotly debated by New Testament scholars for many years. Perhaps what I am suggesting is nearer to what Bultmann calls "self" or "existence-understanding" (Perrin, 1976:222f.). In any case I am not trying to make a pronouncement about his psychological consciousness. However, his whole manner of being, what we have referred to as a Gestalt, indicates a special awareness of his calling and relation to God as his Father, whatever his culturally conditioned understanding of the messianic role and his relation to it may have been. The sense of filial devotion, confident trust, and obedience to the one he called Father (Abba) are clear indications of a self-identity.

T. W. Manson summed it up well when he said of Jesus that "the Father was the supreme reality in his own life." And he adds, "The experience of God as Father dominates the whole ministry of Jesus from the Baptism to the Crucifixion: that is, it fills the whole period for which we have certain and detailed information" (1963:102). Also note the sensitive and insightful treatment of Jesus' call and awareness of filial relationship to God in connection with his discussion of Matthew 11:17 (1963:107ff.).

15. This would be the position of Francis Schaeffer who has vigorously defended or-

we know ourselves to be persons. Indeed, we might plausibly argue that we have more reason to be certain of our own personal being than we have of so-called objective data.[16] One real danger of the rational analogy of being is that it leads to a false sense of certainty, as though we had somehow proved the reality of God in Christ by our logic! A personal analogy frees us from the pseudoempirical illusion of rational ontological categories which tempt us to substitute a rational theological belief in Jesus' deity for a genuine commitment of our whole self to Jesus as Lord.

Further, we may add that the analogy of persons does not involve us in the ontological subjectivity of mysticism. Knowledge of ourselves and others as persons is not mystical. The so-called *experience* in mystical religion is indeed a subjective one in which there is no relation to any other object/subject outside of oneself.[17] But quite in contrast to mystical awareness, the knowledge of ourselves as persons is the result of being confronted by another person. The personal experience is an experience of another personal being over against us in relationship. In this sense our experience of others as persons qualifies as a phenomenal experience. It is not merely a subjective psychological state or mystical consciousness which has no objective referent.

An analogy of personal knowledge, then, offers an alternative to rationalistic and subjective theories of knowing. It grounds the personal relationship of subject to subject in God himself, and it opens the possibility of a genuinely social religious experience. The social-personal paradigm for the encounter of God and his people is the genius of the biblical tradition, and it provides the analogy for Jesus' relation to both humankind and to God.

Specifically, it gives us an analogy which, as we have just said, makes it possible to conceptualize Jesus' relation both to us and to the Father and to understand our own relationship to God through him. When incarnation is understood in terms of the personal analogy, the focus is on Jesus as the one who reveals the Father—not on written prophecy, theology, or command. Indeed, one must also add that the focus is not on the Spirit as an inspirational influence from God but as God's own self present and at work in Christ. A personal self-revelation cannot come to us as a written or oral report about another person nor as ecstatic inspiration from that person. It can come only in a historical relationship to us—an actual being present among us and living with us. It comes to us as a self-giving which can be mediated only through a genuinely personal relation. And for us, of course, that can only mean a historical *human relationship*. Thus we are concerned with the total historical portrait of Jesus, the human being as the Christ of God.

On the other hand, if such a human relationship is a genuine

experience of God's presence, it must somehow be essentially God's relationship to us. By definition the author and content are one in a self-revelation. We need to know that this one who mediates God's presence is one
with him. It is not enough to think of shared spiritual or rational divine
substance. His unity with the Father must be such that we can be confident
that he represents God's inner character and attitude toward us. This, of
course, was the essence of apostolic faith in Christ, and our theological language struggles to express adequately the content of this faith.

Last, when we think of Jesus' relation to God as the personal unity of a
self-identity, we have a paradigm for our own relation as children of God.
His union with God *was given* to him in history. It was his as the gift of selfhood—his own personal identity as God's Son. His deity was not a
preexistent divine substance which was transported to earth and combined
with human flesh and rationality to produce an independent divine-human
being. It was God's work in and through Jesus. The Gospel of John makes
this unmistakably clear in the words of Jesus about his complete and utter
dependence upon the Father (John 5:19, 30). From the human side, then,
his identity as God's Son was achieved in the full submission to his Father's
will and in unreserved participation in *God's being in the world*. In this
same way we become children of God through faith in Jesus Christ.

Contextualizing the Language of Self-disclosure

The language of personal being—"person," "self"—has been highly
developed in Western cultures and has been closely associated with the
development of individualism (see Kraus, 1979:96-101). But the language
of spirit and soul, rational and mystical being, still predominates in Asia
where Hinduism and Buddhism have been the major religious influences.
This significant difference in the mode of conceptualization and language

thodoxy against neoorthodoxy by attempting to reinstate the Aristotelian rationalism that
provided the philosophical base for it. See his *The God Who Is There* (1968) and the many
books that followed.

16. William Hordern argues that the paradigm for all our knowing is our knowledge of
persons. Following the suggestion of John Macmurray, he writes, " . . . it is obvious that the
child first comes to know other persons, particularly the mother. Only slowly does the child
come to see that some entities in his environment are not persons but things. Primitive people,
with their animistic world view, demonstrate that it was only after great effort that man
developed the ability to recognize things as being inanimate" (1964:145-46).

17. The "self" or soul as the rational principle of self-knowing is a mysterious essence hidden behind the layers of phenomenal existence. Newbigin refers to the *Taitiriya Upanishad*
(II, 1-5) as an example of this view. There "it is taught that in order to find the real person one
must go behind the material ('food'), the vital ('breath'), the intellectual ('mind') and the
spiritual ('understanding') [to find the ultimate self]. The real person, the ultimate self, is hidden behind all these" (1983:38). And this "ultimate self" is the one mystical reality that can be
called god or soul (Brahman or Atman). Thus to discover the ultimate self is to discover
nothing outside of one's own mystical essence.

has caused continuing difficulty in the contextualization of the Christian message in Asia.

How shall we proceed in light of this difficulty? How shall we present Jesus as the revelation of God in cultures where mythical-symbolic images and mystical experience are the assumed norms for religious discourse? The traditional missionary assumption has been that the ontological language of the early centuries of orthodoxy is closely parallel to if not identical with the language of ontological mysticism. Therefore, proceeding on this assumption, Evangelical missions have relied entirely on the orthodox language of the analogy of being to make the cross-cultural transfer.[18] Others have attempted to adopt the categories of myth for purposes of dialogue with Asian religions. Notto Thelle, writing in the journal *Japanese Religions*, has suggested that in Japan at least we might try holding the two kinds of language (personal and nonpersonal) in a balance.[19]

Biblical Personalism

First, we must recognize that the biblical picture of God is anthropomorphic. The biblical writers quite unselfconsciously speak of the high God as jealous, angry, repentant, pitying, loving, and the like. They freely attribute human personality traits to God. Of course they recognize that this one is the invisible transcendent mystery; nevertheless there is a direct conceptual correspondence between the anthropomorphic metaphors and the mystery which they describe that is not characteristic of the mythical symbolism of Asian religions. While God is understood to be "beyond personality," as C. S. Lewis aptly put it, he is related to his people after the analogy of historical-personal relationships.

According to our Christian understanding, we experience God in the context of our human community, and the analogy of our relationship to him is that of two people in social discourse. We begin from the concrete relationships of humans which transcend the sentient consciousness also characteristic of other life. In *personal* experience we are aware of our own selfhood, and we know and relate to others not just as "things," that is, not just as objects of desire or revulsion, but also as *subjects who share our self-awareness*. There is a mutuality of recognition in the personal relationship. In this sense God is understood as personal, i.e., one who confronts us in a moral-social relationship which we describe with words such as acceptance, respect, responsibility, and love.

To say, then, that God is personal means that in our experience of God there is a mutuality of personal recognition. We experience God as a "Thou" who knows us as persons, respects our individual self-identity, and holds us responsible in the context of a loving relationship. When we say that God is personal, we are recognizing that he is the ultimate source of our own personal self-awareness.

Speaking of Jesus in Asian Cultures

The personal language of biblical religion with its direct correspondence between the human metaphor and its unknown referent seems to the Asian religious mind to reduce God to the level of human personality and *self*-centered concern. The images and mythical nature symbols that one finds in Hinduism and Buddhism have a much more general and indirect correspondence to their mysterious referent. Human life is seen in the context of environing nature, and the conceptual images are those of cosmic mystery such as the mysterious power of life itself,[20] the triumph of light over darkness, and the benevolence or justice of the cosmic process (*karma*).

Further, personal and emotional categories are not clearly distinguished. The self is associated with the source of desire and thus of selfishness. Therefore a personal God is one with a human personality which is inevitably caught in the conflict of emotion and passion.

In such a cultural context perhaps the first and most seductive temptation is to interpret the historical Jesus as a mythical symbol of that ultimate reality which is identified with the nonpersonal. But if we do so, we pay a high price. Such a conversion of conceptual modes removes God from the

---

18. The fact that the orthodox tradition has felt comfortable with the less personal language of ontological metaphysics is revealing in itself. Has not our Western orthodox tradition with its emphasis on a metaphysical dualistic transcendence attempted to bridge the gap between divine and human with an "en*flesh*ment" and a *physical* death and resurrection rather than a personal confrontation in which transcendent love is revealed in the immanent historical process? And is this not precisely the theological root for the dissatisfaction of the "charismatic" movement within orthodoxy? The question, of course, for charismatics, especially the Pentecostals, is whether the concept of ecstatic inspiration is the highest expression of the personal experience of God.

19. See Thelle's article, "Doing Theology in a Buddhist Environment" (1983:49ff.). He refers to Keiji Nishitani who seems to associate the personal self with concepts of selfishness and wants to break out of personal categories to the selfless and self-emptying "non-differentiating love of God" expressed in impersonal categories. Thelle himself seems to equate concepts of transcendence with personal, and immanence with the impersonal. He suggests simply trying to hold the two sets of language, personal and impersonal, together in a more creative balance. "It is my conviction that they do not point toward two separate worlds or realities. If they are held together, they can enrich our understanding of God's presence" (p. 59).

20. By and large this power of life is represented by sexual symbols such as the phallic symbol for Siva mounted on the female *yoni*, and in cultic prostitution which has been practiced widely among the world's religions. This is sex as a physical, nonpersonal modality. By way of contrast, in the Bible God is related to us in a personal mode of parent and not in a sexual mode of power and fertility, whether that power is represented as male or female. God may be portrayed as pitying father, consoling mother, or offended husband, but never as copulating male or pregnant female. And clearly in the New Testament God's relation to Jesus as "Father" is in this nonsexual, personal mode.

sphere of moral-social relationships and relates him only to our cosmic environment as a symbol of benevolence. He loses his spiritual power to be present in the midst of his people as a living person. In a Buddhist context he may become another Bodhisatva with his own distinctive accent. Or in a Hindu context he may be an *Ishta-devi*, i.e., preferred god-symbol, but he loses his authority as the immediate personal Lord of life in whose presence our own identity and destiny are achieved.

In the article referred to earlier, Thelle also notes that while the church and its theology are a "stranger in the land" to the Japanese, many of them consider Jesus a "friend." If this is so, may not this interest in Jesus be the key to introducing the language of personal analogy and self-disclosure? Jesus as the self-disclosure of God is both immanent and personal, while at the same time he is the complete opposite of selfishness. In him we experience the presence of transcendent (completely unselfish) love which is the hallmark of the personal.

To say that Jesus is the self-revelation of God to us means that in him we have a disclosure of the ultimate nature of personal existence and a fully personal relationship. In his life of steadfast, consistent *agapē* we begin to understand that to be fully personal, even humanly so, does not mean to be the victim of human emotions and passions. Indeed, the Ultimate Person (God) completely transcends such personality characteristics in a fully personal relationship to people. Thus as the "image of the invisible God," Jesus is not only the revelation of a personal God, but he becomes for each of us the other in whose presence the nature of our own selfhood is disclosed.

In conclusion then, both in the interests of accurately presenting the unique biblical concept of "God in Christ" and to avoid a covert syncretism hidden under the apparent agreement in metaphysical and mystical language, it seems best to continue to use the personal-historical metaphors to speak of the deity of Christ. We must, however, give considerably more attention to explaining such metaphors adequately. At stake is not only a theoretical concept of God and Jesus' relation to him, but also our understanding of (1) the nature of human personhood and personal relationships and (2) the nature of our religious experience as a social relationship of God with people. In Christ we have the fully personal paradigm of God-in-relation to us.

Part Two

THE MISSION OF
JESUS, THE MESSIAH

Defining the Mission

Chapter 6

Introduction:
Prophet, Priest, and King

Traditional Protestant Approach

From Reformation times Protestant theology has discussed the work of Christ under the triple heading of prophet, priest, and king.[1] As prophet Jesus is the revelation of God, the Word. As priest he represents humankind to God, making atonement for sin; he is the mediator. As king he is our Lord, the one who has authority in our lives.

In the first two cases, of course, Jesus is viewed as fulfilling and surpassing the prophets and priesthood of Israel. He not only speaks God's Word; he is God's Word to us. He is not only officiating priest-mediator making sacrifice for sin; he is also the perfect offering for sin. In the case of his kingship he is viewed as our spiritual Lord.

According to Protestant theology the first two "offices" of Christ, as they are called, were the focus of his earthly ministry and death on the cross. Except for his continuing priestly intercession, they were fulfilled in his incarnation. But his kingship is generally treated in a different manner. As Calvin put it, Jesus' eternal kingship is "spiritual" in nature. Calvin quotes John 18:36 to mean that Christ's kingship was not of this world but pertains to the age to come, and it brings spiritual, not earthly, blessings.[2] It

---

1. Calvin is the one who introduced the *threefold office* into Protestant theological interpretation of Christ's work. Earlier theologians had recognized a twofold work (priest and king), and in some cases a third was implicit. But Calvin and the Geneva Confession are the source for the prevalence of the threefold concept in Protestant Orthodoxy (see Calvin, Bk. II, XV, 1960:494ff.).

2. Calvin's concern was to refute the idea of an earthly reign of glory either in this age in the church or in a future millennium. He rejected on the one hand the Roman Catholic concept of the church triumphant, and on the other hand the millenarians, whom he considered fanatics (Calvin, Bk. III, XV, 1960:3).

is generally held that his official kingship was kept secret during his earthly ministry. He was, as it were, the king in disguise. As its King and Creator he was in the world, but the world did not know him. He announced the kingdom of God, but the manifestation of that kingly rule lay in the future. It was not manifested in the ministry of Jesus.

In this manner Jesus' kingly office is retained for him in his divinity. According to traditional Lutheran doctrine his kingly office manifests itself in three forms of lordship: He is the eternal Creator-Sustainer of the world; he is the Lord-Redeemer of the church; and finally at the end of history he will be manifest as King over the world (Thielicke, 1977:422). All of these are, to use Calvin's category, spiritual and theological.

Each of these ways of describing Christ's role implies a model for—or at least an approach to—understanding the manner of our salvation. When Jesus is viewed primarily as prophet, his saving role is that of disclosing God's will and calling us to repentance. When viewed as priest, his atonement as a sacrifice and purification of sin is given priority. But Christ's kingly office has not been so directly associated with the salvation of individuals. Certainly the relation of kingship and sacrifice has been given little attention. Of course, the one who is King is none other than the Jesus who died as our Redeemer on the cross, but his earthly mission as Savior is priestly and prophetic in essence, not kingly (Melanchthon, 1965:12-13).[3] However, the emphasis on *Christus victor*, and deliverance from the slavery to sin and Hades clearly points to kingly activity.

In a similar fashion definitions of the work of Christ and the work of the church follow parallel patterns. Protestant church life focuses on the preaching and sacramental ministries of the church. In liberal Protestantism preaching has generally focused on the prophetic moral example of Jesus, while orthodox Protestants have emphasized theological aspects of the atoning work of Christ. Through its sacramental ministry the church plays the role of accepting counselor who helps us to find freedom from inhibiting weakness and fears so that our best selves can find fulfillment. Christ is presented as consoling priest and mediator to hear our confession and speak for us as advocate. For Protestants, of course, he plays this mediator role in heaven and is spiritually present in the sacraments of the church, while for Roman Catholics he provides this saving service more directly through the mediation of the church.

For reasons that are understandable in the context of historical developments, Protestants strictly limited Christ's kingship in the church to a spiritual and heavenly authority. Within medieval Catholicism his kingly authority in and through the church had been used to justify the political imperialism of the church. Protestants wished to reject explicitly such re-

ligious imperialism.[4]

There were also contemporary radical movements within the reformation which interpreted Christ's kingship as temporal and political, and called for violent revolution in his name.

But unfortunately, by merely limiting the kingship to the spiritual realms instead of redefining the essential nature of Christ's kingship as that of a suffering, earthly king, Protestant theology only restricted the cultural imperialism of the church as a religious organization. It did not define adequately the nature and scope of Christ's authentic authority in and through the church (Eph. 3:9-10).

Just as the kingly aspect of Christ's earthly mission was muted, so his effective lordship for our everyday life in the world was blunted. The perimeters of his ethical authority were restricted to the individual's private life, and then largely to the realm of intention.

Otto Weber argues that this threefold interpretation is necessary to guard against "one-sided" concepts of Christ's work for us, and thus our relation to him as Savior. If he is seen only as prophet, Christ becomes the teacher and we those who receive his new teaching. If the priestly office alone is emphasized, then "it is very easy for a passive inwardness to develop." We simply appropriate the sacrifical work he has done in our place and for us. If the work of Christ is seen one-sidely as lordship, then a new legalism tends to develop as we emphasize subordination and obedience to his rule (Weber, 1983:172ff).

Our point here is that in fact orthodox Protestantism's use of the threefold office to interpret Christ's soteriological work has not given a balanced picture. Rather, it focuses primarily on the priestly and secondarily on the prophetic; the kingly is assigned a spiritual and eschatological role which in actuality minimizes the impact and scope of his present lordship.

By way of contrast the Anabaptists emphasized the lordship of Christ. Menno called Christ our "true Emperor," and he admonished kings and rulers as well as common citizens to give him uncompromising obedience. Again and again he refers to him as "Prince of peace" who rules by love and the "sword of the Spirit." His throne is the cross, and his crown is made of thorns. And this cross, according to Marpeck, is the "universally hallowed

---

3. In this passage Melanchthon speaks of Christ as "second person" of the Trinity and emphasizes his present role as "preserving the office of preaching."

4. "Wherever this [spiritual, 'not earthly or carnal' aspect] is not acknowledged, talk about the kingship of Christ rapidly is transformed into the lordly claims of 'Christianity' to which Christians are supposed to commit themselves, and it is not very far from there to the view that we are the ones who must establish the lordship of 'Christianity' " (Weber, 1983:175).

cross . . . by which in the innocence of Christ all followers of Christ overcome . . ." (Klaassen, 1981:96). Thus the one who sheds his blood on the
altar of the cross is in fact none other than the priest-king who suffers as innocent martyr and calls us to follow him in bearing the cross of martyrdom
in faithful witness to his cause. His "spiritual kingship" is not merely an inner, "spiritualistic" authority but a call to faithful participation in his salvific
mission.[5]

We need to find theological categories which say clearly that the one
who was designated to be *lord* is the crucified Savior, and that until we
recognize him as Lord, he cannot save us either by his death or life. We find
reconciliation through the death of one whom we relate to as Lord.

New Testament Emphasis on Kingly Role

This shift of emphasis in Protestant theology is a most interesting
theological development in light of the fact that Jesus was introduced onto
the stage of history as one "born to be king" and he died on the cross under
the sign, "King of the Jews." The birth stories of both Luke and Matthew
present the newborn baby as the Messiah-Savior and Son of God, all of
which are kingly titles. Matthew says that the Magi inquired about the one
"born king of the Jews" (Matt. 2:2). The angels who announced his birth to
the shepherds called him "Christ the Lord" (Luke 2:11). Further, Jesus'
lineage is traced through the tribe of Judah and the house of David, not
Levi and Aaron.

Then when Jesus began his ministry he came announcing the "reign
of God" which was in sharp contrast to the scribal-priestly teaching. The
crowds who heard him and were fed by him tried to force him to become
their king (John 6:15). They did not mistake him for a priestly pretender.
And on his last visit to Jerusalem he entered the city as a king to the accla-
mation of the crowds as "Son of David" (cf. Luke 19:38; Mark 11:10; Matt.
21:5, 9).[6] He was accused by the Jewish leaders as a kingly pretender; and
when Pilate asked him if he was a king, his reply can certainly be taken as
tacit assent (John 18:33-37). The Jewish and Roman leaders crucified him
because they perceived him to be a real political threat to their interests. He
was not stoned as a heretical priest but crucified as a political pretender,
"King of the Jews." Were the leaders completely wrong in their perception
of him and his mission?

On the face of it it does not seem likely that all those who heard and
saw Jesus completely misunderstood him. The idea of kingship is inherent
in the very word Messiah. We fail to see this because we use the Greek
translation *Christos*, and this has come to be used as a synonym for *Savior*.
In the New Testament when Jesus is referred to as a prophet, it is as the

prophet-king after the Davidic typology. When the writer to the Hebrews speaks of him as priest, the prototype is Melchizedek the priest-king, and not the Aaronic priesthood (6:20). The full theological and ethical meaning of the crucifixion can be seen only if we understand clearly that here a king is dying in shame and disgrace. And in the resurrection this kingly one is raised to the "right hand of God"—the place of ultimate authority—to continue his mission of salvation on a universal scale (1 Cor. 15:24-25). The priestly metaphor is an explanatory device to help us understand one aspect of this king's death for his people.

The question then which needs to be answered is "What kind of a king was Jesus?" An answer to that question will help us to understand the nature of his mission and of the salvation which he offers. To see the kingship of Jesus in its proper perspective we must see it against the background of Jewish expectations. He did not fulfill these expectations, but he formed his own convictions in dialogue and tension with them. Jesus did not develop his understanding of his mission in the private study. His concept of the kingdom of God does not have the marks of a theoretical utopia. Neither did it come to him in a revealed blueprint, as the temptation story makes clear.

We will begin, therefore, with a reconstruction of the historical scene in order to sketch the picture of this new politics of the kingdom of God.[7]

5. Menno wrote, "These regenerated people [who are flesh of Christ's flesh and bone of His bone, the spiritual house of Israel] have a spiritual king over them who rules them by the unbroken sceptre of His mouth, namely, with His Holy Spirit and Word. . . .

"They are the children of peace who have beaten their swords into plowshares and their spears into pruning hooks, and know war no more. They give to Caesar the things that are Caesar's and to God the things that are God's.

"Their sword is the sword of the Spirit, which they wield in a good conscience through the Holy Ghost" (Wenger, 1956:94).

6. Each Gospel presents the entry as that of a king, but Matthew presents it as the fulfillment of the messianic prophecy of Zechariah (9:19) and Isaiah (62:11). He makes the crowd's acclaim explicitly the welcome of a king with the words, "Hosanna to the Son of David," and Luke follows this with the words, "Blessed be the King who comes. . . ." Both of these readings go beyond the more veiled language of Mark and indicate the church's clear and overt confession of Jesus' kingship.

7. Albrecht Ritschl (1822-89) was the first Protestant theologian of note to emphasize the kingly role of Christ. Instead of a threefold office he spoke of a twofold work, namely, "kingly Prophethood" and "kingly Priesthood." His emphasis was on the first. The vocation of the Christ as kingly-prophet was to reveal and establish the kingdom of God. He was the "bearer of God's moral lordship over men and Founder of the kingdom of God" (cited in Franks, 1962:621).

Ritschl rejected as "unbiblical" the orthodox Protestant view of Christ's death as a penal sacrifice to satisfy God's righteousness. Rather, he suggested that "the entire life of Jesus be seen in terms of his kingly Prophethood which has for its aim the manifestation and proclamation of the divine intention to forgive which is grounded in the very nature and purpose of God himself" (Mueller, 1969:91). As kingly prophet Jesus was the perfect revelation of God.

Ritschl viewed this kingly prophet's death as the result of his moral courage and willingness to pursue the goal of God's kingdom to the end with no compromise or disobedience of the Father. Ritschl wrote in his major theological work, *The Christian Doctrine of Justification and Reconciliation* (1966: Vol. III, pp. 483-84): "In so far as the speech and conduct and patience under suffering, which make up the life of Christ, arise out of His vocation to exercise the moral lordship of God and realize God's Kingdom, and are the perfect fulfillment of this vocation, even to the extent of His willingly and patiently enduring the pains of death, it follows from the relation of this purpose of Christ to the essential will of God, that Christ as the kingly Prophet is the perfect revelation of God . . ." (cited by Mueller, 1969:91-92; cf. Ritschl, 1972).

As Franks and others point out, Ritschl subordinated Jesus' kingly priesthood to the role of kingly prophet. Having rejected the ideas of satisfaction or equivalent penalty for our violation of God's law, he also rejected the idea of Christ's priestly role as propitiatory. Rather, he defined Christ's priestly role as simply a representational one. Jesus differs from other priests, however, in that he perfectly qualifies to be our priest by his unbroken communion with God and his unswerving loyalty and obedience unto death.

Ritschl's reinterpretation represents a major Protestant breakthrough in understanding the relevance of Christ's life and death for our life in the world. However, his use of the adjectival form "kingly" to modify prophet and priest really places primary emphasis on the prophetic role, not the kingly role. In the end we can only conclude that his Jesus is the great moral reformer who was kept on his ethical course by a unique religious God-consciousness.

As prophet Jesus both revealed and personified a new and higher moral standard—the new righteousness of the kingdom of God. As prophet the necessity of his death was only the moral necessity of faithfulness to his God in the exercise of his prophetic office. Thus his death is "for us" only in a secondary and representational way. This, at any rate, is the way Ritschlian thought was interpreted and applied in North America by theologians such as Walter Rauschenbusch (see Rauschenbusch, 1917: especially chap. XIV, "The Initiator of the Kingdom of God").

Our present formulation differs from Ritschl's by making the kingship-lordship of Jesus the primary soteriological category. He was a prophet-*king* (like David) and a priest-*king* (like Melchizedek). That is, he exercised a prophetic and priestly role as king. The question is, therefore, the nature of his kingship over us and for us. Our point is that Christ saves us by exercising God's style of kingship. He is the manifestation of God's presence among us in authority and power for our salvation. To be precise, his death and resurrection are the manifestation of God's way of being "for us."

Chapter 7

What Kind of King Was Jesus?

Jewish Expectations

Jesus' Introduction to Public Life

Although Jesus was destined to be a king, he was not born into public prominence. He was born in an obscure home of a carpenter-mason as a private person not likely destined to public ministry. True, there were reports of heavenly portents at his birth, but these remained private indicators. They did not serve to project him onto the public stage, and apparently those of his own village did not see "messianic material" in him. They were the ones that he had the most trouble convincing.

Neither did Jesus come up through the political or military ranks to gain public attention. Nor was he accredited by the recognized educational authorities. The rabbis scorned his authority as a teacher, and the politicians thought of him as a revolutionary and potential rebel. Rather he was introduced by a popular prophet who had dared to criticize the king and call the religious leaders snakes. John the Baptist, who introduced him, was a prophetic maverick whose charismatic authority attracted and impressed the crowds.

John came preaching the imminent judgment and salvation of Israel. "The axe is laid to the root of the trees," he announced (Matt. 3:10). Such preaching raised the question about the coming of Messiah (Luke 3:15). The crowds who went to hear him wondered whether John himself might be the Christ, but he said that he was not. However, he said that the Christ was already on the scene and would be made manifest through his own ministry. According to John's Gospel, the Baptist also used the titles "Son of God" and "Lamb of God" in introducing Christ. The term Son of God, as we have seen, is simply another title for Messiah. The title Lamb of God adds the concept of savior, a concept which was already implicit in the idea of a messiah-king. Lamb of God probably associated the Christ with the Exodus Passover lamb in the minds of the people, and it suggested that he would lead the nation in a new exodus (See John 1:19ff.).

So Jesus was introduced to public life as a messiah-savior by an ascetic, charismatic preacher of judgment who was living in the wilderness. All this understandably led to the idea that here, coming from among the people, was a revolutionary savior of oppressed Israel (see Mary's song in Luke 1:46-55).

When Jesus began his ministry with the announcement that the kingdom of God was about to arrive, it quite naturally strengthened this impression. Jesus clearly identified himself with the hopes and fears of the oppressed masses, and he announced that the kingdom of God belonged to them (Luke 6:20f.). When we remember that it is the poor—the dispossessed—who always constitute a threat to oppressive dictatorial governments like Rome, we begin to understand the implications of such a message. In fact, the lower Jewish clergy and the poor masses gave support to the resistance movement that opposed Rome in the name of loyalty to God and the Law of Moses. We might note parenthetically that many of this class joined the postresurrection Christian movement in Palestine.

Palestine in Jesus' day was a country under military occupation, and in a tightly controlled, martial-law society crowds of people always pose a political danger. In this situation Jesus attracted crowds of people, and he spoke to them about a kingdom. Indeed, John tells us that after the feeding of the five thousand, the crowds wanted to force Jesus to accept a crown (John 6:15).

In addition to this, Jesus had at least one known Zealot among his disciples (Luke 6:15), and probably both Peter and Judas were also associated to some extent with the Zealot movement that offered armed guerilla resistance to Rome. This, of course, raised the suspicion of the Jewish and Roman leaders that Jesus might lead an insurrection against Rome, as it also raised the hopes of the common people. Certainly Judas entertained this hope to the end. In order to force Jesus to betray his sympathies with the Zealots or else explicitly denounce them, the Jewish leaders raised the question about paying taxes to Rome. This issue lay at the heart of Zealotism. In this situation Jesus gave an ambiguous answer, but one that could well be interpreted as agreement with the resistance fighters. Further, he critized the religious aristocracy and the rich who collaborated with Rome, and he even went so far as to drive the money changers out of the temple. All of this unavoidably gave the impression that Jesus was a political as well as a religious leader, and we may conclude that Jesus himself did not entirely reject the political image, although he drastically changed its content.[1]

The Warrior-Martyr Messiah

Many of the more nationalistic-minded people among the Jews clung to the hope that a savior-messiah like the Maccabean leaders of an earlier era would arise to lead an armed revolt against the oppression of Rome. The Maccabean leaders were warrior-kings who had delivered their fellow Jews from the pagan oppression and the desecration of the temple by the Syrian ruler Antiochus Ephiphanes about 165 B.C. After that time, following the example of Judas Maccabees, other Jewish patriots had arisen as messianic pretenders to lead revolts against Rome. For example, Judas of Galilee had led such an insurrection in about A.D. 6, and although his attempt failed, his followers, called Zealots, continued an underground resistance movement. As we have noted, the people seem to have taken for granted that John the Baptist and Jesus were a part of this anti-Roman resistance movement.

We must remember that religion and politics were not separated in this resistance movement. Resistance to Rome was in the name of God and in devotion to the law. The ideal of theocracy (God's rule) lay at the heart of the Zealot movement. God alone was to be Israel's king. In the second part of Zechariah's prophecy (Zech. 9-14) we have a forthright espousal of this ideal. The time will come, says Zechariah, when God will be king over all the earth and peace will prevail—the sword will be banished. But according to Zechariah this will be brought about by the military victory of Israel over its enemies under the leadership of Judah:

> On that day I will make the clans of Judah like a brazier in woodland, like a torch blazing among sheaves of corn. They shall devour all the nations round them, right and left, while the people of Jerusalem remain safe in their city . . . On that day the very weakest of them shall be like David, and the line of David like God, like the angel of the LORD going before them (Zech. 12:6-8, NEB).

This victorious redemption will also mean judgment and purgation of Israel so that it may truly be God's people under a new covenant. Jerusalem and the temple will be exalted. God's covenant with the nations will be annulled, and all nations will come up to Jerusalem to worship under the

---

1. Oscar Cullmann (1956) and S. G. F. Brandon (1967) develop the New Testament evidence for this view of Jesus. The latter carries the argument for Jesus' identification with the Zealot cause much further than most scholars feel is justifiable, but it points up the obvious similarity.

covenant made with Israel. And Zechariah adds the threat that those who do not come faithfully to the temple will suffer drought from the hand of God.

Only after Israel's victory God "shall banish chariots from Ephraim and war-horses from Jerusalem." Then the daughter of Jerusalem will see her king "coming to [her], his cause won, his victory gained, humble and mounted on an ass, on a foal, the young of a she-ass" (Zech. 9:9-10, NEB). This is the passage that Matthew sees as fulfilled in Jesus' entry into Jerusalem riding on the donkey's colt (Matt. 21:4-5), but how different is the context of fulfillment than what one would have expected from the prophecy itself.[2]

In summary the Jewish model of messianic salvation was as follows: (1) The kingdom of God was understood as a political theocracy, and God's people were identified with a particular nation, the Jews. (2) Salvation meant deliverance of this nation both politically and religiously so that they might serve God under a new covenant. (3) The messiah-savior figure was somewhat ambiguous. On the one hand he was the warrior-martyr king who would lead the armed resistance and win independence for Israel. On the other hand he was identified with the redeemed Israel through whom God would judge and save the rest of the nations. In short, this is an imperialistic model of salvation by conquest, and in either case the Messiah wins the victory through the armed might of Yahweh.

This background context is important as we consider the mission of Jesus, the Messiah, because it gives us the immediate context in which both he and his disciples who wrote the New Testament worked and thought. The warrior-martyr model of the Maccabeans continued to be the heroic model for Israel's salvation all through the first century A.D., and the Zealots continued their resistance until they were finally completely destroyed and scattered after the uprising in A.D. 135. This final revolt was led by a messianic pretender, Barkochba. There is also some evidence that the Jewish Christians who lived in Palestine continued to espouse this model of messianic salvation by simply applying it to the resurrected Jesus whom they expected to return shortly in glory to deliver Israel.

Reinterpretation of Messianic Mission

Jesus' Rejection of the Warrior-Martyr Model

Jesus' struggle with the warrior-martyr model is clearly represented in the New Testament accounts as a temptation that recurs throughout his ministry. We first meet it in the temptation in the wilderness at the beginning of his ministry. We see it again after the feeding of the five thousand when the crowds wanted to make him king and again in the Garden of

Gethsemane where he rejected the possibility of using force.

A variety of interpretations have been given to the temptations which Jesus faced immediately following his baptism and anointing as the Messiah, but most agree that they are messianic in import. The temptation to make stones into bread reflects the expectation that the kingdom of the Messiah would be a time of abundance in which the wants of all were fully satisfied. Like Moses gave Israel manna to eat, so the new Moses could be expected to provide abundance of food. The temptation to jump from the Temple heights seems to suggest the apocalyptic expectation that the Messiah would suddenly appear as the Son of Man from heaven. The third temptation—which almost all commentators agree is messianic—to worship the tempter himself offers an alternative way to messianic domination of the world. As Cullmann suggests, this is a temptation to use violent resistance to establish a world theocracy (Cullmann, 1956:9). If the worship of Satan and world theocracy seem to be a blatant contradiction which could not have been a temptation to Jesus, only reflect a moment on how many times since then the church has resorted to violence to further the cause of God's kingdom.

Jesus' rejection of these temptations, his refusal to accept a kingly crown from the masses, and his refusal to "call twelve legions of angels" or to accept Peter's Maccabean-like attempt to defend him in the Garden of Gethsemane with the expectation that God would intervene are clear rejections of the Maccabean-Zealot way of messianic salvation. Rather, Jesus adopted the alternative model of the suffering servant portrayed by the prophet Isaiah. We must now turn our attention to this new concept of Jesus' mission which gave rise to the church as a separate reality from Israel.

Announcing the Kingdom of God

According to the synoptic Gospels Jesus' clearly announced mission was to introduce a new era in the reign of God on earth. Mark says that Jesus came as a prophetic preacher announcing the arrival of the rule of God (Mark 1:14-15). Matthew says that he went throughout Galilee announcing the good news of the kingdom of God and healing all kinds of diseases (Matt. 4:23-25).

The announcement that the rule of God has arrived can hardly be understood to be a *de novo* introduction of God's kingship. The word for new in this case is *kainē*, which means new in kind. Jesus is introducing a

---

2. In contrast to Zechariah Jesus said that the messianic nation was to find its model in Isaiah's "suffering servant." Israel will be scattered and Jerusalem destroyed. Further, he said, the kingdom covenant will be taken from Israel and given to another, and that worship of God will not center in Jerusalem or Mount Gerizim. And, finally, he taught that God sends sunshine and rain on the just and unjust alike.

new state, step, or era, namely, the messianic era which the Jews understood to be the fulfillment of the prophetic promise that the "day of the Lord" and a "new age" would come when Israel would be given a new covenant and would live under God's direct authority (cf. Jer. 31:31-34).

Most of Jesus' teaching focuses on this reign of God. His parables deal with it almost entirely. The collected sayings of Matthew and Luke, which we know as the Sermon on the Mount or Sermon on the Plain, are expositions of its nature and requirements. His ministry of healing, forgiving, casting out evil powers by God's holy loving power are the demonstration of its presence and effect in the world. Matthew points to Jesus' healing ministry as part of his vicarious suffering in our behalf (Matt. 8:17). We should also note that his ministry of forgiveness is part of this inauguration of the kingdom of God. His *salvation* activity as the Messiah was already begun in his earthly ministry. We need not wait for his death on the cross to begin to speak of salvation or the saving work of Christ.

The Mission of Jesus and the Kingdom of God—Alternative Models

This much most Christians recognize and affirm as they read the accounts of Jesus' earthly ministry in the Gospels. But what happened to this vision and the initial reality of the kingdom of God as it was present in Jesus? The Jewish nation obviously rejected it as their understanding of the rule of God. And what about Jesus' death by execution on a cross? How does the cross fit into this understanding of the messianic mission? Are we to conclude that the initial rejection of Jesus' vision of God's kingdom and his own messianic mission in effect calls for a revision of our understanding of the rule of God among people, and therefore of Jesus' messianic mission as well? Most traditional Protestant interpretations imply this when they equate the kingdom with the "invisible church."[3]

At the risk of oversimplifying, we may note three alternatives for understanding Jesus' intention when he announced the arrival of God's rule. First, the rule of God is a spiritual and heavenly reality for which there is no temporal-social counterpart now in the world. Jesus himself was the visible embodiment of the rule of God while on earth, but when he ended his earthly existence and returned to "the Father's right hand" he took the authority with him. That is, the kingdom became a spiritual rule with no earthly visible counterpart. On earth the rule of God remains hidden and a matter of faith. It can be realized at present only as an inward spiritual authority for the individual in the midst of the continuing human rule on earth. The church is the representative of this spiritual kingdom and calls people to salvation which will be realized in heaven.

This was the alternative chosen by traditional Protestant theology. In reaction to millennialism with its definition of the kingdom as a physical reign of Christ on earth prior to the consummation, on the one hand, and to the political glorification of the church on the other, both Lutheranism and Calvinism sharpened the distinction between the spiritual and political realms. While Calvin gave relatively more emphasis to the actual renewal of the Spirit in the life of individuals and expected God's law to be enforced by Christians in political positions, he kept the two kingdoms strictly separated. That which belongs distinctly to the kingdom of Christ is inward and spiritual and does not affect one's social or political situation. For example, he interprets Galatians 3:28 and Colossians 3:11 to mean that spiritual freedom is possible in any social condition. "... the Kingdom of Christ does not at all consist in these things [racial, sexual, economic, social conditions]" (Calvin, 1960:1486).

For both Calvin and Melanchthon the church is the locus of the spiritual kingdom of Christ, but this is the church without political prerogatives or social mandate. Indeed, the church as a social institution is not identified with the "spiritual and inward Kingdom." It is the spiritual or invisible church of faith that represents the presence of Christ's kingdom.[4] Melanchthon wrote that the "spiritual eternal kingdom of *Christ* commences on earth in the Christian Church through the divine word, Spirit, and faith, and it lasts hereafter eternally" (Melanchthon, 1965:278-79).

The second alternative is a variation of the first in that it accepts the interpretation of the kingdom as only a spiritual reality in this present time. It holds that Jesus did indeed offer a literal social-political kingdom to the Jewish nation. The millennialist variant holds that the offer was for a future kingdom, and the dispensationalists hold that it was a present offer, but that the offer was withdrawn when the Jews refused and crucified him. The withdrawal of the offer is only temporary however. The social-political rule of Christ will be reintroduced in the future as a literal historical reality. In any case we must be satisfied with a salvation that gives us peace of mind through Christ's atonement and forgiveness of sins in the midst of human

---

3. Medieval Roman Catholic theology chose this option. The kingdom was understood as a spiritual reality of which the church is the earthly religious counterpart. According to this model the kingdom remains in some sense visible on earth, and the rule of God is exercised in both the spiritual (religious) and temporal (secular) rule of the church. Emphasis on the visibility of the kingdom is clearly in continuity with the New Testament teaching. However, the problem, which modern Catholicism to some extent recognizes, arose when the church in effect became one of the "kingdoms of this world" and attempted to exercise God's rule as a rule of political power. Along with this perversion of temporal authority the "spiritual" realities were expressed in sacramental ceremonies rather than in personal-social relationships which should define the church as the people under Christ's lordship.

4. Calvin's comments are to be found in many places in his *Institutes of the Christian Religion* (1960; see, for example, II,15:3; III,3:19; III,20:42; IV,5:17; IV,20:1-2).

violence and injustice (cf. "The Scofield Synthesis" in Kraus, 1958:127ff.).

A third possibility exists, namely that Jesus meant literally to introduce, that is, announce and inaugurate, the beginning of the new rule of God as a socio-spiritual pattern and that he appointed his followers to continue this mission.[5] Here we must be precise in our statement of his commission. He did not tell his disciples to *complete* what he had begun but to continue the initial phase until God inaugurates the final stage of fulfillment. The kingdom continues to exist in the world just as it was manifested in Jesus' ministry. The Holy Spirit continues to be present and working in and through the disciples. This interpretation would suggest that the rule or kingdom of God is among us as a social-spiritual possibility to be announced and inaugurated following the style of Jesus' own life, death, and resurrection.

Perhaps we should pause here to point out that the "kingdom of God," the "salvation of God," and the "peace of God" are synonyms in the Bible. Insofar as the questions which we have raised above might imply a dichotomy between kingdom and salvation, they are themselves problematic and help to cause confusion in understanding the role of Christ. When Jesus announced that the kingdom of God was at hand, he was understood to be saying that the day of God's salvation had dawned. That was the good news to which people were to reorient their lives. Thus in no sense should kingdom of God and personal salvation be contrasted with each other. This continues to be true of the language of the New Testament epistles. To be personally saved is to come under the rule or lordship of Christ, or as it is said in Colossians, to be brought into "the kingdom of [God's] dear Son" (1:13).[6] Insofar as one is saved, or in the process of being saved, one is a citizen of the kingdom of God and under the rule of his covenant.

When Jesus began to announce the kingdom of God, it must have sounded much the same as the old prophetic promise of the "day of the Lord." Both before and after the resurrection it raised the old question of *when* the kingdom would be restored to Israel. This was clearly implicit in John the Baptist's question to Jesus whether he was truly the Messiah (Luke 7:20 ff.). Even after the resurrection the question was raised by the apostles (Acts 1:6). But it finally became clear that Jesus had something quite new and different in mind. In short, the kingdom he announced was not a restoration of national political power to the Jews. From the outset he rejected the equation of the kingdom of God with a nationalistic theocracy based upon Israel's political restoration and military independence. But he did indeed announce a kingdom!

This is a crucial point, and it has often been misunderstood by the church. Indeed, only a few centuries after Christ's crucifixion and resurrection the church returned almost entirely to the old model of imperialistic conquest for its missionary activity as though Jesus intended the church to establish a religious empire.

The misunderstanding grows out of the fact that Jesus did not simply substitute a spiritual and future concept of the kingdom of God for the political one expected by the Jews. Pilate seems to have been one of the first to misunderstand Jesus in this way, and on that account he would have freed Jesus from crucifixion. This is not surprising, given his background in the Graeco-Roman world of mystery religions and Gnostic philosophy. We must take seriously the fact that neither the crowds who heard him, nor his disciples, nor yet the Jewish leaders understood Jesus to be saying that the kingdom of God is a spiritual, heavenly reality only. To them it was quite clear that he meant a political, social order among humankind under God's covenant. But what kind of order? That is the question. His was a radically new concept of politics and law.[7]

What is the nature of this kingdom or salvation of God? And how is the kingdom or rule of Christ related to the cross? These are the questions we must now pursue as we try to understand the mission of the Messiah.

God's Kingdom and the Cross

In a number of places the New Testament writers say that it was necessary for the Christ to suffer rejection and to die (cf. Mark 8:31). These writers represent Jesus himself as clearly holding this view. Is this necessity to be understood merely as the inevitability of his rejection as Messiah by a politically entrenched, compromising hierarchy? Or is some deeper moral necessity involved in the inauguration of God's salvation? The latter seems to be the case. According to the New Testament the cross is an inherent necessity in the coming of the kingdom of God. How are we to understand this?

---

5. I have developed this implication at more length in *The Authentic Witness* (Kraus, 1978:140ff.).

6. Some would make a clear distinction between "kingdom of heaven," "kingdom of God," and "kingdom of Christ," but the distinction already indicates an interpretation of Christ's mission which tends to distinguish it from the cosmic purpose of God in a way that is biblically inadmissible.

7. The word politics comes from the Greek word for city *polis*, which refers to the art of structuring and regulating human social relationships. Law defines the basis for and the way in which the social order is to be governed. In this generic sense of the word Jesus offers an alternative politics and not a religious system defining life in a spiritual world. Such a politics is spelled out in Romans 12:9-14; 13:8-14 (verses 1-7 give the context and relation to secular governments which the new politics requires) and in Galatians 3:26-28; 5:13—6:5 (see Yoder, 1972).

The Rule of Agapē

The answer lies in the fact that the kingdom of God is the rule of agapē—that kind of love demonstrated in Jesus Christ. Therefore the nature of the love which Jesus taught and demonstrated as the new law of the kingdom is central for understanding both the character of the new thing which he introduced and the way in which he brought it to reality. If the mission of Jesus was to inaugurate the kingdom of God as the power and rule of love, how shall he do it? What is the mystery of agapē which demands that he "must suffer many things and so enter into his glory" (Luke 24:26)?

The overwhelming impression left on the apostles by Jesus' life and death was that God is a God of love and that in Jesus God had reached out to the world in love to reconcile all humankind to himself (2 Cor. 5:19). This is clearly the word of John 3:16. God's sending of his Son, the Messiah, was an act of love; and to enter into the qualitatively new life which he offers, one must put complete confidence in this Son who is the paradigm of God's love. According to Peter, Jesus is our supreme example of suffering love (1 Pet. 2:21-24; 13:8-10). Love is the highest gift of the Spirit of Christ (1 Cor. 13; Eph. 5:22f.).

The Nature of Agapē

But what is this agapē, this new love which can unlock the secret of Christ's mission of salvation? John wrote to Christians at the end of the first century that the command to love was not a new command in the sense of having recently been introduced, but it was new in the sense that Christ had made it true in their experience (1 John 2:7-8, NEB). In this connection we should note that the command to love God with one's whole being and the neighbor as oneself was not new with Jesus. It was, in fact, given by him as the summary of the law and the prophets (Matt. 22:37-40). What is new in Jesus is the radical application of this law to all of life in such a way that it actually fulfills the law's intention.

Matthew quotes Jesus as having said that the new righteousness of love must go beyond the righteousness of the Mosaic Law as the scribes and teachers of Judaism understood it (Matt. 5:20). And we may certainly infer from this that it surpasses the ordinary righteousness of all human systems of justice.[8] These systems at their best can be stated in the negative form of the "silver rule": "Do not do unto others what you do not want them to do to you." Jesus gave the "golden rule": "Do unto others what you want them to do to you."

Thus agapē requires not only that we refrain from returning evil for evil; it requires that we return good for evil. It requires not only that we do not insist on a just equivalent ("an eye for an eye") for ourselves but that we forgive "seventy times seven." As Paul put it, "Love never gives up!" Love requires me to take the initiative to be reconciled to one who harbors hurt feelings or a grudge even when my intentions have been misunderstood. Or again in the words of Jesus, we are to love our *enemies* and pray for those who misuse us. Further, we are to be servants of others; and just as God does not show partiality in his love but sends blessings on friend and foe alike, so those who would live under his rule of *shalom* are to be complete or impartial in their service of love (Matt. 5:43-48). This is the higher righteousness of God's kingdom that we are to seek first (Matt. 6:33).

In summary we can say several things about the nature of this kingdom *agapē*. First, it is *universal in scope and without favoritism in its application*. This is an important difference from human concepts of love. The gods of the various nations all favored their own people, and in turn each blood family was expected to favor its own members. This was even the understanding of many of Jesus' and Paul's Jewish compatriots.[9] Paul reproved his fellow Jews for mistaking God's patience with them for favoritism and approval (Rom. 2:4).

Second, love is *nonimperialistic. It does not force itself on the other person*. On the other hand, love never gives up or becomes indifferent to the other person. It expresses itself as *grace*—encouraging, prodding, correcting, reproving, and warning in a spirit of acceptance.

Third, also as grace love *takes unilateral action* which bears the full risk of suffering rebuff and rejection. In this way it accepts the responsibility for the wrongdoing of others and suffers the consequences of their action.

Last, *agapē* transcends human justice and finally cannot be understood in terms of a just or equivalent penalty. This is perhaps the most difficult aspect for us to accept, but Jesus seems clearly to have taught that we should not demand or expect a just equivalent in the kingdom of God, and

---

8. In his essay, "The Sermon on the Mount and the Justice of the State" (1960), Bultmann points out that the antitheses of the Sermon on the Mount do not mean that the "demand of God," which is *agapē*, stands in contradiction to the "demand of justice" as it was understood by the Old Testament prophets. "Justice," he wrote, "has a legitimate meaning when it stands in the service of the demand of love, or, in practical terms, when it serves the community" (p. 204).

He explains, "Now Jesus speaks in a situation in which it has become clear that the law, whose fulfillment the prophets had demanded as obedience to the will of God, can be fulfilled without a man's actually being obedient, i.e., that one can fulfill the commandment in a formal way without really submitting to God's will. Jesus' demands arise out of the knowledge that one cannot fulfill the will of God up to a certain point, but rather that God demands the whole man. In this sense he sets his, 'But I say to you' over against the ordinances of justice" (Bultmann, 1960:203).

9. Esdras said that the creation itself was for Israel's sake, and all the rest of the nations were "nothing" and as "spittle" in God's eyes (2 Esdras 6:55-56).

that, indeed, God does not operate by those rules (cf. Matt. 20:1-16). (In this way it fulfills the Law of Moses.)

The Righteousness of Agapē

Does this mean that God indulges our sin and turns a deaf ear to the distress of those who suffer injustice? If not, and the answer certainly is "no," how are we to understand the justice or holiness of God's love?

While God does not act according to human rules of penal justice, he does not condone, indulge, or compromise with evil and injustice. God's justice is incomprehensibly more profound than human justice. God's wrath is incomparably more opposed to evil than the moral indignation of the highest human virtue. His love confronts and condemns evil, and it refuses to cooperate in either its methods or selfish ends. This confronting, correcting love, which refuses to return evil for evil, we call God's holiness.

Precisely this kind of confrontation led Jesus to the cross. Jesus is thus the decisive paradigm for understanding God's justice in contrast to human legal justice, giving significance to John's words that God is "faithful and just, and will forgive our sins" (1 John 1:9).

This new righteousness of love, or we might call it a "politics of love," was not put forward as a utopian ideal but as a creative possibility for human society under God's new covenant offered in Christ. It was intended as an alternative for the old power politics of law and order. It fulfilled and superseded the old legal requirements of codified law in the sense that love requires that one go beyond obedience to the legal precept and actually seek the good of the other person. In the new order, relationships are not governed by legal prescriptions which define the limits of self-serving action but by positive good will which seeks the common good.

In this sense Paul says that "Christ is the end of the law . . ." (Rom. 10:4). This is not, of course, in the sense that one is free from the law's true intent (Rom. 8:3-4) but from reliance upon legal definitions and obedience as the means of establishing relationship to God and our fellow humans.[10] In this sense the law was a "custodian until Christ came" (Gal. 3:24). Now we have the new possibility of living in the spirit of Christ (vv. 26-27) as children of God where the old limits and hindrances to relationship are overcome by love (v. 28).

Jesus made it his messianic calling to live by this new standard of love in full obedience to God. That was his mission. Only in this way could a new beginning in human history actually be initiated. Jesus did not come only to provide a means of forgiveness for past sins. Neither did he come merely to teach a new higher moral ideal by which the injustices in the world system might be mitigated.[11] Or, to use Bultmann's phrasing, he did not simply supersede the relativities of law with the absolute demand of God to live each moment under the existential demand of love.[12] He came actually to inaugurate a new beginning. The final purpose of God in Christ was not to give a precise and perfect standard for human systems of justice, or simply to stimulate humans to new heights of trust and greater efforts to achieve the righteousness of love, but rather to *create a new order of relationships in keeping with his own nature and will to love*.

Jesus, the King of Love

So in answer to the question, "What kind of a king was Jesus?" we must say that his kingship was characterized by the authority of love. Taking the righteousness of love as God's way of dealing with hostility and sin, Jesus accepted the Isaianic suffering servant as the model for the messianic mission. Jesus' power and authority were the power and authority of love,

---

10. Again, Bultmann, who has seriously wrestled with this problem in the European Protestant context, has a good word on this. In "Christ the End of the Law" (1955) he wrote: "That means, then, that he is the end of a life, which, sustained by the need for recognition . . . seeks to establish its own righteousness. Christ is the end of the law as the end of sin, self-glorifying, and reliance on the flesh: he is the end of the law as the way of salvation; he is the means of access to the way of salvation through grace for the true believer, that is for the man who gives up his own righteousness and surrenders himself completely to the God who leads man from death into life" (p. 54). Elsewhere in the essay Bultmann seems to recognize that Paul affirmed the new possibility of true holiness (p. 61), but he remains extremely vague in giving it any ethical content. The new possibility remains for Bultmann an existential relationship of absolute trust in God which gives us freedom from the anxious urge to acquire credit and recognition in God's sight.

11. In this sense Reinhold Niebuhr in *An Interpretation of Christian Ethics* (1935) was certainly correct. Jesus did not give us a new prudential standard of justice. "Surely," he wrote of the Sermon on the Mount, "this is not an ethic which can give us specific guidance in the detailed problems of social morality where the relative claims of family, community, class, and nation must be constantly weighed. One is almost inclined to agree with Karl Barth that his ethic 'is not applicable to the problems of contemporary society nor yet to any conceivable society' " (p. 51).

And as a corrective to liberal Christianity's interpretation of Christ as the ideal man, the moral prophet whose teachings and life we can emulate "once the persuasive charm of his life has captivated (our) souls," we can only agree with and applaud Niebuhr's attempt to describe the radicalness of *agapē*. But again, has he not gone too far when he calls the law of love "an impossible possibility" (Niebuhr, 1935:117) and relegates it to the category of an absolute that can only provide an out-of-reach ideal that will agitate our conscience? We must find our social ethical guidance in the more immediate and relevant law of justice according to this view.

12. In his *Theology of the New Testament*, (Vol. I, 1951) Bultmann asks, "What positively is the will of God? The demand of love" (p. 18). Bultmann lays great stress upon the absoluteness of this demand: "Rather, these imperatives are clearly meant radically as absolute demand with a validity independent of the temporal situation" (p. 20). But he insists that one cannot historicize this absolute. It has only an existential and eschatological application. Existentially "only he is ready for this salvation who in the concrete moment decides for that demand of God which confronts him in the person of his neighbor' (p. 21). Thus concretely it is a radically individual and personal ethical demand. Eschatologically it does not allow for any ethical social approximation or aim at individual character formation (p. 19).

not the authority of law or physical might which are the basis of human political organization. He did not see his mission as reforming the old system, that is, establishing a legal system of human justice. He came to start a new movement—a movement which did not have its origins in earthly social systems (Luke 4:18; John 18:36). In the true sense of the words he was a *radical martyr* bearing witness to the new order of God's love to be established now. His conflict with the religious establishment came at those points where it hindered and opposed the initiation of the new order. For example, Jesus would not argue the scribal interpretation of the law; rather he pointed to the law's true intention and sharply criticized attempts to evade or defeat that intention.

Thus Jesus' authority lay in his power to demonstrate the reality of the new order of salvation. He challenged the old religious authority by his salvific actions such as healing on the Sabbath and forgiving sins; he appealed to the power of God at work in his ministry as the basis of his authority (Matt. 12:28). When John the Baptist lay in prison tortured by doubt and sent to know whether he truly was the Messiah, Jesus answered by telling John what he was doing in God's name (Matt. 11:4-6). When he was asked by what authority he could give a new interpretation of the Law of Moses or pronounce the temple of Jerusalem open to all nations, he appealed to creation itself (Matt. 19:4-9) or to the prophetic word in Israel's own history. Thus he identified himself with the direct work and word of God. But in no case did he resort to a threat of violence. He did not threaten the people with God's punitive power which, like Elijah of old, he might have commanded. Neither did he use his own power latent in his popularity with the crowds to justify his actions.

Rather, as he saw with prophetic vision what would be the consequences of Israel's stubborn rejection of God's love, Jesus wept over Jerusalem, calling the city to repentance so that such judgment might be averted. And his words from the cross were, "Father, forgive them, for they do not know what they are doing." As John sums it up, "God did not send his Son to judge the world but to save it" (John 3:17).

This authority of love is the power of life in contrast to the power of death which human governments exercise. It is the power of *intrinsic* goodness in contrast to *legislated* goodness. Jesus' authority was that of one who challenges the injustice of social systems by simply obeying the authority of a higher law intrinsic in creation itself. He refused to recognize the right of the unjust system or to fear its power of death. And as is quite evident throughout history, this is the ultimate challenge to any human system based upon the threat of death because it is precisely this kind of radical affirmation of life against which physical death has no ultimate sanction.

Chapter 8

The Cross as Theodicy: Why Jesus Had to Die

We have noted the New Testament references to the necessity of the Messiah's rejection and death, and our first clue to why it was necessary was the nature of God's *agapē* (Chap. 7). We must now pursue this question of the necessity further.

From the human perspective Jesus' radical challenge to the sociopolitical system seems to be an adequate explanation for the inevitability of his execution by the religious and political authorities. His kind of goodness and power threatened the only order of society in which they could believe. All the accounts agree that the authorities *would not* believe on him. They repudiated his authority by attributing it to Satan. Thus they blasphemed the Spirit of God which was the true source of Jesus' power. Their final judgment was that either he must die or the nation would be destroyed. Thus, from the human side we have an answer to our question why Jesus had to die.

Sin, as Reinhold Niebuhr once put it, is deicidal.[1] Humankind, individually or corporately, cannot tolerate God's goodness because it does not conform to human legal and moral codes. Human beings do not trust the integrity of God's love; and they cannot believe that the righteousness of love can bring liberation to the sinful human order. The cross, as Paul observed, is a stumbling block to Jews and foolishness to Greeks (1 Cor. 1:23).

However, the question of the divine mystery persists, and it can now be stated. Why was it necessary for God to submit himself to this hostile,

---

1. This idea was also expressed earlier by P. T. Forsyth, the British theologian who said, "Sin is the death of God. Die sin must or God" (1917:146).

evil situation in order to save humankind? The question has two closely related facets: (1) Assuming the biblical picture of creation, why should God
concern himself further with rebellious, hostile creatures who refuse to acknowledge his goodness and doubt his intentions? A quick answer that it is
God's nature to be gracious fails to deal with the moral dilemma of evil in a
universe created by a wholly good God as the Bible depicts him. (2) Assuming that God is gracious to forgive our sins, why must he take the way of the
cross? Why must Jesus die for us? Why was it not possible for God to answer
Jesus' prayer for deliverance in the Garden of Gethsemane?

Theodicy a Primary Theological Motif of the Cross

Orthodox theologians since the Reformation, following the lead of St.
Anselm (1033-1109), usually concentrated on the second of the two above
questions. Calvin held that the necessity of an incarnation is not "simple
and absolute" but stems only from God's decree of salvation, and the
"decrees of God" themselves are not open to question. The necessity lay in
humankind's inability to "ascend to God" or to provide a mediator from the
human side (Calvin, Bk. II, xii, 1, 1960:464). Thus also in Calvin and succeeding orthodoxy the focus is upon the question how the cross saves us
from our sins.

Later Protestant theologians, assuming this necessity of grace, pressed
the explanation further to say that God is both just and gracious, therefore
his justice must be satisfied before he can show his grace in forgiving sin.
However, his grace shows its ultimate precedence over his justice in that
God absorbs the just penalty of our sins himself through the punishment of
his own Son on the cross. In effect God pays our debt to his own justice. The
ultimate manifestation of his grace is that he transcends his own law
without disavowing it.

As we shall note later, while this is a serious attempt to deal with the
morality of forgiveness, it makes the mistake of defining morality in terms
of legal justice. Here, however, the point is that it ignores the even more
profound and prior problem of theodicy, that is, the moral justification of
God as Creator and Lawgiver. What ethical right has God who created a
world in which evil exists and in which sin is an inevitable concomitant of
existence to establish a law of perfect justice by which to judge his creatures? In his book comparing the Judaeo-Christian and the Japanese traditions entitled *Mount Fuji and Mount Sinai* (1984) Koyama writes that the
problem of the integrity of the Christian God was already raised for the
Japanese by the preaching of Xavier and his missionaries in the sixteenth
century. It was raised in two settings. The God whom the missionaries said
was all loving and all powerful allowed natural evil to destroy the innocent.

And more painful yet he allowed ancestors who had never had the chance to hear the gospel to suffer in an eternal hell.[2]

This is the primary problem to which the crucifixion of Christ speaks. The ethical justification of God's forgiveness must be understood in the light of the definition and vindication of his holiness in creation. Thus we will begin by asking how the cross is a vindication of God's holiness in creation.

Patterns of Theodicy

Judaism—Law

One of the most difficult questions posed by the biblical view of God and creation is the question of evil and humankind's sin. What is the origin of evil? On the one hand, the biblical view is that God is wholly good and all that he created was good. But we also see evil and suffering in the world. Further, the biblical view seems to be that God created everything from nothing, that is, God is the only power ultimately responsible for what now exists.[3] If that is so, then God must also be ultimately responsible for the evil that exists.

Both Jewish and Christian thinkers have wrestled with this knotty question through the centuries. If God is all powerful and wholly good, how can he be the creator of a world in which there is sin and evil without being ultimately responsible for its evil? And how can we put our faith in a God who has created such a world of suffering, sin, and punishment?[4]

Of course no one claims to have fully resolved the mystery of this dilemma, but in Judaism and Christianity we see two different approaches to

---

2. Koyama says that Xavier thought he had given the Japanese a satisfactory answer, but he continues, "I doubt it. Japanese people were then, and now, not interested in the discussion about 'all have the knowledge of the divine law of nature.' The question is about the 'integrity' of this great God who decided to keep the prison of hell irrevocably shut for eternity" (Koyama, 1984:170).

3. The doctrine of creation *ex nihilo* is not a philosophical explanation of the origin of the universe but rather an affirmation of God's ultimate sovereignty. The most careful statement of this concept is found in Hebrews 11:3 which says simply that "*by faith* we understand that the worlds were made out of that which does not appear."

4. This question is not raised by dualistic systems which posit an eternal conflict between good and evil. Buddhism gives an agnostic answer and simply calls for individuals to overcome desire which is the source of suffering in themselves. Hinduism resolves it with the doctrine of *karma* or fate which in the ultimate cycle of rebirths will bring reality to its final conclusion. Neoplatonism sought to deal with it by positing a number of emanations from the original perfect source. That is, the ultimate perfect source of being gave rise to a series of lesser principles or demiurges, and one of these is the immediate creator of the world in which both good and evil appear. The form and force of the question as we are considering it is peculiar to Judaism and Christianity—the two religions that accept the world view of the Bible. *The Problem of Suffering in the Religions of the World* by John Bowker is a recent (1970) study of this age-old problem.

its solution. The rabbinic tradition tended to justify God's ways with the human race by means of *law*, and the Christian tradition by means of *grace*. These are not completely different or contradictory ways, but a fundamental and significant difference exists between them. And since Judaism is the historical, cultural parent of Christianity and provided the context in which its original views were formed, a comparison of the two can help us understand the meaning of the Christian answer.

Both Judaism and Christianity hold that there is a moral as well as natural or physical order of creation and that this order reveals the Creator's original intention and design for human life. But where does one see this original creation order manifested? The patterns in nature itself are ambiguous and have been read many ways. Indeed, most of the world's religions reflect different ways of understanding nature.

Rabbinic Judaism held that the fundamental order of creation is definitively revealed in the Law given through Moses. *Elohim*, the God of creation, is the same God as *El Shaddai* who covenanted with Abraham and *Yahweh*, the covenant God of Moses. This same God spoke the Ten Words of law on Sinai. Thus the *dabar Yahweh* spoken at Sinai is the identical word of creation. Indeed, the rabbis could say with some poetic license that Torah was God's agent in creation. The Law of Moses, therefore, is not an addition to the creation order, but the very explication of it. *It defines God's righteousness in creation.*

In this manner *law*, and specifically the Law of Moses, was given authoritative precedence over creation to define justice and to regulate human behavior.[5] The law justifies God's action with humankind in history. It provides the principles of judgment by which God will judge the world. One can appeal to no higher principle or authority in order to explain the enigmas of human history.

The Jewish theodicy, then, says that God is justified by his law which he has revealed to humankind.[6] God, by virtue of being Creator, has the right to define the nature of moral goodness, and he has done this in the Law given to Moses. In a social order where the king by virtue of his power defined justice, this kind of assumption could easily be accepted. After all, following the analogy of kingship, God, the true King of heaven, was so far exalted above human kingship that human beings had no ground or right to question him. The only approach to the mystery is through examination of the law of the covenant, which, as the Psalmist wrote, is "perfect" (Ps. 119). God's law is the definition of justice, and God is justified by the perfection of his law.

Further, God has graciously informed all humankind of his law and given them every chance to live in obedience under his beneficent covenant. But every human being has perversely and wickedly rebelled against God's law. Still God offers forgiveness to all who will repent and live according to his law. In addition he uses the suffering which results from human sin to induce repentance and to purify those who have repented. Thus God is doubly justified in rejecting and punishing those who will not repent, even though it is the greater part of humankind. God's grace is shown in rewarding the righteous who have kept his law and have been refined like gold in the fire of suffering.

New Testament—the Cross

The writers of the New Testament came to a different conclusion when they substituted the authority of Jesus for that of Moses. According to the Gospels Jesus reversed the Jewish order of priorities in defining the moral order of human relationships. According to the Gospel of Matthew he appealed to the original intention of God in creation as a precedent for interpreting and applying the Law of Moses. When the scribes argued that Moses had allowed a man to divorce his wife, Jesus countered with, "From the beginning it was not so" (Matt. 19:3-9). On this question about a basic human social relationship Jesus dared to say that there is a law of personal moral relationships implicit in creation which human systems of law, even the Law of Moses, only bear witness to but do not ultimately define. This same reversal of authority from law to creation is also implied in Jesus' saying, "The sabbath was made for man, not man for the sabbath" (Mark 2:27).

Following this lead, Christians rejected law as the final justification of either humankind or God. In its place they put the revelation given through Jesus Christ. According to Hebrews 1:1-4 Jesus was God's Son through whom the decisive word has been spoken. All past revelation through the prophets, including that of Moses, has been surpassed. Again, Paul said that the law was neither God's first nor last word but that it had been introduced into the scheme of things as a kind of educative device preparing humankind for the disclosure of God's final word in Christ (see Gal. 3:19ff.; Rom. 3:21-22). The Johannine approach was to identify the Word of creation with the Word revealed in Christ (John 1:1-14). God's very nature is disclosed in the *Logos* of creation that gives life and light to all humankind; and this *Logos* became embodied in Jesus the Christ. In him God's true

---

5. In rabbinic literature the law and wisdom are personified as agents of God in creation. The Christian comparison to this is John 1:1-14 where the *Logos* or Word spoken in Jesus is the personification of God's righteousness.

6. Second Esdras, written about A.D. 100 by a Jewish author, wrestles with this question and makes a case for justification, both of God and humankind by law. See especially Esdras chapter 7.

God's last word is love not law - Seems much of "orthodoxy" again turned it around + made God's last word law + not love ↘justice

152

THE MISSION OF JESUS: Defining the Mission

glory shines, and that glory is at its highest radiance in the cross (see John 13:31-32). Thus while the law bears witness to God's nature and intention, it does not ultimately define it. God's first and last word is love and not law, and this word was spoken with climactic forcefulness in the life, death, and resurrection of Jesus Christ.

The Christian approach, then, attempts to understand and justify the way of God with the human race by pointing to his love which is most fully displayed in the life and death of Jesus (Rom. 8:31-39). This does not resolve all the mystery, but we are asked to put our trust in God who does not stand aloof from us in our suffering but who rather takes upon himself responsibility for our hostility, identifies with us in our suffering, and overcomes sin and death for us.

The answer which this approach gives to the question why God involves himself in the sin and suffering of humankind is that God is love. Even as God fully shares our humanity in death, his death is a judgment upon our sin because it was caused by our sin. The cross, which is both the symbol of our execution of God and of God's self-sacrifice, is itself love's judgment on sin and revelation of God's way of overcoming evil. The crucifixion shows us the true character of sin and the righteous love of God in dealing with it, namely, not by violent punishment but by self-sacrifice.

Creation itself is a work of love, and only the full disclosure and victory of love over sin and death can justify God in his creation of humankind. The cross is the highest manifestation of God's kind of love—the love that is at work in creation, and as Paul wrote in Romans 5:8, somehow in the cross itself as a "proof of [God's] love" (NEB) he is justified in his dealings with humankind.[7]

Thus the final justification of God is not manifested in the last judgment which punishes lawlessness with violent retribution and rewards righteousness, but in the resurrection which overcomes the consequences of sin. The new movement of thought in the New Testament is not from cross to final judgment, although traces of this remain in its apocalyptic portions, but from the cross to resurrection and to the final defeat of death and the powers that hold humankind in bondage because of sin (1 Cor. 15:20-28; Col. 1:18-20; Rom. 11:32-33). Judgment is not denied, but the judgment is given into the hands of the Christ who is Savior of the world (Rom. 8:31-34; Rev. 5).

This new approach is not fully developed in the New Testament writings. It emerges like many other explosive, powerful new ideas that point to the possibility of God's kingdom coming on earth as it is in heaven, and it beckons us toward the future with the Spirit of Christ as our guide. This approach does not resolve all of the vexing questions about the final outcome of individual sinners, and that seems to be a major problem for many who feel strongly the need to rationalize and justify a particular "Christian" morality or find some satisfactory resolution to the problem of injustice suffered by individuals. For such people a God whose love is defined within the limits of justice or is "balanced by his justice" seems more comprehensible and consistent with moral law.

Esdras and the Jewish-Christian Synthesis

To such people who think of God as ultimately a just lawgiver and judge, the idea that God is justified by his involvement and suffering with his creatures in a process of redemption is far from self-evident. Esdras, a pious, deeply concerned Jewish writer who lived about A.D. 100, developed the Jewish view of God as just lawgiver and attempted to justify God according to the Law of Moses. His apocalyptic visions in which the angel of God explained God's judgments were much appreciated by some Christians of the period, and they clearly influenced Christian thinking about this question. Esdras came to the conclusion that it is precisely God's law which must be justified, and therefore painful and obscure as it may be, we must judge that God is most fully vindicated in condemning the greater part of humankind to torment because they have knowingly despised his law. Indeed, the angel told him: "When the Most High was creating the world and Adam and his descendants, he first of all planned the judgement and what goes with it" (2 Esdras 7:70, NEB).

> He [angel] said to me: "You are not a better judge than God, nor wiser than the Most High. Better that many now living should be lost, than that the law God has set before them should be despised! God has given clear instructions for all men when they come into this world, telling them how to attain life and how to escape punishment. But the ungodly have refused to obey him; they have set up their own empty ideas, and planned deceit and wickedness; they have even denied the existence of the Most High and have not acknowledged his ways. They have rejected his law and refused his promises, have neither put faith in his decrees nor done what he commands. Therefore, Ezra, emptiness for the empty, fullness for the full!" (2 Esdras 7:19-25, NEB).

This same Esdras prophesied about a future Messiah for the Jews, but he saw no reason why he would have to suffer for his people. How then could Christians have been so impressed with the writings of Esdras that they translated them and even wrote several introductory chapters for them? Quite simply they identified Esdras' Messiah who was yet to come as

---

7. The whole passage, Romans 5:11-16, follows this line of argument.

a heavenly warrior and judge (2 Esdras 7:13-32) with Jesus who would return in a second advent as warrior and judge.

This joining of Jewish apocalyptic with its view of final judgment and the emerging new understanding of God's salvation in the cross and resurrection became fairly standard in Christian theology. One finds this basic solution of cross *and* final vengeance in major theologians like Augustine (fifth century), whose theology endorsed the Constantinian synthesis of Christendom and justified violence even in the cause of the church where judgment and punishment of heretics was required, and of John Calvin (sixteenth century) who justified the same kind of violent punishment for heretics.

But we must take careful note of the change that occurs in the reasoning when these two conceptions are joined in this fashion. By identifying Jesus who died on the cross with the Messiah of Esdras in a final act of vindication and judgment they circumscribed God's love disclosed in the cross by God's punitive justice as his final word. According to this understanding the cross justifies God in his punitive judgment of most of humankind by demonstrating the divine lengths to which he has gone to save them. He has far superseded the demands of justice in his offer of salvation.

Nevertheless according to this formulation, the cross justifies the law of God in a fashion not much beyond the argument of Esdras. Love meets and supersedes the demands of retributive justice which remains the moral norm for God's action. It does not transcend the justice of *lex talionis* as a moral norm.

To see the significance of this for discipleship we must keep in mind that on the social-political level this is the formulation of a Constantinian synthesis of the crucified Christ and Caesar, of cross and sword. It exalts the love of God as paradoxically and infinitely above justice simply by an infinite (and illogical) extension of love. Justice remains the rational standard. And since human systems cannot achieve the infinite solution of love, they remain justified in operating within the rational limits of punitive justice. Christians too exercise their Christian callings (discipleship) within these limits but with the recognition that it is not the ultimate solution. Therefore, they seek ways to restrain the harshness of justice with love in the faith that God's infinite love will finally balance the scales of justice.

Let us briefly follow this line of historical development before we attempt to formulate an alternative.

Anselm and Classical Protestantism

Saint Anselm of Canterbury undoubtedly has had the most pervasive influence on orthodox theories of Christ's atonement up to the present time.

He formulated his theory in the context of the medieval society wherein vassals owed their lords honor and obedience; and in turn the lords owed them protection. God, Anselm said, who is the infinite Lord deserves *perfect* loyalty, obedience, and honor, but humankind has fallen far into debt on all counts. Because God is infinitely perfect he cannot simply cancel what is owed to himself. He must have proper "satisfaction."[8] Since humankind owes the debt, God sent his Son to become human and to live a perfect life of obedience. Thus Christ first fulfilled his own individual human obligation; and then in humankind's place he bore the undeserved punishment of death. Of course if Jesus were only a human individual his life and death would redeem only one other individual. But because he was also God his life and death have infinite merit to pay the debts of the whole human race. An equivalent payment has satisfied God's demands, and he is free to forgive with honor. This was Anselm's answer to the question, "Why the God-Man?"

Anselm's immediate concern was to preserve the honor or holiness of God's love. For Anselm love and justice are in tension with each other, and this tension must be resolved within the being of God himself. God is *both* loving *and* just, and he must maintain his moral honor when he exercises his forgiving love. He must satisfy the moral demands of his own nature.

This theory, sometimes called the satisfaction or objective theory, became the basis for Reformation and post-Reformation restatements of the atonement theory in a more juridical form. These seventeenth-century theologians pictured God in the metaphor of a just-yet-merciful judge rather than an honorable-yet-kind lord.[9]

With this shift in metaphor Protestant orthodoxy returned to the basic assumptions of Esdras. Indeed, many of the same kinds of issues with which Esdras wrestled are raised in the writings of John Calvin and the Reformed theologians who followed him. Their atonement theory assumed that God's law as revealed through Moses is the standard of justice for God himself. Further, they defined justice to mean punitive justice, that is, giving equivalent violent punishment for violence committed. Therefore God must mete out violent punishment in order to satisfy his own nature. However, because God is also ultimate love he cannot be satisfied within himself to act merely as a just judge and executioner. He longs to forgive and be reconciled. He must by his own nature also be Redeemer. Therefore

---

8. The idea of satisfaction first arose out of the early church's requirement of a token of the penitent's sincerity. The satisfaction required was in proportion to the seriousness of the sin. Later it came to mean the "temporal punishment" due to sin which must be met even though the eternal consequences had been canceled.

9. In his chapter 16, "The Demand for Justice," H. D. McDonald traces this emphasis from Martin Luther to A. A. Hodge (1985:181-195).

his love must find an adequate way to satisfy his justice.

This formulation of the atonement theory goes far beyond the direct statements of the Bible itself in explaining the rationale of atonement. Only when "bearing sin" or "becoming sin for us" are interpreted as taking our legal punishment, an interpretation which is by no means evident, can such a theory be extracted from Scripture.

For Protestant orthodoxy, then, the problem of the vindication of God becomes the problem of vindicating the legal justice of his love. Mercy and love must not be defined in such a way as to undercut the demands of justice when God forgives the guilty criminal. Thus orthodoxy holds that Christ was punished in our place as the "Greatest Criminal." To remain morally righteous in his forgiveness God himself fully satisfied the demands of his own justice. He paid the legal penalty for disobedience required by his own just law. He did this by sending his Son, who is himself deity, to bear the violent punishment, namely, death, for our sins. Because Jesus has paid the full penalty God is morally free to act in grace and mercy toward us. This theory, therefore, is usually called the penal substitutionary theory.

Again, according to this theory the cross demonstrates God's love paying the legal demands of the law's punitive justice. Thus again love is circumscribed by justice.

This attempt to vindicate God through an objective atonement wrestles with a real moral problem, but by simply equating the categories of holiness and justice it reduces God's holiness or goodness to legal categories. But, as we have noted, law does not define God's holiness. It only defines human justice. At best it bears witness to God's holiness. The moral holiness of God's love transcends law and justice. Thus if we want to grasp the astonishing newness of the love of God disclosed in Jesus, we must find a better way to understand the holiness of God's love than is suggested in these theological approaches.

The Cross as Symbol of Solidarity

Consummation of Incarnation

The cross has become the special event and symbol of God's solidarity with us in our sinful existence and his atoning love for humankind. But we must understand that the cross is the consummation of the incarnation itself. The Apostles' Creed sums up the incarnation with the words "born," "suffered," "dead and buried," and this clearly follows the lead of Paul in his letter to the Philippians (2:5-11). The cross as a discrete act or event cannot be separated from the whole of Jesus' life as though it contained a separate meaning in and of itself. Rather it is an integral, completing part of the whole revelatory incarnation event. *Thus to be precise we should say that God is justified by an incarnation which finds its consummation in the cross, and not by a legal transaction which took place on a cross.*

The incarnation, and especially the cross, indicates God's solidarity with us even in our sinfulness. The biblical writers do not hesitate to interpret the significance of Jesus' life in this way. In Romans 8:3 Paul wrote that God's Son came "in the likeness of sinful flesh" in order to condemn sin in the flesh. In Galatians 4:4-5 he says that Jesus was "born under the law" in order to redeem those under the law. In a number of other similar statements, for example, 2 Corinthians 5:21, Jesus was "made . . . to be sin who knew no sin"; and Hebrews 2:14-18 says that he "partook of the same nature," i.e., flesh and blood, "that through death he might destroy him who has the power of death." Such statements indicate clearly the nature of God's identification with us in our sinful condition. Jesus, who was called Immanuel, was "God with us" even unto death.

Such an act of solidarity tells us that God accepts fully his responsibility for creation. He is not a cynical or insincere Creator who created human beings vulnerable to evil and death and then placed sole responsibility on them when they failed. He did not abandon them to destruction in resentment or indifference. Rather God is a patient and loving Creator who continues to complete what he has begun. Or again, he is not a God who arbitrarily makes laws for his creatures which have no basis in his own nature. Indeed, he calls upon his creatures to be holy *as he himself is holy.* He has accepted his own responsibility for the creation which he made "out of nothing," and he continues to sustain and "save," or recreate it even in its perversity.

Cross and Resurrection the Creative Pattern

This kind of incarnation reveals that God is still at work creating humans in his image. The traditional picture of a fully completed creation at the end of six days followed by a time of rest for God and of testing for humans is an oversimplification, as both the writings of John and Paul indicate. God has never ceased his work of creation. Indeed, the incarnation of Jesus itself has always been understood as a special creative act; and Paul does not hesitate to speak of the continuing work of God's Spirit as a "new creation" (2 Cor. 5:17).

Jesus clearly indicated that his own work was a disclosure of the nature of God's ongoing work (John 5:17-24). Thus the incarnation also shows us how God is at work, namely in the way Jesus himself was at work. *The way of compassionate, life-giving service is the way of creating humankind in God's image.*

Finally, we must remember that the ultimate outcome of Jesus' death on the cross is resurrection. The incarnation culminating in the cross and resurrection reveals to us the way in which God is at work finishing his creation. In the face of human failure and evil it is the process of vicarious death and resurrection. It is a process in which the freedom of humans is fully respected and yet not allowed ultimately to defeat the original intention of God. And as we noted above, it is a process of re-creation, that is, of re-forming the deviant and restoring that which has been prostituted by sin. It is not a process of discarding the imperfect and beginning each time *de novo*. Even the original creation of Genesis 1:1-2 suggests a process of the Spirit of God working with darkness and chaos to bring light and cosmos. God, as Paul put it, is now in the process of recreating humankind into the image of Jesus Christ who is the perfected image of God.

To know that God is still at work in the process of creation postpones the question of his final vindication to the completion of his work. And our attention shifts in the present from a legal justification to the resurrection as the guarantee of a final successful outcome. The resurrection is evidence that God's love will triumph over the darkness and chaos to complete his creation. Thus Paul appealed to the God who raised Jesus from the dead in justification of his gospel.

Here too we must speak of the Holy Spirit who is also called the guarantor of our salvation now in process (2 Cor. 5:5; Gal. 5:5). The connection between the Holy Spirit and the resurrection is made quite explicit in Romans 8:11 where Paul speaks of the Spirit that dwells in us as "the Spirit of him who raised Jesus from the dead." The new life which the Spirit gives to those who are "in Christ" is also called the firstfruits or down payment of the completed redemption of creation (v. 23). Thus the final recreation or reunification in Christ (Eph. 1:10) and the vindication of God are coincidental and future.

In the present the Spirit's indwelling power to bring life out of death, reconciliation in the midst of hostility, and joy even in travail and futility are the *arabon* or guarantee of God's self-vindication. Christ's cross and resurrection and the Spirit's enabling presence in the lives of those who own the risen Christ as Lord are indicators or signs of God's righteousness and faithfulness to forgive sin. We are saved in hope.

Chapter 9

theory metaphor -	God	Humanity
legal	Righteous Judge -	criminal
Moral	Divine Legislator	law breaker
Political	King who rescues	fallen into slavery
Personal Familial	Parent - Father	child

Love and Sin: Why the Way of the Cross?

Abelard and the Personal Metaphor

We have come now to the second question which we raised in the introduction of chapter 8: Why must God take the way of the cross and resurrection to reconcile and recreate his creatures?

We have seen how legal and moral metaphors predominate in atonement theories. According to the legal metaphor God is the Righteous Judge, and the sinner is a criminal against the laws of the universe. In the moral theories God is the Divine Legislator giving a just law, and the sinners have dishonored God in their willful transgression of his law. A third, less frequent metaphor pictures God as a king who rescues subjects who have fallen into slavery under a foreign power through their foolish rebellion against him.

The legal and moral metaphors, as we have seen, clearly lead to the idea that an equivalent payment for sin is necessary before God is morally free to forgive sinners. The kingly metaphor, which seldom if ever appeared alone in theological statements, is not so clearly ethical in its orientation. In this metaphor a payment of ransom is made to the enemy who holds humankind captive. Or the rescue is simply the outcome of the king's victory over his enemies.

Another metaphor drawn from human experience is frequently used in the Bible, but it has not been given prominence in the theological discussions of the atonement. This is the parent-child metaphor. In fact, this metaphor and the kingly one are related since in the ancient societies the king was the father of his nation. The lack of the parental metaphor's use was probably due to the Western bias that associates morality and law. But

Is it interesting that for 1,000 years Xtans lived without a theory to explain this?

if we consider that morality is based fundamentally on the nature of personal relationships, then the most intimate and responsible personal relationships surely become the best context for interpreting God's relation to humankind.

The best-known individual attempt to use the personal metaphor was that of Peter Abelard (1079-1142). Abelard rejected both the idea of ransom and the moral necessity of a legal equivalent to satisfy God's justice and used a personal analogy of God as the eternal loving Father. The cross, he said, is merely the manifestation in time of the reality eternally present in God.

Abelard's objection to the idea that God accepted the death of his own Son as a penalty for sin and was placated by it seems warranted. To think of Christ's death as satisfying a legal requirement which changed God's response to sin and the sinner beginning in about A.D. 30 calls for a moral change in his nature that is highly problematic. God has not changed from a morally indulgent to a morally responsible judge, but, as Paul wrote, Christ has shown what the true nature of God's righteousness has always been. The problem had been that the nature of his righteousness was seriously misunderstood by both Jew and Gentile, thus limiting the effect of God's saving acts in human experience.[1]

God didn't change — we just didn't get what God's nature really was

However, Abelard's conception of God as an eternally loving Father did not adequately deal with the righteousness of God's love; and he did not explain how God's forgiveness is grounded in his own righteous parental love as it was disclosed in Christ. Rather, he made the genuineness and perseverance of humankind's responding love the moral basis for receiving forgiveness.

Searching for "Objectivity" in a Personal Metaphor

In the foregoing discussion I have attempted to show how the life, death, and resurrection of Jesus manifest the inner moral consistency of God's love in creation and redemption. When we deny the adequacy of the so-called objective legal metaphor to explain the vicarious element in Christ's passion and death, we need not simply ground forgiveness upon the responding love of humans (Abelard) or upon an existential human decision (Bultmann). God's forgiveness is by grace, but grace is not an ethically ambivalent indulgence. God fully accepted the ultimate ethical responsibility for his creatures' sinful behavior as was demonstrated in Christ's life and death; God demonstrated his power to accomplish his original purpose in creation when he raised Christ from the dead. Thus God's forgiveness is grounded in his own righteous, all-powerful love, and not simply conditioned upon a genuine ethical repentance. As John wrote,

Salvation not up to us

"He is faithful and *just* and will forgive our sins and cleanse us from all unrighteousness" (1 John 1:9).

Parent-Child Analogy

The true nature of genuinely moral responses is best seen in our most intimate human relationships; this is why the parent-child metaphor has potential for illuminating God's way with his children. Thus perhaps our best approach to the subject is to give several examples from experience before making a more formal analysis of the experience of ethical pardon.

New Testament scholars generally agree that Jesus' special name for God was the Aramaic *Abba*. This is significant, as Kittel points out, because the use of this term "far surpasses any possibilities of intimacy assumed in Judaism, introducing 'indeed something which is wholly new" (Kittel, 1964:72).[2] Following Jesus' example the early church also used this familial designation for God, who was known as "Father of our Lord Jesus Christ" and "our Father." Thus, however we explain what Jesus did on the cross to reconcile us to God, we must remember that he and we are dealing with our true *Father*.

In light of this it seems somewhat strange that so little use has been made of the parent-child metaphor to illuminate the relation of God to his erring, alienated children. If we follow this New Testament precedent and

---

1. The crux passage to this effect is Romans 3:21-26. Paul begins by stating that God's righteousness "has been manifested" in Christ apart from law. This sets the context for the following explanation. In verses 25-26 he explains that up to the present God has not dealt with humankind strictly according to the Mosaic Law. Thus his leniency in overlooking sins according to the law might appear to be indulgence. Now the true nature of his eternal righteousness has been disclosed in Christ. This is a "faith-righteousness," not "law-righteousness," and to this kind of righteousness there can be no exceptions. Nor, one might add, have there ever been exceptions to it. From the beginning God has required a *faith* relationship. Thus these verses do not necessarily teach a change in God's manner of dealing with sin but rather a clarification of his action which changes the subjective situation of humankind.

2. This point was developed by Joachim Jeremias in *The Lord's Prayer* (1964:17ff.), and Ferdinand Hahn also discusses it in *The Worship of the Early Church* (1973:21f.). Jeremias writes: "*Abba* and *imma* are thus the first sounds which the child stammers. *Abba* was an everyday word, a homely family word, a secular word, the tender filial address to a father: 'Dear father.' No Jew would have dared to address God in this manner. Jesus did it always in all his prayers which are handed down to us, with one single exception, the cry from the cross: 'My God, my God, why hast thou forsaken me?' Jesus thus spoke with God as a son would with his father, simply, intimately, securely, filial in manner. But his invocation of God as *Abba* is not to be understood merely psychologically, as a step forward in a growing apprehension of God. Rather we learn from Matthew 11:27 that Jesus himself viewed this filial form of address for God as the heart of that revelation which had been granted him by the Father. In this term *abba* the ultimate mystery of his mission and his authority is expressed. He, to whom the Father had granted full knowledge of God, had the messianic prerogative of addressing him with the familiar address of a son . . ." (1964:19-20).

attempt to understand the work of Christ as the expression of a loving father who is deeply offended at the rebellion, alienation, and foolish hurtfulness of his children, we immediately find ourselves in a setting of profoundly ethical dimensions.

In the case of moral delinquency within the family we applaud the responsible resolution of offenses that result in reconciliation and the maintenance of the family unity. We do not expect families to deal with internal moral problems on a legal basis. In fact, in such cases we consider a legal solution, even if just according to the law, a lower rather than a higher solution. For example, in a marriage the offended innocent partner who bears the brunt of moral infidelity and forgives the repentant partner is highly respected. But, of course, such an action goes beyond the legal definitions of justice and, in fact, cannot establish a legal precedent. The ethically right action is not in this case established or defined by the law.

Four Examples

Consider and compare the following four examples of parental responses to their children's serious moral and legal offenses. In his book, *Too Late the Phalarope* (1953), Alan Paton tells the story of the seduction of a young, married, white police officer. The setting is in South Africa, and the scandal is heightened by the fact that the woman is a black. Paton draws a poignant picture of the old, morally inflexible father's response to his son's indiscretion. He disowns the son, then goes into his house, locks the door, and pulls down all the blinds. He leaves his son to pay the full legal penalty which he himself fully approves.

Our second example comes from an incident in which an irresponsible teenage son caused an automobile accident by his drunken reckless driving. In the accident several young people met a fiery death, but the boy who caused it was unhurt. In this case the father, a wealthy, influential lawyer, responded by using his money and legal skills to help his son evade the legal consequences of his deed. Perhaps the father considered the futility and negative consequences of subjecting his son to prison for many years and thus justified his action.

In a third example, traditionally quite common in Japanese society of the past, the father suffers the social disgrace and is expected to take upon himself responsibility for his child's crime.[3] In an attempt to atone for the errant behavior of his son the father might even commit suicide to show his profound disapproval and shame. Thus he offers a sincere apology which could be accepted as the basis for forgiveness.

Our last example is a case where the child's offense was an act of rebellion both against the family and the neighbors. A young man and one of his friends stole money from his family; then they stole more money and a car from the neighbor and ran away from home. When the young man was arrested in another province, the parents would not press charges, but he was tried and sentenced to prison for the theft from the neighbor. Not only did the parents suffer the disgrace of social disapproval, they also were themselves profoundly offended at what their son had done. However, they remained open to forgive and continued their attempts to reconcile and rehabilitate the child, and they allowed him to keep the money he had stolen from them.

The first two examples represent attempts to resolve a moral-personal crisis by defining it in only legal terms; however, the fathers made opposite responses. While we may recognize that the action of the first parents represents a more ethically justified response than the indulgence of the second, we are also agonizingly aware of the moral tragedy in the first father's legally justified rejection of his son. The last two examples depict the inner pain and shame borne by those who have been betrayed and offended by the actions of one for whom they have natural responsibility. While we cannot recognize suicide as a "saving" solution to the problem, we cannot but respect the father's moral sensibility and his acceptance of responsibility in solidarity with his offending son.

In the last example the parents reached out both to the offending child and to those who with themselves had borne the brunt of the offense. They disapproved of their son's immoral action and accepted its social-legal consequences without rejecting their son. They recognized their own continuing responsibility and solidarity with their child even in his moral blunder and alienation, and all our deepest moral instincts tell us that they are fully justified in doing so. *The acceptance of responsibility in solidarity with the offender and the "vicarious" suffering of the moral shame of the offense are in fact recognized as a moral ground for forgiveness on the part of parents.*[4]

Following this analogy, God as Parent has declared solidarity with us through his human embodiment in Jesus. He has fully identified with us in our human situation and borne the consequences of our fault (sin). He has accepted both the shame and guilt of our offenses, and without condoning

---

3. For example, as late as 1983 when a Japanese young man who was a student in Europe killed a Dutch girl in a fit of passion, his father in Japan resigned his job because of the disgrace.

4. Solidarity is a word quite commonly used in the social sciences to describe the social unity or togetherness of groups in their pursuit of their goals. It means to join or stand in sympathy and participation with.

The New Testament word which approximates this concept is *koinōnia.* This word is translated with a variety of English words such as participation, fellowship, in common with. I am using solidarity as a general synonym for *koinōnia,* for example, "Christ's solidarity with us," or "our solidarity with and in Christ."

or excusing our fault he has taken upon himself the responsibility to nullify our guilt as defined by the law and to reconcile us to himself. Thus he has made possible a new moral beginning beyond the alienation of shame and the burden of guilt.

The moral vindication of God as Father-Creator, which includes a vindication of his justice in forgiving our sins, is a more basic and profound problem than we can define within the prescriptions of legal justice. The *genuineness* and *integrity* of God's love must be vindicated, and its *power* to overcome sin and death must be demonstrated. The objective proof of the atonement is to be found, therefore, in the power of the cross and resurrection actually to bring reconciliation and newness of life, and not in satisfying legal justice. This is the gospel of the cross which Paul boldly proclaimed to the ancient world as "the power of God for salvation" even though by human standards of power and justice it was a "stumbling block" and "foolishness" (Rom. 1:16; 1 Cor. 1:18ff.; Eph. 2:11-14).

We have already seen that God's final solution to evil and sin is love *(agapē)* and not justice as it is understood in human legal systems *(dikē)*. And we have examined the nature and moral quality of that love. Now we are in a position to explore further the mystery of the divine necessity that moved God to intervene in humanity's sin and suffering and to consider why Jesus chose the way of the cross in order to accomplish his messianic mission.

We have seen that the cross-resurrection is the vindication of God's holy love. Now we must examine love's response to human fear and rebellion. In brief we can say that the divine necessity of Jesus' death is inherent in the nature of God's love on the one hand and the nature of human sin on the other. In order to accomplish his mission as the Savior the cross was inescapable, for, as someone has so beautifully put it, "Where love and sin meet there a cross is set up, and the one who loves must bear the cross."

Why the Cross?

Agapē as Unconditional Love

God's love is his unconditional and unqualified concern for the welfare of his creation. The full implications of such love can only be seen in his relation to his personal creatures because these creatures "in his image" can accept or reject his love.

When we say that God's love is *unconditional* toward us, we mean that its quality and constancy is not changed by our response. It does not turn to hate or anger or apathy when the response is negative. Jesus said that God's love is constant in its concern for enemies as well as friends (Matt. 5:43-48).[5]

Thus God's love takes the initiative to approach not only friends from whom it may expect a loving response, but also to be reconciled to enemies, that is, those who have hostile feelings and ill intentions (Rom. 5:6-8). In this latter case love makes itself vulnerable, taking the risk of rebuff and rejection. And because it is *unqualified* it does this without the option of withdrawing its offer. "Love never gives up; and its faith, hope and patience never fail" (1 Cor. 13:7, TEV).

Further, God's love is by its very nature *self*-giving. In our human relationships we readily recognize the difference between receiving gifts from a person who remains aloof or detached from the gift and a gift of the self in a genuine relation of caring acceptance.

People have many motives and reasons for giving gifts. Some are given because we owe a debt of gratitude; others are a social courtesy or duty. Some gifts are given in order to put oneself in the good graces of another person or even to put that person in debt to us so that we may ask a return favor. In each of these situations the gift frees the giver from the obligation of fully giving oneself. Such giving acts as a means of detaching the giver from the one who receives. By contrast *agapē* is a genuine gift of oneself to the other person.

Therefore *agapē* is the dynamic that creates personhood. A gift of oneself gives self-worth and self-identity to the recipient. We understand and act on this principle in our human experience of family. In a real sense the self, or self-identity, is a gift of parent to child. Children need the loving attention of their parents in order to develop self-identity and self-respect. If they do not get the caring attention which they need, they often aggressively demand it by boisterous and even naughty, rebellious behavior. "Presents" to keep them quiet and occupied are not enough; children need the parents themselves in order to develop a sense of self-worth.

Using this personal analogy we can say that God's love gives us ultimate self-worth because God gives himself to us. He did not come simply to instruct our ignorance, to show pity on our weakness, or to set a high moral example. He came to be with us. He came to give us a new name, that is, a new identity and a new sense of dignity as children of God by sharing his own identity with us (Rom. 8:29). This is our salvation that we are called children of God, and John adds, "and such we are" (1 John 3:1, NEB.) That is the message of the embodiment of God which was climaxed in the ultimate self-giving of Jesus, namely, his death on the cross.

---

5. Sometimes the word "indiscriminate" has been used to describe the impartiality of *agapē*. If this word is used, it needs to be pointed out that the goal (*telos*) of *agapē* is not indiscriminate. Thus it cannot be indulgent or permissive of wrongdoing, i.e., action that defeats its *telos*.

In such self-giving there can be no manipulation or coercion. The perfect gift of love must be completely free of ulterior motives or threats. There must not even be a deferred or an inferred threat. There must be no threat to abandon, to ostracize, or to take punitive revenge. Otherwise such a gift ceases to be *agapē*. Thus in the showdown between God's love and human hostility, Jesus, as the one sent by the Father's love as a gift of himself, could neither run away and hide nor resort to violence.

And in conclusion, this kind of unqualified, unconditional self-giving does not, indeed cannot, stop short of complete self-giving. We have often heard that God *demands* absolute trust and obedience from humankind; but God demands nothing that he himself is not ready to give. *Agapē* is self-sacrificial love. At no point can it withdraw the offer to care without denying itself, and God cannot deny himself. The only way to stop *agapē* is to kill the one who loves, and in Jesus' case even that did not work. There was a resurrection.

Thus the cross is to be seen as the climax of Jesus' life and not to be separated from it. The cross is for him the *end* both in the sense of *telos* (purpose) and *eschatos* (finish). When he gave his life—and it was a gift— he gave all he had. It was the last and complete act of love, and as such it completed and defined the nature of his life. As John wrote, "Having loved his own he loved them to the end" (John 13:1). If he had died any other way than at the hand of sinners in an act of execution, his life would have a different meaning.[6]

Sin the Rejection of Love

Sin is popularly viewed as a crime against God's law. Indeed, in Japanese the character used to translate sin usually means crime. When sin is viewed this way it can be dealt with within the framework of the judicial system's definition of a just penalty. The requirements are acknowledgment of guilt and restitution or commensurate penalty, and they presuppose future obedience. When the just requirements of the law have been met, the judge is free to be merciful and to forgive. In the case of moral transgression where legal definitions are not specific, the judge may show leniency when a proper spirit of repentance is displayed by the offender. The major conservative theological theories of atonement for sin, as we have seen, are based upon this legal-moral definition of justice.

But in the biblical perspective sin is a much more serious problem than this. The problem is not simply a broken law but a broken relationship. It is characterized by alienation, hostility, fear, and spiritual blindness that separate us from God who is the very ground of our being. In Ephesians sinful humanity is not only referred to as "disobedient children" but also "wrathful children" who have separated themselves from the covenant of God (2:2-4, 12).[7]

The New Testament describes sin in various ways: Sin is a slave master, a power within us, a perverse selfishness that will not acknowledge the authority of God. Its manifestation within our lives is an irrational resentment and blindness that disables and inhibits the will so that we cannot even do what we recognize as right (Rom. 7:13-23). The hostility and blindness of sin is such that it does not recognize genuine love when it sees it. It mistakes the sacrifice of love for a self-serving gift and thus reacts in fear and distrust. Because of this it rejects and even tries to destroy the one who loves (John 10:31-39). Death is its solution to fear. Death is its ultimate weapon and power.

When we see the problem in this light we begin to understand why the cross was necessary. The goal of God's love is to restore the broken relationship. In order to do this, God must break through the fears, hostility, and resentments that cause the continuing alienation. He must heal the blindness that disables and inhibits loving response. His goal is not to destroy the wicked person, not even to see that a *quid pro quo* justice is

---

6. "Salvation is the fruit of the whole incarnate life of Jesus Christ, including his death and resurrection; consequently it is revealed in all his actions. The miracles in particular show figuratively what salvation is—the curing of the sick, the feeding of the hungry, the giving of sight to the blind, and the raising of the dead. Salvation, that is, means the healing of the ills of mankind, and the imparting of light and life; in other words, Jesus deals with sin, and gives men knowledge and life. These aspects of salvation are seen from time to time in the course of the gospel, but appear preeminently in the death and resurrection of Jesus" (Barrett, 1960:69).

7. The Greek phrases "children of disobedience" and "children of wrath" are exactly parallel, and the grammatical problem is whether we should use them as objective or subjective genitives. The first phrase is fairly clear, but the second is not so clear. The phrase "wrath of God" used elsewhere might suggest the objective genitive, thus reading "children of [God's] wrath." But the meaning of the immediate context which juxtaposes God's rich mercy and love with human nature (disobedience and hostility) strongly indicates an adjectival usage of "wrathful children."

This interpretation seems fully warranted when we understand wrath as the rage which is the reflexive response of one who has been shamed. "Rage," writes Gershen Kaufman, "protects self against further exposure and further experiences of shame by both insulating the self and keeping others away" (1974:571). God has been dishonored (shamed) by our irrational, unjustified rejection of his goodness. Thus his natural response, as it was understood by the ancients, was rage (wrath). But Paul says that God has overcome his rage, and again in Christ seeks communication and a renewal of covenant relationship. The problem is that humans in their ignorance and superstition still blame God whom they view as a God of wrath. Feeling caught in a fateful (*karmic*) situation they experience shame and rage against God. They are "wrathful children" who have refused the gracious overtures of the God who overcomes his justified rage to renew contact and relationship.

So the situation described here with the phrase "children of wrath" is the vicious circle of shame and rage which God has broken through from his side but from which "wrathful children" are still unreleased. This assumes that the cultural context of the passage is more oriented to shame than to legally defined guilt.

We will return to the whole analysis of shame and guilt at a later stage of the discussion.

done. God is not ultimately interested in judgment which results in a perfect balance of retributive justice. Jesus said that he had come not to judge but to heal. God's ultimate goal is reconciliation, restoration of relationship, reintegration, and unification of the created order (John 3:16-17; Eph. 1:9-10). Or to put it another way, God's goal is victory over the frustration, bondage, and death caused by sin (Rom. 8:18-25). Salvation is not the gift of paradise, a gift detached from God himself. Salvation is a relationship to God.

Therefore, given the nature and goal of love and the character of human sin, the death of Christ was both inevitable and necessary for the advance of the kingdom of God in the world. From the human side it was inevitable because we are sinners caught in the shame and frustration of our sin. From the divine side it was necessary because God is love, and love cannot deny itself. Love finds its vindication in unhesitating faithfulness to its purpose. Love is ultimately its own justification.

The New Testament language of atoning love and vicarious sacrifice for us and instead of us—a love which asks only that we give our trusting, obedient response (faith) as an acceptance of its gift of a new self—surely must be understood within the framework of this personal analogy. Other metaphors of the battlefield or law courts must play a secondary and circumscribed role in its interpretation.

How Jesus' Life and Death
Make a Difference

Chapter 10

Metaphors of Salvation: What Kind of Difference?

Thus far we have spoken quite objectively about the nature of Jesus' historical mission of salvation as his mission to inaugurate the "reign of God." We have seen how his death and resurrection were integral to that mission. Now we turn our attention more directly to the way in which his mission as Messiah-Savior affects our lives today. Of course, much of what we have said thus far has a direct relation to this, but now we want to look at our topic from the subjective side.[1] How are we to understand the meaning of salvation for our life in the twentieth century? How does it affect our lives both personally and in community? And how can we actually participate in the mission of Christ? Note the double meaning of this word "participate" in the last question. How do we claim Jesus' work in our behalf and thus participate in its benefits? And how do we become part of the ongoing mission of Christ?

How we understand the relation of Jesus' life and death to the meaning and destiny of our lives depends in large part upon our understanding of salvation itself. Indeed, these two questions, namely, how Jesus' life and death are related to us and how salvation affects our lives, are really two sides of the same question. However, for discussion purposes we must separate them. We will look first at the meaning of the Christian concept of salvation. It is a complex and many-faceted concept with many assumptions

---

1. Vincent Taylor shows "how intimately the appropriation of the work of Christ by the believer is related to the understanding of the doctrine of atonement. And he concludes, " For purposes of thought it is most useful to isolate Christ's deed and man's response, but in practice without both there is no 'at-one-ment' and, in consequence, no satisfactory statement of the doctrine" (1940:262).

about the world and the human race involved in it. Then we will examine how we appropriate this salvation which Jesus offers for our own benefit.

The Concept of Salvation

Words and Metaphors

The word "salvation" itself in both its Hebrew and Greek forms carries the basic idea of rescuing from some peril. The peril may be from human enemies, physical peril or death, or some demonic power or disease. In the last sense it is a synonym for healing, and it is often so used in the Gospels. It is also used in a more technical religious sense as deliverance from sin and its power.

The New Testament uses a number of different metaphors to describe salvation from sin and its power.[2] This variation of metaphors depends on the different ways in which sin is represented. When sin is characterized as a kind of uncleanness or taboo, salvation is depicted as a washing with water or a purging by blood. Salvation is thought of as freedom when sin is viewed as bondage or slavery to alien powers. In this case God's saving action is described as redemption from bondage to sin and law, or ransom from slavery to Satan, the adversary. Where the focus is upon the intrinsic consequences of sin, namely, death and powerlessness, salvation is spoken of as new life—new birth, resurrection, new creation, and regeneration. When sin is viewed as waywardness or rebellion against God, salvation is a change of direction or turning around called conversion. It is a renewal of the mind and a reorientation of one's whole way of life toward God. When sin is viewed as hostility, salvation is reconciliation; and when it is guilt, salvation means forgiveness and justification.

Salvation is not exclusively a *spiritual* phenomenon. That is, it is not simply a theologically defined change in the way God regards us. (In some theologies this is called our "standing before God.") Neither is it merely a *future* possibility for which the present age of suffering provides a continuing time of preparation and testing. It is a real—although at present incomplete—change in the human condition including all its dimensions—spiritual, social, and physical.

The present human condition of frustration, fear, and hostility in which we are all participants is understood in Christian theology to be a deviation from God's original intention for creation. It is a result of humankind's rejection of responsibility to God and dependence upon him. This rejection is mirrored in our selfish assertion of the ego against our fellow humans. In rejecting God's authority we have accepted the authority of powers such as taboos, traditions, ideologies, military force, scientism, economic consumerism—all "idols" which are foreign to our human well-being and destiny. Thus out of harmony with God's intention and covenant, we are caught in self-defeating frustration and finally death (cf. Rom. 1:18ff. and chapter 7).

The Christian concept of salvation is that Jesus significantly changed this picture. Through his passion and resurrection we are offered new possibilities for a quality of life and personal relationship here and now. In a real sense God's future has already manifested itself in the present as a radical, new possibility; and we may participate in it now in the midst of the old. This new life is called "eternal life" in John's Gospel because it has the quality of eternity in it and lifts us above the fear and bondage of death.

Interpretative Priorities

The Bible, as we have noted, uses a number of metaphors rather than a simple rational definition to describe God's salvation. These metaphors are often directly attached to a concrete application. For example, Paul says that we have been raised from the dead with Christ (metaphor), therefore we should act like a person who has been radically changed (moral application). However, no comprehensive theological analysis of salvation is to be found in the Bible. Furthermore, the Bible does not standardize the metaphors. Different writers seem to prefer different metaphors.

For these reasons the theological task calls for classification and assigning of interpretative priorities as well as simple explanation of the metaphors. Theological differences appear in this process of assessing meaning and assigning priorities. In traditional Protestant theology reconciliation and justification have been given the hermeneutical priority. In Eastern Orthodoxy, by way of contrast, deliverance and immortality have been given priority. *In Anabaptism salvation was understood as the genuine possibility for a new life under the lordship of Christ*, and this will be our present approach.

This understanding of salvation as a radical possibility for a new life in the midst of "this present age" requires yet another set of interpretive priorities. In biblical terminology these are: (1) the restoration of covenant relationship to God and each other; (2) deliverance from powers which defeat God's original intention for the human race; (3) renewal of "the image of God" in genuine righteousness and truth, that is, the fulfillment of our true human destiny. And to this we may add (4) the eschatological aspect, namely, the ultimate abolition of death.

---

2. In his most recent book, *Understanding the Atonement for the Mission of the Church* (1986), John Driver has enumerated the various New Testament approaches and metaphors dealing with salvation and the atonement. I am in basic agreement with him, and I must assume much of what he has said as background. Those who are not acquainted with this biblical material will find his work most helpful.

Salvation as Restoration of Covenant Relationship
Concept of Covenant Nation

The restoration of covenant relationship is perhaps the most comprehensive interpretive category used in the Bible to describe God's saving activity in humankind's behalf. The paradigm, of course, is God's covenant with Israel. The Hebrew slaves of Pharaoh were rescued from slavery and given a new self-identity and peoplehood as Israel under God's covenant law.

The covenant form which we see in Exodus 20-24 follows the pattern of the ancient Hittite contract between the king and his subjects. But several fundamental differences make the Israelite concept of covenant unique. First, the one making the covenant with Israel is God, the Creator, and not the king of the nation. Indeed, the covenant was made before they had a human king. God himself was perceived as Israel's king, and under him were judges and prophets who represented his will to the people. When a human king was chosen to head the nation, he also, along with his people, stood under the covenant.

This is an important distinction in cultures where the gods have been depicted as the ancestors of the people and the ruler was thought of as a living manifestation of the gods. Indeed, this concept of a natural or blood-relationship to the gods symbolized in the sacralized kingship was the view of many nations that surrounded ancient Israel, and the Mosaic conception of covenant is a self-conscious refutation of it.

In the Japanese Shinto tradition, for example, the lines between heaven and earth—"heavenly *kami*" and "earthly *kami*"—are not clearly distinguished. They provide little or no sense of a transcendent creator whose relation to humans must be defined by covenants such as we have in the Bible. Rather, the relation to the gods depends upon heredity and the privilege which goes with being descendents of the *kami* (gods), and this relationship is epitomized in the emperor who was said to be the descendent of *Amaterasu omikami*, the Sun-goddess. Thus societal relationships, even to the present, tend to be viewed in terms of family dependence and expectations. In fact, the whole socioeconomic structure is formed on this pattern.

During the Tokugawa Shogunate the conception of the emperor as the divine titular head of the nation was promulgated.[3] This gave a basis for what Joseph Kitagawa has referred to as an "immanental theocracy" to develop (Kitagawa, 1966). The government itself was invested with divine authority. And this concept of governmental authority was continued in the Meiji era. Emperor Meiji was invested with divine status and authority, and he related to the people as the family head. Thus the whole life of the

people—moral and religious as well as political, social, and economic—
came under the direct authority of the "divine" government which was the
manifestation of the ancestoral gods.

In contrast to this Shinto tradition and experience where the nation's
relation to *kami* is based upon natural rather than contractual ties, the
twelve tribes of Israel were not bound together by ancestral family ties but
by a common covenant with the God of Abraham, Isaac, and Jacob (Exod.
12:38). God and king were not related by blood ties, and Israel could not
assume that their authority and rights were the same.

The New Testament concept of the church as the "new Israel"
parallels this covenant relationship of old Israel. Thus we who through baptism recognize and attempt to live under the covenant that forms the
"people of God" do not recognize the political and social authorities as ultimate divine authorities. Political government—and, indeed, institutional
ecclesiastical authority also—is a human authority, and God's *covenant*
people must subordinate it to the authority of God's covenant.

The christological significance of this becomes evident when we
remember that Jesus is the one who has the status and authority of *lord* for
us. He is the one who has made the covenant and defined our relationships
to God and to each other. If we use the ancient pattern of sacral kingship as
a comparative metaphor, *Jesus is the King who is invested with the authority of God to make the covenant with us.* Thus he is our final authority
for life, and all religious, ethical, and political-social authorities must be subordinated to him in the believer's life. For the church he is "Lord of lords
and King of kings" even in this present era when his lordship is not
recognized by the world systems of authority.

The second fundamental difference between God's covenant with Israel and typical political covenants was that *God's authority over Israel was
based upon his love and faithfulness, not on his power.* In the biblical
covenant God bound himself to fulfill his promise before he stipulated the
regulations. This is explicit in the covenant with Abraham (Gen. 15:17ff.),
but it is also implicit in the introduction of the Mosaic covenant (Exod.
20:2). God reminded Israel that he had been faithful to his promise to Abraham and had saved them from Egypt.

---

3. The Tokugawa Shogunate repressed Christianity and stressed the Confucian virtues of
loyalty and filial piety; the interest in Confucianism led in turn to revival of historical studies
that took scholars back to Shinto myths of ancient Japan. Reischauer writes, "The interest of
historians and Shinto scholars in the early days of Japanese history naturally revealed the high
place the imperial family had once held in Japan, and the nationalists tended to emphasize the
divine ancestry of an unbroken imperial line as one of the unique virtues which accounted for
Japan's supposed superiority. Together with the greater attention and more adequate support
the Tokugawa gave to the imperial court, this made most Japanese aware again that there was
an emperor in Kyoto, and that in theory he was the supreme ruler of the land" (1971:110-11).

Here, then, already in the first statements of covenant the authority of grace takes precedence over power and fear. The pattern is not law enforced by threat of power. Nor is the covenant a *quid pro quo* bargain struck between God and Abraham. God did not make his own faithfulness conditional on humankind's obedience. To Abraham God showed himself to be the God of love, and his covenant was a covenant of promise and hope to which Abraham was invited to respond. The promise was fulfilled in Christ who inaugurated the new covenant.

Third, on the basis of his own essential goodwill and faithfulness toward humans, God states the obligations of the covenant binding on Israel. That means that the obligations of covenant are not legal and extrinsic to our good. Rather, they spell out the conditions for our human fulfillment in community. The covenant is a "covenant of life and peace" (Mal. 2:5).

And last, Israel was required to accept the lordship of God. They accepted him as their *King* (ultimate authority) and pledged loyalty to live under his rule in obedience to his covenant, i.e., they pledged to keep faith with God as his loving children. According to the same pattern we live under the lordship of Christ.

Covenant as Offer of Salvation

In both Testaments the plight of the unsaved Gentiles is described as being outside the covenant relationship with God. To be outside the covenant meant to have no sense of peoplehood under the true God. It might even be described as being "strangers to the covenants of promise," and "without God in the world" (Eph. 2:12). In modern psychological parlance we might speak of this as attempting to find one's social and personal identity in a goal that is less than ultimate, i.e., an idol which is too small to fulfill the human potential, whether individual or national.

To find salvation, then, is equated with inclusion under the covenant authority of the only true God, i.e., the God who alone can give life and peace. The covenant of God with Israel provides the normative pattern for God's saving relation to all humankind. Therefore we need to look briefly at the nature and contents of this covenant relationship.

As we have seen, Israel's relation to God as his family was a relationship of faith. Their sense of identity depended not so much on heredity as upon their common loyalty to the God who had rescued them from Egypt.

This relationship to God was established by God himself through his miraculous deliverance of Israel from slavery in Egypt. It was defined in the agreement that God made with them at Sinai. The covenant stated both God's promise and their obligations. In their common allegiance to the covenant they found their new identity. They were God's *covenant people*.

Thus the "mixed multitude" (Exod. 12:38) of former slaves was given a new cultural and religious self-conciousness as a nation. They became "sons of the living God" (Hos. 1:10), i.e., they received full status as children, not by birthright but by accepting the covenant offered to them by God.

For Israel this national covenant which identified them as Yahweh's people was their present salvation. But they recognized that this salvation was still incomplete, and they waited for a new covenant. Thus the completion of God's salvation might be spoken of as the giving of a *new and better covenant* (Jer. 31:31-33; Heb. 7:22; 8:6ff.).

Although God remained faithful to the covenant, Israel constantly broke it and sought salvation by "other gods," depending on her own armies and upon political alliances with neighboring nations. Israel's unfaithfulness interrupted the covenant relationship, and thus salvation could also be spoken of as *restoration of covenant*. But the promise was that God would establish a new kind of covenant which would more effectively internalize and personalize the relation between each Israelite and God.

Christians understand that this prophetic promise was fulfilled in Christ who is called "the mediator of a new covenant" (Heb. 9:15). The church is understood to be the community of the Spirit formed by the new covenant offered in Christ. According to Peter's sermon at Pentecost, one can be saved by identifying with this new community of the Messiah through baptism (Acts 2:38). And in this community one receives the identifying presence of God's Spirit, the Spirit which Paul later called "the Spirit [that] makes you God's children" (Rom. 8:15, TEV).

In this new "household of God" or "one new humanity," as the church is called in the Ephesian epistle, those who had been "strangers to the covenants of promise" and "without God in the world" have now been reconciled both to God and their fellow humans (see Eph. 2:12-19). All those who by faith are a part of this new reality have now become children of God in Christ Jesus (Gal. 3:26), and the old obstacles and hostilities that had made *shalom* (peace) impossible have been abolished (see Gal. 3:26-29; Col. 3:9-17). All this has been accomplished through the new covenant sealed with the blood of Christ; and the new community of salvation is a community of faith and freedom empowered and guided by the Spirit of Christ rather than a new law. Such is the governing picture of salvation in the writings of Paul.

Content and Nature of Original Covenant

We have spoken of salvation as the restoration of covenant between God and humankind. While the concept of God's relation to Israel as a covenant relationship was based upon Israel's historical experience, the prophets also conceptualized God's relation to humankind in creation as a covenant relationship. They viewed humans as God's vassals who were charged with responsibility to him for the care of the earth as the "garden" of the Lord (Gen. 1:27-31).

To see the full significance of this concept we need to remind ourselves of the nature and content of that original covenant (Gen. 1:28). First, it was *not conceived of as a national covenant* establishing kingship over one nation. Thus it did not give one nation special precedence or privilege of standing before God. It was a *covenant made with all humankind*.

Second, it was *not a cultic or religious covenant*. It made no provisions for ritual worship or spiritual devotion. When Israel attempted to satisfy the covenant's requirements by cultic sacrifice, the prophets reminded them that the Lord did not need anything to eat and that justice—and not sacrifice—was the first requirement of the covenant (cf. Luke 11:42).

In the first instance the covenant required humans to recognize God's ownership of the earth and care for it as his custodians. Thus the selfish exploitation and waste of the earth's resources is a breaking of the covenant between God and humankind. In theological terms it is sin. Implicit in this first requirement is the second command, namely, to deal fairly and in good faith with one's fellow humans, recognizing that they are children of the same Father and made "in his image." Thus selfish exploitation of poor nations of the earth and war are also sins against the covenant. Third, to these ecological and social commands in the covenant the prophet Micah adds what we may properly designate the spiritual requirement, namely, "to live in humble fellowship with our God" (Mic. 6:6-8, TEV.) And these are all summed up in the New Testament with the dual commandment to love God with all one's heart and the neighbor as oneself.

Finally, we are told that the ultimate goal of the new covenant ratified in Christ's cross is none other than the realization of the original covenant intention in an actual universal reconciled community under God (Eph. 2:14-16). God's cosmic goal is the reunification of everything in heaven and on earth *in Christ* (Eph. 1:9-10). Thus speaking of salvation as renewal of the covenant is the theological way of saying that God is working for the healing of human relationships, the achievement of spiritual and moral righteousness, and the final attainment of his original purpose that the earth shall be the generous, fecund home of his creatures.

Salvation as Forgiveness, Justification, and Reconciliation

Forgiveness

Some of our most important ways of describing the restoration of relationships grow out of this covenant symbol. Foremost is the Christian concept of *forgiveness*. Forgiveness is God's canceling of the debt and pardoning of the offense incurred by our default on the covenant. Forgiveness is God's generous initiative in clearing the ground for a new beginning of relationship.

The only requirement for receiving this pardon is *repentance*, which in this setting means the full acknowledgment of the debt which is being canceled. Of course, one cannot receive a pardon without accepting the implication of guilt, but repentance is more than tacit admission of responsibility. It is the free admission of guiltiness together with the full intention to change henceforth the inappropriate pattern of response.

Reconciliation and Justification

The concepts of reconciliation and justification should also be interpreted in the context of the covenant metaphor. *Reconciliation* is a more comprehensive term than forgiveness, indicating that covenant relationship has been reestablished. The Christian doctrine of reconciliation through Christ is simply another way of saying that God has taken the initiative to reconcile erring and alienated humankind to himself and to each other through the work of Christ. In Christ he offers to bind himself in covenant for the good of all humankind. He has crossed all racial and national barriers to establish a universal community of peace. In Ephesians Christ is said to have made peace between "Jew and Gentile," and through him Gentiles, that is, all humankind other than Jews, have been included under the covenant of salvation as part of God's household (2:17-19).

Thus reconciliation is viewed as both horizontal (human to human) and vertical (human to God). God's salvation covenant binds us to other people and to himself.

Justification views salvation from the perspective of covenant law and speaks to the individual's standing in the community before God's law. The Jews had insisted on precise legal obedience as the means of obtaining a right standing with God. But the new covenant sealed in Christ's blood (1 Cor. 11:25) speaks of "justification by faith" in him. Indeed, Christ himself is said to be our justification (1 Cor. 1:30) in the same way he is also called our sanctification and "our peace" (Eph. 2:14).

The Christian doctrine of justification by faith stands in opposition to the concept of salvation by legal observance of the law. However, at the outset we must add that it does not mean that one can regain standing before God in the community without a changed attitude toward the commandment and a reorientation toward others.

During the period of Jewish history following Ezra respect for the Law of Moses had increasingly turned into a pursuit of legally precise obedience to its precepts. The law was considered to be the supreme revelation of God's will and purpose, and obedience to its commandments was the way to maintain proper relationship to God. While this was a sincere attempt to honor God through honoring his law, it led to a formal legalism which all too often defeated the true intention of that law.

Already in the prophetic tradition before the time of Ezra voices were playing down the legal and cultic aspects of covenant obedience and pointing to the intention of the covenant law, namely, justice, mercy, and love (Mic. 6:8). Others saw clearly that Israel's relation to God did not depend upon literalistic, contractual obedience but upon love and faithfulness toward him. Under the new covenant in Christ this prophetic tradition is heavily underscored in light of the teaching and example of Jesus. Through his perfect submission to the Father's authority and his faithfulness unto death he became the paradigm for justification by faith rather than law. And through participation in his faithfulness we are justified (Rom. 3:22, 26).

Justification by Participation in Christ

In a later section we will examine at more length the way in which the salvation offered in Christ is appropriated (see chapter 14), but here may be a good place to explain briefly the meaning of "participation in Christ's faithfulness" or "faith in him."[4]

Fundamentally, justification by participation in the faithfulness of Christ means four things. First, it is the recognition of Christ as the true Son or "image of God" and, therefore, of his life as the true pattern of faithfulness to the covenant. This involves the renunciation of our own attempts to achieve self-justification by legal obedience. We put our trust in another as "pioneer and perfecter of our faith" (Heb. 12:2). Second, participation involves a pledge of loyalty to the covenant which is offered to us through him in his death and resurrection. Third, faith in Jesus is participation in his Spirit of love for God and our fellow humans. As Paul plainly put it, "Any one who does not have the Spirit of Christ does not belong to him" (Rom. 8:9). And fourth, faith in Christ means sharing "his sufferings, becoming like him in his death" (Phil. 3:10), by which Paul meant participating in Christ's mission to bring salvation to all humankind even at the cost of suffering and death.

Thus by implication the Christian doctrine of justification by faith defines the covenant of God not as legal precepts but as the promise of love. It does not make faith a substitute for obedience, but it removes the law as a standard and establishes the promise of God in Christ in its place. *Faith is the response of obedience to God's love rather than his law.*

Limitation of the Justification Metaphor

When we speak of reconciliation between God and humankind, we must note that this includes a much broader concept than the individual settlement of guilt feelings and fear of God's just wrath. In moralistic or legalistic cultures alienation is often experienced as strong feelings of guilt in the presence of God, the Righteous Judge. In such societies emphasis on reconciliation as justification, that is, the removal of guilt and guilt feelings, is understandable and important. This, of course, has been the predominant theological motif in Western theology which inherited both the Roman tradition of justice and the Hebrew concept of theocratic law. But in those cultures where individual guilt before God is not emphasized, the alienation is nonetheless present and real even though it takes different forms; and reconciliation to God is in no way less necessary.

In many tribal cultures the anxiety of fear is much stronger than that of guilt. In such cultures the fear is caused not so much because God is conceived as a just judge, but rather as an arbitrary tyrannical force, or perhaps multiple forces which are inconsistent and undependable. In such situations reconciliation must come through a clear identification of the *Almighty* as the Father of Jesus Christ, the source and ground of love. People in such cultures must be assured that their true destiny also is found under the "covenant of life and peace" (Mal. 2:5). And they must see the power of the cross actually overcome the powers of magic and darkness. Early Christian leaders such as Ignatius of Antioch understood this far more clearly than do we who live in secular, scientific cultures. In his letter to the Ephesian Christians he exclaimed that when the Savior came into the world all the powers of sorcery were destroyed (Lightfoot, 1898:68).

In cultures where individuals find their self-identity and approval through inclusion in the group, exclusion and alienation from the group are the most dreaded results of wrongdoing. Shame, experienced as feelings of embarrassment, unworthiness, and remorse, follows the realization of wrongdoing. Again, the biblical concept of reconciliation clearly speaks also to this kind of alienation which sin has caused.

Reconciliation Through the Blood

We can also best understand the references to Christ's blood in the

---

4. In 1969 Marcus Barth published his article, "The Faith of the Messiah" (1969:363-70), in which he pointed out the exegetical evidence for translating the phrases *ek/dia pisteōs Iēsou Christou* (Gal. 2:16, Rom. 3:22,26) as "the faith [or faithfulness] of Jesus Christ" rather than our "faith in Christ." Since then considerable literature has debated the issue. Barth includes a bibliographical footnote on the literature prior to his article. For a further elaboration of Barth's position see Luke Timothy Johnson, "Romans 3:21-26 and the Faith of Jesus" (1982:77-90). I had come to similar conclusions on theological grounds and find these corroborating exegetical discussions convincing.

context of the covenant relationship. Romans 3:25, for example, says that Christ's blood is the means of forgiveness for our sins.[5] In the Hebrew cultic system blood had a variety of uses, and its symbolism depends upon the context in which it is used. Romans 3:25 alludes to the ceremony on the Day of Atonement when the high priest sprinkled blood on the lid of the ark of the covenant (the "mercy seat") to purge the people's accumulated transgressions against the covenant.[6] The people's failure to keep covenant with God dishonored (shamed) him and filled his house with shameful pollution. Especially where the shame of sin's pollution implies that the sinner must be removed from the sacred presence, i.e., put outside the sacred realm of the covenant relationship, blood rather than water was used as the cultic cleansing, restorative agent. The blood was a covering or cleansing agent to expunge the shame of the people's transgressions[7] and thus preserve the bond of the covenant.

But blood was also used in the making of covenants and is sometimes referred to as "the blood of the covenant" (Heb. 10:29; Exod. 24:8).[8] This is the meaning alluded to in the sacrament of the Lord's Supper where drinking from the cup of wine is understood as a participation in the covenant offered to us in Christ's blood (see 1 Cor. 11:25; 10:16-17). Thus Christ's death on the cross, or as it is sometimes worded, "the blood of the cross" (Col. 1:20), is seen as God's provision for and solemn promise to keep the new covenant offered by Christ. This is a covenant that goes beyond the old agreements ratified with animal blood both in scope and in character. This covenant is one of *grace* offered to *all humankind* (Eph. 2:13-14).

Deliverance from Alien Authorities

Redemption (*apolutrōsis*) and ransom (*lutron*) also provide an important metaphor of salvation in the Scriptures. In the first instance the metaphor alludes to Israel's rescue from bondage in Egypt, but slavery was also a common experience of the first-century Roman world. Captives of war were used as slaves in the households of the victors. Even people of noble birth might be brought into such bondage. Such captives might be rescued from their captivity either by a victorious army or by ransom. In Israel's deliverance from Egypt no payment of ransom was made; this was simply an act of God's saving power. Both the ransom metaphor and the victor metaphor are used in the New Testament. The emphasis does not seem to be on the *method* of deliverance but on the *fact* of deliverance.

Deliverance from Sin

Following this metaphor sin is viewed as a foreign master to whom we have been sold (Rom. 7:14). Just as the slave was captured and sold to masters outside his or her family or native country and made to serve the pleasures of a foreign master, so the powers that dominate our lives in sin are alien and unnatural to our own self-fulfillment as God's children.

While the metaphor derives from the objective social experience of slavery, it is also true to our interior experience. Sin is not experienced as a genuinely free act of the human self but as a kind of impotence. Paul does not equate the ego itself with the evil power but pictures it as captive. The problem as he sees it is not ignorance, as suggested by the Greek philosophers, but the inability to do what we acknowledge to be right. It is as though the ego (self) is enslaved and therefore unable to control its own actions. The natural authority which is appropriate to our own best interests is exchanged for a foreign, unnatural authority which is experienced as bondage.

In other passages Paul associates the power of sin more closely with the

------

5. The word found in Romans 3:25 which I have translated "means of forgiveness" is *hilastērion*. It is used in the LXX to translate the Hebrew *kapporeth* which means "mercy seat," or the lid of the ark of the covenant where the high priest sprinkled blood once a year to purge the sins of the people (cf. Heb. 9:5; Exod. 25:16ff.). Thus Christ on the cross is called our "mercy seat"—the one through whom we find cleansing and restoration to the presence of God. In my judgment one should not attempt to read any theory of atonement from this. Certainly nothing penal is indicated.

The related word *hilasmos* used in 1 John 2:2; 4:10 has a broader usage and means to cover, cancel, or make ineffective the consequences of sin. This is the meaning of the technical word *expiate*. As Büchsel says, "[For John] the subjective results of *hilasmos* in man is *parrēsia*, confidence before the divine judgment, 4:17; 2:28, or victory over the consciousness of sin" (1965:317). In any case the word does not imply the pacification of God but rather the removal of that which separates us from his loving presence.

6. Some passages refer to our being "justified in (*en*) the blood" (Rom. 5:9), "redeemed" through (*dia*) the blood of his cross" (Col. 1:20), "ransomed" with his precious blood. And in Revelation 5:9 we are said to be "bought" (*agorazō*) by blood. These last two references come from the practice of purchasing the freedom of slaves, either by a divinity—a form followed in which the temple priests transferred the money in the name of the god—or by secular manumission. God set us free by buying us as his slaves with Christ's blood, i.e., supreme sacrifice (see Büchsel, 1964:124f.).

In Romans 5:9-10 the phrase "justified by his blood" seems clearly to be parallel to "reconciled by his death." The point here is not a theory of atonement but the exaltation of "our Lord Jesus Christ through whom we have received our reconciliation" (v. 11).

In the other passages "blood" often seems to stand for Christ's vicarious death or "the cross." The full phrase is found in Colossians 1:20—"the blood of his cross" (cf. Eph. 2:13, 16. Especially in Ephesians 2:13 "the blood of Christ" means blood of the covenant.)

7. The imagery of the book of Hebrews seems to substantiate fully this interpretation of the use of blood as a purgative. As the author says, "[Under the old covenant] almost everything is purified with blood" (9:22). See also Hebrews 1:3; 9:12-14; 10:19-22; 1 Pet. 1:2; 1 John 1:7 (cf. McCarthy, 1962:14f.).

8. This blood of the covenant refers to the ancient practice of sealing a contract by blood. The form of this sealing varies, but it is found in many cultures (cf. the covenant between Abraham and God, Gen. 15:7-21). In some cultures the blood of the two parties is ceremonially mixed, signifying the new bond of union. In the Hebrew tradition an animal life was sacrificed and the blood was sprinkled on the people. Afterward a meal was eaten together (Exod. 24:3-11).

perverted desires of the self. These selfish desires for power and pleasure are objectified as "the flesh," that is, passions, fears, and desires that grow out of the existential human situation of limitation and dependence. These passions also may overwhelm us and become masters of our actions (Titus 3:3). Again, the source of sin is not pictured as human nature itself. Sin is not experienced as the free exercise of our energies to satisfy our desires but as the domination of "the flesh," or what is the same, the idol of greed.

Thus the power of sin is understood as unnatural and detrimental to authentic human self-fulfillment. Whether the power of sin is viewed as an exterior authority or the domination of "the flesh," it is unnatural and alien to our human nature.

The metaphor of redemption from slavery is used as a parable to make the main point of deliverance from sin's power without elaborating the details of ransom as later post-Apostolic theologians such as Origen did. The highly existential and realistic evaluation of human weakness and perversion in itself urges us to move beyond the legalism of insisting that the ransom be interpreted within the framework of juridical equivalence. This is a dynamic and graphic portrayal of salvation as deliverance from the power and domination of sin itself, and not simply its penal consequences.

Indeed, this is only one metaphor used to describe our freedom from the impotence which results from sin. Another metaphor is our ultimate powerlessness in death which is the final result of sin. Salvation is the power of God which was displayed in the resurrection of Jesus also raising us from death to new spiritual life and vigor (Rom. 6:4; Eph. 1:19). Paul actually mixes these two metaphors of sin and death in Romans 7 when he says that the slavemaster, "Sin," killed the ego (the I).

The power of sin lies in the inhibiting guilt, fear, and anger that weaken our determination, blind our rational insight, blunt our best impulses, and thus frustrate our efforts. Deliverance from such bondage must be understood in terms of personal dynamics. Here the categories of forgiveness, reconciliation, and deliverance converge in our experience of salvation. Forgiveness and acceptance create the possibility of freedom from sin's power.[9]

Indeed, this is the word of Paul in the Romans 7—8 passage. The "no condemnation . . . in Christ" of Romans 8:1 is the turning point between the frustrating inability for self-control described in chapter 7 and the freedom to keep the law's true intent (8:3-4). Forgiveness and reconciliation provide the nexus for the radical new possibility of grace. Thus deliverance or redemption must be described as both forgiveness (loosing from guilt and shame) and at the same time freedom from sin's illegitimate authority and power.

Bondage to the Demonic

Salvation as deliverance from alien authorities also includes deliverance from *demonic* powers. This category which has often been dismissed as mythological in our rationalistic age plays an important role in the New Testament descriptions of salvation.[10] Jesus himself is depicted as an exorcist as well as religious teacher and healer. The demonic is portrayed as both an individual and a social malady, and it seems to be clearly distinguished from the power of sin although the debilitating consequences of sin leave human society vulnerable to demonic powers.

In contrast to the power of sin the demonic in the New Testament seems to define those powers which destroy selfhood and self-identity. Under the domination of sin the self is pictured as intact but in submission to idolatrous authority. Sin's hallmark is selfishness. Under the domination of demons the self is pictured as disintegrated and displaced by powers and influences exterior to itself. The demonical symptoms in the Gospel accounts of Jesus' ministry include profound withdrawal and inability to communicate, loss of self-identity, fear of health and healing, self-hatred and suicidal tendencies, fearfulness, cynical anger, and malevolence (Mark 1:23-26; 5:2-9; etc.).

Demonic violence in contrast to sinful violence is the uncontrolled violence of chaos rather than purposeful violence directed toward selfish ends. While modern Western medicine treats these conditions only as interior morbid states of the personality, it still recognizes the power of an external authority figure to bring healing and reintegration into the lives of those thus afflicted. The saving power of the Christ is such a loving, authentic authority which can heal the wounded, tortured self. His lordship offers an authority under which authentic self-integration and fulfillment can be achieved, which is one modern way to say that the demonic is subject to his power.

The powers of the demonic are also referred to with such terms as "rulers of darkness in high places" (Eph. 6:12), "rulers of this age" (1 Cor. 2:6), "prince of the spiritual powers of the air" (Eph. 2:2), "principalities and powers" (Rom. 8:38; Eph. 3:10; Col. 1:16). Or again in Colossians 2:8, 20 and Galatians 4:3 they are called *stoicheia*, or elemental nonpersonal

---

9. The American psychologist Carl R. Rogers especially has emphasized that acceptance by another person is the nexus for change in personality problems (see Rogers, 1966:126-41).

10. Rollo May has observed, "It was entirely right that the Enlightenment and Age of Reason, in the flush of their success in making all life reasonable, should have thrown this out [the belief that we are taken over by little demons flying around], and have regarded it as a deteriorated and unproductive approach to mental illness. But only during the last couple of decades has it been clearly impressed upon us that in discarding the false demonology, we accepted, against our intention, a banality and a shallowness in our whole approach to mental disease" (1969:125).

powers of taboo and superstition that keep whole societies in bondage.

These "rulers" represent those super-individual, super-human powers of political, economic, and social institutions which control societies, cultures, and nations. Their demonic character is most immediately recognizable in societies dominated by black magic and sorcery where overt appeal is made to irrational evil powers and people are subdued by superstitious fear. But such character may also be seen in those modern totalitarian governments, whether of the left or right, which control their citizens by repression and death. They impose an unstable order in society based upon fear of death. Insofar as the order they impose furthers human development they are provisionally legitimatized, but their demonic nature is seen in their lack of self-control and abuse of rational authority. Their power is limited by a balance of destructive power, not a rational self-control. Thus they too represent a demonic element in human society from which Christ came to set humankind free.

The New Testament writers have various approaches to the meaning of salvation from such powers, but all agree that the resurrected Christ has been given authority over them (Eph. 1:19b-21). In 1 Corinthians 15:24-26 Paul writes that the heavenly Christ now rules at God's right hand conducting the battle against all such powers until they are defeated. In Colossians he says that on the cross Christ "made a public spectacle" of the powers (2:15, NEB) and that by Christ's victory God has "rescued us from the power of darkness and brought us safe into the kingdom of his dear Son" (1:13, TEV).

Such passages are hardly an adequate foundation on which to build a theology of deliverance from the powers, and the relation of Christ's death and resurrection to the powers is not immediately evident in history (Berkhof, 1962). However, the disclosure of the authority of love as God's way of achieving true justice is the beginning of the end of power based upon fear and death, although as yet there seems to be little historical evidence of the worldly powers withering away. And today in the last part of the twentieth century our world skirts total destruction by a balance of demonic terror. Indeed in this respect our situation is not greatly improved over that of the first century when the cross was raised on Golgotha as an ensign to the nations.

What we can say with confidence is that Christ offers us deliverance from the fear of such demonic powers. To those who know the "power of the resurrection" and live in that hope death has lost it terror and thus its power to control us. Under the lordship of Christ we have been "transferred to the kingdom of God's beloved Son" and given the opportunity to live under the authority and control of love.

Chapter 11

Salvation as Renewal of the Image of God

Understanding the Metaphor

To understand renewal of the image of God as a way of talking about Christ's work of salvation we must first examine the meaning both of the word "renewal" and the phrase "the image of God." Especially in an evolution-oriented culture we must explain and justify renewal as a valid conceptualization of human experience. Why, some might object, should we speak of renewal rather than continuing growth and development? By way of preface then, we must briefly introduce the Christian concepts of (1) humankind made in the image of God and yet (2) experiencing existence as a state of "original sin."

The conception of humankind in God's image is found throughout the Bible. This conception is first used to describe the unique capacity of humankind in contrast to other animals in the Genesis account of creation (1:27-28). It stems from the metaphor of humans giving birth to children "in their own image" (Gen. 5:3) and speaks of the special covenant relationship which humankind has with God as those who belong to his family. It is used in the New Testament to describe both Jesus, whom the writer to the Hebrews says "bears the very stamp of God's nature" (Heb. 1:3; cf. Col. 1:15) and all those who through the renewal of their minds have put on the "new nature, created after the likeness of God in true righteousness and holiness" (Eph. 4:23-24).

This doctrine of the image of God is a way of saying that human beings have a special capacity for responsibility under God and that authentic human identity and selfhood is established in a freely chosen relationship to God as Father. Our lives find their fulfillment in the recognition of our dependence upon God and free acceptance of responsibility to him.

Perhaps we can better see the significance of this conviction that authentic selfhood is achieved through acknowledgment of ultimate responsibility to God if we contrast it to other options chosen by humans. To begin with, the ancient Greeks, for example Aristotle, held that self-identity and fulfillment are found through the acquisition of rational knowledge. For him the highest authentic expression of humanity was to be seen in the male philosopher. The hedonists held that fulfillment is found in satisfying our human desires. The ascetics, on the other hand, said that denying our desires and living according to a strict discipline is the only way to find one's true self. They identified the self as a spiritual substance which is smothered and diminished by material existence. Many others have held that human identity is found in gaining and exercising power over one's environment and especially over other people. By way of contrast, the cultures of Asia have by and large emphasized harmony with nature and submission to the social group as the way to realize authentic selfhood or enlightenment.

In contrast to all of these, Christianity holds that human beings have been created in God's image, that is, in a likeness of God which enables them to participate in the life of God as his children. Accordingly, authentic self-fulfillment is found in what Martin Buber called an "I-Thou" relationship to God (Buber, 1958) such as we see portrayed in Jesus himself.

The concept of original sin is a way of describing our experience of selfhood as always tinged with selfish egoism and the fear of other selves. And especially it describes the experience of feeling ourselves threatened by God, the ultimate source and fulfillment of all selfhood.

The original sin was and is the rejection of the image of God as an authentic self-image and the attempt to find an identity and selfhood independently from God. The image of God implies a likeness to God which involves humankind in responsibility to him as well as dependence upon him. And the rejection of the image is not only an assertion of independence but also a renunciation of responsibility. The result is that the sinful self-image has become an introverted perversion of the image of God as intended in creation. Indeed, it is a prostitution of that image for selfish human ends. This turning away from God as the source and goal of our life, and the enthronement of the ego, is what is referred to as the *fall* from original innocence.

Whether or not we interpret the fall of humankind into sin as a historical event in world history, it does represent a profound insight into our human experience of self-knowledge. We not only know ourselves to be something less than we have the potential to be, but we experience the personal development of self-knowledge, which may be described as a movement from innocence to responsibility, as an evasion of or rebellion against responsibility to and for others. The question of Cain, "Am I my brother's keeper?" is the question of all fallen humans. We want to be responsible only to and for ourselves.

Further, we realize that our quest for knowledge and control of our environing universe involves us in increased evil as well as good—and evil of our own making at that. Neither our individual nor universal development moves us in a straight line of upward progress, but indeed, each new invention or discovery results in new dimensions of irresponsibility, failure, and guilt. Each improvement is at the same time a fall, that is, an increase in potential and real evil along with the negative consequences that flow from it.

This experience has led to and seems to justify the concept of God's continuing work as a *re*creation and *re*newal according to the original intention of God. The question of salvation is how to escape from this dilemma of escalating evil in the quest for authentic human selfhood. Paul describes the dilemma as the "circle of sin and death" (Rom. 8:2, Phillips) and says that it can be broken only by God through Christ (cf. Rom. 7:1—8:4).

In this context, then, salvation is described as the restoration of the true image of the Creator and renewal of our nature in that knowledge (Col. 3:10) or as a restoration of "true righteousness and holiness" according to the image of God (Eph. 4:22-24). This is also called a "renewal of [the] mind" (Rom. 12:2), and the pattern for this renewal is the "mind of Christ" (1 Cor. 2:16; Phil. 2:5; Rom. 8:29). Christ, the true "image of the invisible God" (Col. 1:15), is the exemplar (Rom. 8:29) into which likeness, Paul says, we are being progressively changed (2 Cor. 3:18).

Traditional Interpretations of the Image Metaphor

This language of renewing the image of God has been interpreted in a number of ways in the various theologies of the church. Three major motifs have surfaced in the Catholic and Protestant traditions.

Redivinization, Early Greek Fathers

Early in the Greek tradition and continuing today restoration of the image was interpreted as *redivinization and restoration of immortality.* For example, Ignatius of Antioch wrote that release from the old nature is release from transitoriness and death. For such an understanding he could appeal to 1 Corinthians 15:47-49. Paul calls Adam, whose sinful image we now bear, the "man of dust," and he promises that by contrast we shall share "the image of the man of heaven."

From this perspective Christ's mission basically is the overcoming of death for us so that we may regain the immortality which was forfeited by sinning. Fourth-century Greek church fathers such as Gregory of Nyssa and Gregory of Nazianzus held that the divine image included not only reason, wisdom, free will, and moral goodness but also immortality by which humankind shares the divine nature. In contrast to Augustine they held that sin did not destroy free will, although it weakened and corrupted human nature. On the other hand, God did deprive humans of immortality—that mark of participation in divinity. Sin may be thought of as a sickness unto death. Through the incarnation, death, and resurrection of Christ our sinful nature is purified, and immortality which enables us to participate in the divine nature is restored.

How the incarnation effects this was described in various ways, but the general explanation is that through the enfleshment of *Logos*, divine being joined with the human body and soul. In this manner God's purity and life touched our sinfulness and death and began to purify and rejuvenate our corruption and weakness. Christ, the Great Physician, began to heal us and bring us back to life (Nyssa). Nazianzus spoke of the incarnation as a union of the divine with "all parts of human nature, in order that they all might by this union be consecrated and sanctified, and that *the Divine Nature united with the human nature might penetrate the latter as the leaven does the mass*, strengthening and ameliorating it" (Ullmann, *Gregor von Nazianz*, 1825, quoted by Franks, 1962:59. Emphasis mine. See Kelly, 1958:375ff. for an excellent summary of fourth-century views). Thus Ullmann concludes that Nazianzus conceived of salvation "as the sanctification, beatification, and deification of man."

According to this motif, then, salvation means the restoration of immortality and life with God in the Spirit. God has defeated death and the devil, not by a simple act of omnipotence, but as a human being subject to death. In this way through solidarity with us in our humanity he initiated a new potential for all humans to be renewed in the divine image. At present this renewal is experienced only sacramentally through the church, but Christ's resurrection guarantees ultimate restoration (1 Cor. 15:45; 1 John 2:3).

Restoration of Status, Calvin

A second interpretation which is common in Protestant theology emphasizes the change as a change of spiritual position or status. It involves a change in what John Calvin following Augustine called the "supernatural gifts"—faith and love which are restored "sufficient to attain heavenly life and eternal bliss." But the "corrupted natural gifts"—understanding, judg-

ment, and will—are not restored to their former condition (*Institutes*, Bk.
II, 2, 12, 1960:270). Calvin does speak of a new birth, regeneration, and a
"conversion of the will" which he describes as changing our evil will into a
good will (II, 3, 6, pp. 298f.). However, he is so concerned not to give any
credit to human volition and effort that in effect the "new creature" is in no
way intrinsically new, but only the puppet of God's grace.[1] We have been
restored to the status of children, but we wait for the time when we shall
actually be changed into his image. At best in this life we begin to be
transformed into the moral image of Christ, but the process is perfected
only at physical death when the spirit is divested of the body.

Calvin's problem with the metaphor of the divine image renewed in us
inheres in his concept of the image itself. His presentation is confused by
the fact that his philosophical and psychological assumptions are basically
Platonic (*Institutes*, I, 15, 1960:6-8), but his theological hermeneutic makes
the "renewal [of the moral image] through Christ" the key for understanding the original meaning of the divine image (I, 15, pp. 4ff.).

On the one hand Calvin speaks of the image of God as that "true
piety, righteousness, purity, and intelligence" which were perfectly
displayed in Christ (I, 15, p. 4). When it is so understood, then he can speak
of the "new birth" as "the beginning of our recovery of salvation . . . that
restoration which we obtain through Christ, who also is called the Second
Adam for the reason that he restores us to true and complete integrity" (I,
15, p. 4). In this context Calvin is careful, however, to say that the reforming
of God's image in us is the *end* of regeneration."[2] He is careful to describe
the beginning as an adoption into the inheritance of life—a *status* concept.

On the other hand, Calvin speaks of the divine image as the faculties
of understanding and will which the human soul possesses in contrast to
other animals.[3] Originally, he says, the soul, and the organic body as well,

---

1. I think Calvin does not intend this conclusion, but he so assiduously presses his point of
election and grace that he allows no room whatsoever for a genuine change of will and
character in the believer. All our righteousness remains an "alien righteousness," to use
Luther's term. Or to quote Calvin, "The first part of a good work is will; the other, a strong effort to accomplish it; the author of both is God" (II, 3, 9-10, 1960: 302ff.). God's work of redemption is done "quite alone" by God himself. The human will is "first actuated through
grace." It is "bent, formed, and directed" (II, 3, 3-7).

2. In a later passage entitled "Rebirth in Christ," Calvin equates repentance with
regeneration and speaks again of the restoration of the image of God as its "sole end" (III, 3,
1960:9). The renewal of the moral image is a slow and uneven lifetime process. Calvin wrote:

. . . indeed, this restoration does not take place in one moment or one day or one year; but
through continual and sometimes even slow advances God wipes out in his elect the corrup-
tions of the flesh, cleanses them of guilt, consecrates them to himself as temples renewing all
their minds to true purity that they may practice repentance throughout their lives and
know that this warfare will end only at death (III, 3, 1960:9).

3. The soul is an incorporeal, immortal substance which "dwells in the body as a house"
(Calvin, I, 15, 1960:6). It has been "engraved with the image of God."

were perfect and "rightly composed to obedience." Adam not only had free will but also the power to attain what he willed (Calvin I, 14, p. 8). This concept of the original image includes both a capacity of the soul and a level of perfect attainment in understanding and will which have been "corrupted and frightfully deformed" through the sin of our first parents.

If this conception of the image were consistently followed, then a renewal of the image would entail a substantial change in the soul which in turn would restore the powers of understanding and free will. This Calvin was loath to grant. He roundly criticized this idea as the error of Osiander, a contemporary Lutheran theologian who tried to define Christ's righteousness in us as more than an "alien righteousness."

In the end Calvin makes the renewal a change of our *spiritual position in Christ*, i.e., we are reinstated into God's family as children through election. However, there is little or no substantive change. The image of God in the newly formed Christian remains debased and deformed. The renewal of the image is not an actual restoration in humanity but an "imputation" to us of Christ's achievement in our behalf.[4]

From this perspective Christ, who is the perfect image of God, is the representative human and Mediator between God and humans. The overwhelming emphasis remains upon what Christ has done for and instead of us and not what he has done in and through us. To use traditional terms, Christ is the justifier through his substitutionary death. Although Calvin mentions regeneration and rebirth which are life metaphors, his controlling concept remains the death of Christ as a legal satisfacton. How the salvation of the resurrected, living Christ who is the "source of . . . life . . . our wisdom, our righteousness and sanctification and redemption" (1 Cor. 1:30; Rom. 5:10b) effects an *ethical transformation in us* receives relatively little attention.

Although Calvin does not use Luther's term, "alien righteousness," his own term, "imputation," makes the same point. Luther had observed that the "old Adam," i.e., the old nature, is still very much alive in Christians, and they must depend upon the "external righteousness" of Christ for salvation (Luther, 1961:88ff.). This insistence upon the continuing priority of grace and God's enabling power in the life of Christians is well-taken, but the question is what kind of change in us that divine power effects.

Calvin was deeply concerned to foster a life of discipleship to Christ, but such a definition inevitably defeats his purpose. Where there is no freedom to choose joyfully the way of Christ, discipleship can only be a matter of submission to the law of Christ. It is quite understandable that with his definitions Calvin could only see the Anabaptists' *Nachfolge Christi* as perfectionism and legalism.

Moral Renewal, Wesley

A third interpretation is represented in the Wesleyan or Holiness tradition. This position puts more emphasis upon Christ's work *in* the lives of believers. As John Wesley himself put it, salvation through Christ means "a restoration, not only to the favour but likewise to the image of God, implying not barely deliverance from sin, but the being filled with the fullness of God" (Wesley, 1954:84).

Wesley is rather more specific than Calvin in his definition of the divine image which distinguishes humans from other creatures. He taught that humans were created in God's image in a threefold sense. The *natural* image of God consists of "understanding, will, and freedom." The *political* image is seen in the human domination of the earth under God, and the *moral* image is a reflection of God's own goodness. The first human couple, he said, were "full of love . . . full of justice, mercy, and truth," spotlessly pure from sin (Wesley, 1954:111). When the first humans sinned they lost the moral image of God and in part the natural image.

The new birth or regeneration reverses these consequences. It does not, of course, restore the Edenic situation and perfection, but it effectively recreates the divine image in the believer. "By new birth," Wesley wrote,

> [We experience] a change from inward wickedness to inward goodness; an entire change of our inmost nature from the image of the devil (wherein we are born) to the image of God; a change from the love of the creature to the love of the Creator; from earthly and sensual to heavenly and holy affections—in a word, a change from the tempers of the spirits of darkness to those of the angels of God in heaven (1954:141).

Salvation means not only deliverance from guilt and fear of punishment (justification); it also rescues from the power of sin (sanctification). New birth is the beginning of sanctification just as the birth of a child is the beginning of its nature and family identity. The new birth restores the

---

4. Wilhelm Niesel insists that this difference between the actual restoration of the image in humankind and its imputation to us through participation in Christ's achievement is crucial in Calvin's theology. He writes: "In these considerations one point must be carefully noted. The role of Christ is not simply to set in motion a process of salvation within us when we encounter Him. No, He alone has died the one decisive death and He alone has overcome death with the effect that in Him the divine image in man is restored. Our part is to share in His death and resurrection. In speaking of what Christ bestows upon us we may never speak merely of the gifts in themselves or of our own lives in so far as they are remoulded by those gifts, but we must ever keep well in view the *ex Christi participatione* . . . . It is not we who die and it is not we who are renewed, it is only in Christ that that can happen to us. Just in this teaching about rebirth, where we are most readily inclined to speak only of man, of his gifts and newness of life, Calvin's theology is strictly revelational" (Niesel, 1956:128).

moral identity and potential. "But it is by slow degrees that he [Christian] afterwards grows up to the measure of the full stature of Christ" (Wesley, 1954:172).

This tradition, then, understands the restoration of the image to be a moral renewal in "holiness and true righteousness" (Eph. 4:22-24; Titus 3:5b). Not only is the saved person given a restored status; the old nature is removed and a new nature is given which enables Christians to keep God's law of love. Accordingly Christians are expected to "have the mind of Christ" and "walk in newness of life." They are called by God's enabling grace to be "perfect" in their desire to love him and to follow Christ in "righteousness and true holiness."

Wesley's interpretation highlights Christ as exemplar and authority (Lord) for the Christian life in a new way, but he did not materially change his conception of Christ's redemptive role. His heavy emphasis remained upon Christ's atoning sacrifice for the guilt of our sins. In this he was entirely within the orthodox Protestant tradition. He strenuously opposed the deistic opinions current in eighteeth- and nineteenth-century England which muted the atoning work of Christ.

Following Calvin's lead, Wesley spoke of Christ as Prophet, Priest, and King, and he gave first place to his priestly work. However, he pointed a new direction when he related the prophetic and kingly roles directly to the restoration of the image of God and the governance of sinful passions in humans. As Prophet, he said, Christ gives knowledge and understanding to the regenerated believers. He hinted that this prophetic work continues in the work of the Spirit "guiding us into all truth." As "king forever" he gives laws, restores the image of God to those "reinstated in His favour," and reigns "in all believing hearts until He has 'subdued all things unto Himself' . . ." (Wesley, 1954:86).

This theme is not carried through in Wesley's Christology. Rather, his Trinitarian assumptions lead him to separate the work of the Son and the Spirit and to give a large place to the Spirit's operation in our present experience of salvation. We are saved by the *merit* of the Son and the *power* of the Spirit (Wesley, 1954:92-93).

An Anabaptist Understanding of the Image Metaphor
Restoration in God's Image

The language of renewal, re-creation, and restoration of humanity in the image of God is a powerful way to speak of salvation as the possibility of a radically new life in the midst of the old. Among the Anabaptists this renewal was considered the hallmark of true Christians. For example, Peter Riedeman said, "Therefore faith is a real divine power, which renews man and makes him like God in nature, makes him living in his righteousness, and ardent in love, and in keeping his commandments" (quoted in Klaassen, 1981:64).

In a similar vein Dirk Philips wrote:

> Through this promise, yea, through this gracious gospel of Jesus Christ, man is again comforted, yea, renewed in the image of God, and is born again to eternal life. In the beginning God desired to have people who are made in his image, and still does. Therefore he created man in his image and in his likeness in the beginning, as it is written: "God created man for eternal life in his image that he should be as he (that is God) is" (Wisdom of Solomon 2:23, quoted in Klaassen, 1981:67).[5]

When we speak of salvation as a new creation or re-creation of the image of God, we must first note that creation is God's work. So the metaphor itself speaks of the renewal as a work of God in us. The change is not self-generated but is received as a gift. It is spoken of both as a gift of divine life (the Spirit) and as a work in our lives by the Spirit (Rom. 8).

The Anabaptists were accused of "works righteousness" and called "heaven stormers." But this metaphor which was so central for them speaks of the work of God in us through Jesus Christ. Christ is the image exemplar, and the Spirit of Christ renews the living image in us. The Spirit restores in us the family identity, gives us assurance of family relationship, and creates new attitudes and character. Also this "Spirit of sonship" (Rom. 8:15) motivates us to live a life patterned according to the new order of creation—a life in "imitation" of God, our Father (Eph. 5:1).

Second, the metaphor of creation in God's image is closely related in meaning to the metaphor of our birth as God's children (John 3:6). Indeed, as we have seen, the metaphor originally came from the birthing of children who have "the image" of their parents. That this is only a metaphor seems to be indicated by the use of words such as create and re-create and not others such as procreate. The biblical writers are quite careful not to make God one of the ancestors no matter how exalted. What then is the meaning of the image-of-God metaphor?

The metaphor is clearly used to suggest both a restoration of family *identity* (status) and also family *character*. The new status or position is em-

---

5. Calvin is critical of what he calls the Anabaptist "illusion of perfection." He says that they teach that "the children of God are restored to the state of innocence, [and] now need not take care to bridle the lust of the flesh, but should rather follow the Spirit as their guide, under whose impulsion they can never go astray" (*Institutes*, III, 3:14, 1960:606f.). There were, of course, many varieties of Anabaptists, but this was certainly not the main or centrist position. Rather, they might be blamed for rather more moralism and emphasis on self-discipline that even Calvin might approve.

phasized when we, both men and women, are called "sons of God." In a culture where the family name and inheritance were the privilege of the sons, Paul could describe our new relationship "in Christ" as the full family status of sons (Rom. 8:14; Gal. 3:26; 4:5; Eph. 1:13b-14).

But to be called a child of another person, e.g., of Abraham or David, also meant sharing the family characteristics. Thus Jesus told the Jewish leaders that if they were truly Abraham's children, they would act like their father, Abraham (John 8:39). To be born into the family means to share the character image of the parents. So Jesus as the Son and image of God reveals his character, and we as his "brothers and sisters" also are called to disclose God's love and grace. While we should probably avoid the language of divinization, we must stress that salvation means sharing in a qualitatively new kind of life. As John puts it, we have "eternal life," namely, that quality of life that participates in the eternal. Or as Paul might say it, we have "life in the Spirit."

Further, to speak of the uniquely human quality as the image of God indicates that our human self-fulfillment can be achieved only in a loving, responsible relationship to God. We find our authentic fulfillment in our self-identity as children of God. This fulfillment cannot be achieved by identification with any national or tribal image. Neither can we expect the fulfillment of our human image and destiny through scientific grasping for knowledge and power over our world. Because we are in God's image and not merely the image of earthly parents, we can never find the fulfillment of our destiny (salvation) through submission to any human culture and tradition.

In conclusion, the metaphor of salvation as a renewal of humanity in the divine image speaks of a genuinely new possibility for the integration and fulfillment of our lives and the life of our world as children of God. Paul uses the figure of birth pangs to describe the struggle and agony of creation as the human race is being formed into the image of God (Rom. 8:18-24). He looks forward in hope to the final revelation of that image in the children of God and to the freedom that will come with it for the whole creation. His confidence is grounded on the experience of the Christ whose suffering and death was prelude to the glory of resurrection and life with God.

Christ's Role in the Restoration

How, then, shall we understand theologically the role of Jesus Christ in the formation of humankind into God's image? Certainly his role as the *one who has initiated the new humanity* must be accentuated. He is the "first-born among many brothers and sisters" (Rom. 8:29), the "first-born of all creation" (Col. 1:15), the "first-born from the dead" (Col. 1:18). In him the goal of sonship already has been reached. In him we have been created for righteousness (Eph. 2:10). In him the new creation order has begun (1 Cor. 5:17). We have been chosen and called to be conformed to his "image" (Rom. 8:29). Or he is the "second Adam," "the man of heaven" whose image we shall bear just as we have borne the image of the "first Adam, the man of earth" (1 Cor. 15:45-49; cf. 1 John 3:1-2).

Of course this medley of related metaphors does not create a theological description of Christ's role, but it does suggest a personal-social dynamic in which Christ is the paradigm, exemplar, or role model who stimulates, trains, and encourages us to share his achievement of the image of God. At the time of this writing, the twenty-third Olympiad is being held in Los Angeles. Time and again the television announcers have commented on the empathetic bond that develops between coach and athletes-in-training. Perhaps we can use this as one modern metaphor of the relation between Christ and the Christian-in-training, which is a good translation of *mathētēs* (disciple).

The relation between the ancient master and disciple was far deeper than that of the modern teacher and student. This relation can probably be best understood today in terms of the relationship of the Hindu *Mahadevi* or *Rishi* (Divine Teacher) and the Zen Buddhist masters and their devotees. Such "divine" masters initiate their followers into the revelations and disciplines of their ancient traditions, and they virtually become "lord" for the devotee.

This would suggest that more attention needs to be given to the life of Jesus as exemplar. Here we are not interested in a literalistic imitation. That is not in the spirit of Jesus. Rather, it is the "mind of Christ," the spirit or style of Jesus, who attained the glorious image of God through death and resurrection. Jesus qualified as the "second Adam," not in the manner of the "first Adam" who through selfish aggression grasped for the image, but through faithful obedience to the will of God (Phil. 2:5-11). Precisely this one, who washed his disciples' feet, we call "Master and Lord" (John 13:12-15), and his is the mind or attitude we are called to emulate (Phil. 2:1-4).

Salvation as Eschatological Renewal

Finally, salvation is spoken of as *hope*, a hope which we have in Christ and for which we are waiting (Rom. 8:24-25; 2 Pet. 3:11-13). When taken in the larger context it seems clear that these passages should not be interpreted to suggest a totally future salvation. Rather our hope is for a consummation or completion of what Jesus has already begun. The biblical word *eschatos* (end) and the concept of the two ages clearly suggest historical movement toward a consummation.

Here our purpose is not to develop a full eschatological description of the consummation but to note how it is described in relation to Christ and to inquire how the future salvation is related to our present experience of Christ. Our main focus will be upon the *eschatos* (end) as the conclusion of the mission of Jesus. How is he as the Messiah related to a yet-future consummation of salvation?

Apocalyptic Restoration

The writers of the New Testament approach the eschatological implications of Christ's cross and resurrection in two ways. On the one hand they attempt to fit Christ's mission into the framework of an earlier apocalyptic vision. On the other hand, they interpret the consummation as a projection based upon the knowledge and experience of Jesus Christ which we already have.[6] These are not entirely irreconcilable, but they do give us two quite different pictures of the final salvation.

The descriptions of 2 Peter 3 and 2 Thessalonians 1, for example, clearly follow the conventional patterns of apocalyptic judgment and vengeance when they speak of Jesus' manifestation at the end of history. The one who came as the suffering Lamb of God the first time will return to mete out violent justice on the wicked and to comfort those who have suffered for their faith. Little in these passages suggests that Jesus' revelation of God as the Father and his rejection of violence and vengeance has made any intrinsic difference in the writers' views of the end-time victory of Christ.[7]

If we use the book of Revelation as an example, we can see how the gospel impregnates the older apocalyptic patterns. First, Jesus as "the Lamb who was slain" is the "Lion (warrior) of Judah" (5:5). And in spite of the violent imagery that follows throughout the book this figure of the sacrificial self-giving Lamb commands the action (5:9; 11:15; 13:8; 17:14; 19:13). Indeed, the contradictory symbolism is pressed almost beyond the point of reconciliation. For example, this Lamb treads "the wine press of the fury of the wrath of God the Almighty" and rules the nations "with a rod of iron" (19:15).[8]

Second, the New Testament apocalyptic gives a significantly different view of the end result of salvation. The nationalistic elements which are so pervasive in earlier apocalyptic are gone. Jerusalem, the capital of the "new heaven and a new earth" (Rev. 21:1), is not the national capital of a victorious Israel but the "new Jerusalem which comes down from God out of heaven" (21:2). This is a faithful presentation of a universal salvation by faith which we see so clearly in Paul's writings. The radical newness is underscored by the rule of God as the Lamb who dwells with humankind (22:1-5).

Third, the saints who are the "followers of the Lamb" are not depicted as warriors in the midst of the martial violence that surrounds them. They are martyr-witnesses who follow the example of Jesus and are the victims of the political violence and economic repression. They overcome by the blood of the Lamb (Rev. 12:11; 7:14).

Having noted all this, we see that the metaphors of violent political retaliation and vengeance so characteristic of apocalyptic still dominate the accounts. Even the souls of martyrs under the altar cry out for vengeance (Rev. 6:9-11). At best the apocalyptic imagery is esoteric and ambiguous, and it is of limited use in conveying the message of God's salvation through Christ. Precisely these characteristics have led many Christian interpreters to give a highly spiritualized interpretation of the imagery much as they do the violent language of the Psalms.

The Christian apocalyptic vision of salvation, then, describes Jesus as the resurrected Messiah who has already conquered the powers of death and leads the continuing struggle against evil. At the consummation he will be the victorious judge to whom all humankind will have to answer. He will

---

6. This inescapably raises the question of how these two quite different approaches and different conclusions are to be reconciled. Those who insist on a verbal-plenary concept of inspiration that results in the perfection of every apostolic opinion recorded in the New Testament insist that both of the pictures be given equal value and that they can and must be "harmonized." This has led, on the one hand, to "spiritualizing" the apocalyptic imagery, or on the other to classifying the different "dispensational" approaches of God in the various stages of revelation and salvation. But is this the only possible way to respect the authority of Scripture as the true Word of God to us? I think not. Rather, we have here a good example of the new wine of the gospel bursting the old wineskin. The old apocalyptic which served a useful purpose in the process of revelation proves inadequate to contain the new wine of the gospel. After all, we should realize that the apocalyptic interpretation was formed before Jesus came as the Christ and without clear knowledge of his radically new conception of the Messiah's mission.

Jon Sobrino states it well when he says, "Jesus' own preaching was *formally* apocalyptic, but he superseded its *material* side in so far as he proclaimed God's coming in grace" (Sobrino, 1978:243).

As a vehicle of communication, especially for a Jewish audience, the apocalyptic interpretation was used in a transition period, but it does not give us the final word. As in so many cases in the New Testament, a new word, a deeper understanding—an advance into further truth directed by the Spirit as the apostles reflected more deeply on the significance of Jesus—is spoken in the midst of the old. Indeed, we are privileged to have not only the final product of the apostles' most mature reflection but an insight into their "theological method" as it were. And the method as well as the final insight is highly instructive for us. As for them also for us, Jesus and his cross-resurrection must remain the touchstone for our theology.

7. We might note that the Thessalonian epistles are among Paul's earliest writings and that he makes a more reflective approach in later writings. As for 2 Peter, its canonicity has been questioned from the earliest period. This does not mean that we reject its validity as a witness to Christ, but we certainly must attempt to understand it within its context.

8. Vernerd Eller has attempted to read Revelation as a tract for nonresistant martyrdom. His interpretations emphasize the "new wine" which seems to burst the old wineskins of apocalyptic. See his *War and Peace from Genesis to Revelation* (1981) and *The Most Revealing Book of the Bible* (1974).

then be manifested as final authority meting out rewards or punishments as they are deserved. Perhaps if we remember that this victorious judge is the Lamb whose wounds are still evident, whose discernment is represented by seven eyes (Rev. 5:6ff.), and whose word of judgment is the word from the cross, we can still find meaning in this Christian revision of the apocalyptic imagery.

Renewal as Completion of Christ's Mission

The second approach, which seems to have more potential for theological development, attempts a reinterpretation of the *eschaton* in light of what has been disclosed in the incarnation. Making Jesus Christ the starting point and touchstone, it seeks to describe the consummation as the extension and completion of what he began in the cross and resurrection.

Two special words are used to describe this consummation in the New Testament. The first word, *epiphaneia*, which occurs in the pastoral and Thessalonian epistles[9] refers to the *eschaton* as the "*manifestation* of Christ." In the end it will be made incontrovertably clear to all that the truth lies with Jesus Christ. His *epiphaneia* will be the final vindication of his claim to be the true and living way. And as the manifest truth he will appear as the judge. (Compare the concept of judgment in John 3:19-20; 12:48-49.)

The second word, *parousia*, has a broader usage. It is a synonym for *epiphaneia* (cf. 2 Thess. 2:8), but it puts emphasis on Jesus' coming and presence as manifest Lord. In the *eschaton* Jesus will come and will be fully present to all and in all. As Paul seems to say in 1 Corinthians 15:25-28, at that time Christ's reign, i.e., his authoritative command of the battle with the forces of evil and death, will be finished, and he will at last be known to all as the very presence of God who will then be "all in all" (cf. Rev. 22:3-5).

When we speak of the end as consummation of what was begun in Christ, we use a number of events and metaphors which first describe Jesus' revelation of God and eternal life and our present experience of Christ in salvation. For example, we move from his resurrection as the firstfruits to the final victory over and abolition of death (1 Cor. 15:25-28, 51-54). We move from his cross as the manifestation of God's judgment upon sin to the final manifestation and judgment. We move from Jesus' birth as the Son of God to the fulfillment of our own adoption or birth as children of God in his likeness (Rom. 8:23, 29; 1 John 3:2-3). In our experience we know him as Lord in the church, and we hope for the time when he will be "Lord of lords and King of kings"—when everything will be subject to his will. We know him as the one who reconciled the warring human families to God and to each other, and we anticipate the completion when he will have reconciled and reunited all things in the universe (Eph. 1:9-10; Col. 1:20).

Each of these approaches is expanded in the New Testament, but our main point here is to note that the culmination of salvation is the completion of what Christ has already begun. Thus we speak of it in categories of transformation, re-creation, redemption, resurrection, and reconciliation. And the relation of these to Jesus' mission is clear. He is the "pioneer and perfecter" of our salvation. Or as another version puts it, he is the one on whom our "faith depends from start to finish" (Heb. 12:2, NEB).

9. These references are to 1 Timothy 6:14-15; 2 Timothy 1:10; 4:1, 8; Titus 2:13; and 2 Thessalonians 2:8.

Participating
in Jesus' Salvation
"For Us"

Chapter 12

The Cross of Reconciliation: Dealing with Shame and Guilt

The gospel is the message of Christ crucified (1 Cor. 2:2). Of course when we speak of the cross, it is the cross of the resurrected Christ. His salvation "for us" includes both death and resurrection, as we have seen. But it is through the cross that reconciliation and peace are achieved (Eph. 2:13-16). Christianity has from the beginning been the message of the cross. But how has the cross become the instrument of God by which we are freed? And how specifically does the death of Christ on the cross release us from the burden we call guilt and the social disgrace which we call shame? What does it mean to say that he "bore our sins in his body on the tree" (1 Pet. 2:21-25)?

To explore these questions we will first need to look more carefully at the meaning of *guilt* and *shame* and how they are related to our experience of sin. (These are the words that refer to the inner moral stigma and the social offensiveness of our mistakes.) How is the imputation of blameworthiness, either by oneself or by others, related to our experience of inability to live in love as God's children? In understanding these connections we can begin to see how Christ's suffering of shame and guilt is related to our experience and how it can provide a remedy for sin.

The Nature of Shame and Guilt

In the Christian view shame and guilt are more than subjective feelings conditioned by a relative cultural situation. They must be defined in terms of an ultimate authority which defines the true nature of human existence and relationship. The biblical concept that humans are created "in the image of God" means that their true nature and responsibility must be defined in a relation to God. This gives both shame and guilt an objective moral status which must be taken seriously in the act of moral pardon.[1] Acts against the very nature and ground of existence cannot be resolved by escape from one set of cultural mores to a society with different patterns and definitions. Sin is a universal objective moral offense, and pardon must be morally justified. Both its objective (social-moral) and subjective (individual-psychological) aspects must be dealt with.

Traditional resolutions based upon the legal metaphor have proved inadequate to the profound nature of the problem. It is not a matter of "paying a debt to justice" as defined in the law of talion, i.e., "an eye for an eye and a tooth for a tooth." The shame and guilt of sin are antecedent to legal evaluation and penalties and cannot be equated with them. Legal metaphors only bear witness to a more primal reality of personal relationships. They do not define the essence.

Experienced as Defilement and Blame

Shame is associated with concepts of sin as defilement or *uncleanness,* and it is experienced as a sense of embarrassment or unworthiness in another's presence (Isa. 6:1-5; Luke 5:8; 7:6). Shame is a fundamental aspect of the moral response, but its full ethical character depends upon an ethical perception of the *holy* one in whose presence it feels defilement. Subjectively shame is experienced as embarrassment, feelings of unworthiness, loss of selfhood, and despair. Objectively it is suffered as social disgrace, exclusion, or ridicule which the group projects onto the "defiled" individual. Shame is used in many cultures as a deliberate deterrent to or penalty for conduct of which the society disapproves.

Guilt is experienced as a burden of responsibility that one must bear for what has been done.[2] Subjectively guilt is felt as blame or self-accusation, a sense of sin when the offense is recognized as *my fault.* Guiltiness suggests inexcusability and implies that the offensive action was deliberate, and this inexcusability of the act gives guilt its condemning force. By way of contrast, defilement and its shame are no less severe when they are inadvertent and even unavoidable.[3]

Objectively guilt is fault or culpable error for which society may hold the offender responsible. Such responsibility is objectified in formulas of restitution or legally prescribed penalties. As objective moral fault guilt is an intentional offense against other people; and raised to the spiritual level it is an offense against God (sin). Because it is intentional it causes hostility and alienation. These consequences are intrinsic, not legal; and left unchecked, guilt results in the final alienation which we call death.

Cross Related to Both Shame and Guilt

The Christian doctrine of forgiveness and reconciliation, then, must deal with the social disgrace and exclusion (objective shame) as well as the subjective feelings of failure and unworthiness. Further, it must deal with the intrinsic consequences of guilt—both its internal and external consequences, and it must do this in such a way that it does not condone or augment the objective fault.[4] The intention of forgiveness is to nullify shame and guilt so that reconciliation and a new beginning become possible. The shamed person must find new identity and personal worth. And the guilty person must find expiation. Both the objective alienation and hostility which have been institutionalized in our social and legal systems and the subjective remorse and blame that so inhibit personal fulfillment in human relationships must be overcome.

Western approaches have dealt almost exclusively with the relation of the cross to guilt, and, as we have seen, they have explained it as the moral ground for forgiveness, i.e., as equivalent penalty to clear the debt of guilt, or as a moral influence to induce penitence for guilt. Undoubtedly this bias developed from Roman concepts of justice and law which dominated medieval Christendom. In the modern era with its heavy emphasis on feelings and psychological conditions guilt *anxiety* has become the focus of attention. The cross as a means of dealing with guilt feelings has been underscored. Accordingly the consequence of forgiveness purchased by the blood of Christ is relief from the anxiety of anticipated punishment and internalized blame, i.e., "peace of mind."

Our contention is that the role of the cross in reconciling us to God must be seen in broader terms as an answer to both shame and guilt. And

---

1. The ancient Stoics grounded such an ethic in reason and a universal law which transcends its national and tribal expressions. Christians have tended to identify God with this reason, and God's law as expressed in the Bible with the universal law. This rather too-easy identification of reason and God left out much of the personal dynamics involved in "law," but we seek precisely this kind of absolute ground as an ethical basis for our experience of Christian forgiveness.

2. Paul Ricoeur's comment that "guilt designates the *subjective* moment in fault as sin is its *ontological* moment" is a most helpful distinction. But his statement a paragraph later that "guiltiness is never anything else than the anticipated chastisement itself, internalized and already weighing upon the consciousness . . ." seems a bit superficial (Ricoeur, 1967:101).

3. For example, in the tragedy of Oedipus his fault is not only unintended but results from his own attempt to avoid the prophecy of his fate that he would kill his father and marry his mother. Even so he suffers all the disgrace and remorse of his acts.

4. One of the earliest objections to Paul's doctrine of grace was that it not only condoned but encouraged sin, and Paul felt at pains to answer the objection. See Romans 6. At this point we should also compare the Amida Buddhist tradition which not only forgives but excuses and permits continuation in sin as a result of ignorance. The grace of Buddha seeks to deal with this problem by providing alternate paths to salvation, some of which are so disguised that the sinner will not even be aware that he or she is being saved.

further, the resolution of the shame problem—both the problems of social exclusion as a moral sanction and the inner anxiety of failure that shuts us off from others and paralyzes moral response—provides the context and paradigm for understanding the resolution of guilt, not vice versa.

A Social-Psychological View of Shame

The significance of shame has not been generally recognized in modern Western analyses of the human social-psychological problem. Freud generally associated shame with sex inhibitions and tended to confuse it with guilt. Post-Reformation theologians also have assumed that human feelings of unworthiness and shame are the simple consequences of guilt and have explained the work of Christ almost exclusively as the pardoning of guilt.

Both the secular disciplines of psychology and anthropology as well as theology have taught us to think of shame as a morally inferior reaction to wrongdoing. Psychologically it was described as a stage in development prior to a fully mature individuality (Erickson, 1950:222-24). Anthropologically it was described as an "external sanction" indicative of a culture which has not yet advanced to the stage where inner moral sanctions, such as we have in the West, would be effective (Benedict, 1946; Mead, 1937).

Theologically shame was associated with cultures of primitive groups having inferior ethical traditions. Its motivation was considered self-serving (face saving), and thus it was assumed to be an ethical sanction far less worthy than conscience. Based upon such an assumption the latent conscience must be stimulated and guilt anxiety raised through the preaching of God's law before the gospel of forgiveness could be effective.[5]

More recently a number of psychoanalysts and psychologists have attempted to delineate more carefully the differences between guilt and shame and have shown that shame is the more primal and disruptive instinct of the two. Shame plays a major role in the alienation and antagonism that afflict the human race. From these observations and analyses emerge several insights that are most helpful in understanding how the crucifixion of Christ can reconcile alienated humans.

Exposure to Oneself

First, shame is not experienced merely as exposure to others but also as exposure to oneself. As Helen Lynd in a comment on Dostoyevski "who knew so many hidden aspects of shame," says, "the deepest shame is exposure to oneself even though no one else may pay any attention to or even know of it" (Lynd, 1961:31). Gerhard Piers, a psychoanalyst, points out that shame is experienced when we fail to meet our "ego ideal." Shame anxiety accompanies failure to meet one's own self-expectations and not only those of the group.[6] And after a careful review of different kinds of data Lynd observes that "there is a particularly deep shame in deceiving other persons into believing something about oneself that is not true"—a very interiorized norm and anxiety to say the least (Lynd, 1961:31).

Milton Singer, an anthropologist, agrees with this. He shows how the older definitions which attempted to distinguish between guilt and shame cultures by defining guilt as an internal moral sanction and shame as an external, face-saving sanction simply do not fit the realities (Piers and Singer, 1971:63-70). He points out that both guilt and shame are experienced similarly in the presence of others, and vice versa in the privacy of one's own psyche. Shame, not only as fear of group ridicule and exclusion but as disappointment and disapproval of one's own weakness and failure to meet the ideal, can be an internal sanction.

This reassessment and redefinition of shame anxiety as an interior— and potentially serious—moral reaction to shortcomings or failure to meet one's ideals opens the way for a reevaluation of it as an appropriate reaction to sin. And it also calls for serious theological reflection on its ethical resolution as both a spiritual and psychological block to personal relationship with God and others.

Failure to Attain Ideal

Second, shame anxiety occurs as a result of not living up to an ideal. However the ego ideal is formed, and apparently it is a complicated psychological process, it includes both individual and group ideals. Theologically it also includes the ideal implied in the concept of humanity in the divine image. Again, Piers says that in contrast to guilt anxiety which

---

5. Even a classic study like H. R. Mackintosh's *The Christian Experience of Forgiveness* (1927), which moves far beyond the legal understanding of guilt and sensitively explores the way in which it is related to fractured relationships, seems totally unaware of the shame factor. For Mackintosh the gravest *penalty* (a legal term) for sin is "forfeiture of fellowship," and in this manner he introduces the personal-moral factors of forgiveness through Christ's cross onto center stage (Mackintosh, 1927:25ff.). In his chapter on atonement he wrote, "We ought to fix it in our mind that the atonement is only relevant to the *guilty and alarmed conscience*, that we must look at it with penitent eyes" (p. 194; italics mine).

6. Piers differentiates guilt and shame as follows:

a. Shame arises out of a tension between the ego and the ego ideal, not between ego and superego as in guilt.

b. Whereas guilt is generated whenever a boundary (set by the superego) is touched or transgressed, shame occurs when a goal (presented by the ego ideal) is not being reached. It thus indicates a real 'shortcoming.' Guilt anxiety accompanies transgression; shame, failure.

c. The unconscious, irrational threat implied in shame anxiety is abandonment, and not mutilation (castration) as in guilt.

d. The Law of Talion does not obtain in the development of shame, as it generally does in guilt" (Piers and Singer, 1971:23-24).

is focused on "active punishment by superiors" for transgressions, it is the "all-seeing, all-knowing eye which is feared in the condition of shame, God's eye which reveals all shortcomings of mankind" (Piers and Singer, 1971:29-30).

Our major concern here is not with the psychological origins of the two responses in the development of personality but with their characteristics and their effects on human relationships. If the above analysis is correct, it suggests that where shame is a major factor in psychological and cultural development, *relationships and ideals will be more important and persuasive than law and punitive threats.*

Isolating Anxiety

Third, shame anxiety, if unresolved, becomes a potentially more serious disruptive force in personal relations than guilt. It is an isolating, alienating experience which inhibits communication. Gershen Kaufman calls it a "total experience that forbids communication with words" (1974:568-74). Shame anxiety includes but goes deeper than the fear of abandonment or excommunication which may enforce conformity to the group norm. Kaufman describes its effect as rage in contrast to anger. "Rage," he writes, "protects self against further exposure and further experiences of shame by both insulating the self and keeping others away. Anger directly invites contact in order to get one's needs met" (1974:571).

By way of contrast, guilt results from a measurable offense. People experience guilt as anticipation of deserved punishment, and since such an offense is measurable and pardonable, the offender remains relatively open to communication with others, whether in confession and forgiveness or in defiance and punishment. Lynd notes, "Guilt, at least in our culture, can be a form of communication. There is communication of a sort not only between penitent and confessor, but between criminal and judge. Condemnation or punishment is itself a form of communication, relation to one's fellows" (Lynd, 1961:66).

This is an especially important insight for understanding the nature of human alienation from God. The cause of our hostility and defiance against God is not merely our fears of deserved retaliation. Not even the inner recognition of our own fault alone prompts us to avoid his presence. Our shame of the weakness that led us to betray the trusting, loving Friend causes us to hide and blame our Maker. Fear of being discovered in our nakedness or exposed in our uncleanness makes us hide in resentful embarrassment. Chagrin and inferiority feelings trigger the projection of self-justifying blame onto God and others. The instinctual resentment of being humiliated, not only in the eyes of others (God) but in our own eyes, creates this anxiety, irrational alienation, and hiding from love. Our rage against God is the projection of our self-loathing. We must be reconciled to ourselves as well as to God. Therefore, God must deal with the "vicious cycle of shame and rage" which makes us "children of wrath." This is the nature of the human problem to which a theology of atonement must address itself.

Not Eased by Punishment

Fourth, in no way can shame be expiated through substitutionary compensation or retaliation. As Piers observed, it does not respond to the law of talion. No payment such as a "debt to justice" can balance accounts and thus restore lost honor. Suffering punishment for the mistake may screen the feelings, but it cannot genuinely relieve the anguish of shame. Only a forgiveness which covers the past and a genuine restoration of relationship can banish shame.

What is needed is a restoration of communication. The rage which isolates and insulates must be overcome. Reconciliation and restoration of mutual intimate relationship through a loving open exchange is the only way to heal resentment and restore lost self-esteem. Kurt Riezler believes that "mutual love banishes shame."[7] And Helen Lynd says, "The very fact that shame is an isolating experience also means that if one can find ways of sharing and communicating it, this communication can bring about particular closeness with other persons and with other groups [who have experienced similar social humiliation]" (Lynd, 1961:66). Her point is slightly different from ours, but she does underscore the possibility of converting a mark of shame into a badge of honor through breaking out of isolation and sharing with others who have experienced similar painful discrimination. Shame is banished when open communication is established through loving identification and the worth of each can be mutually affirmed.

Forgiveness and Shame

Nature of the Problem

Now, how does this analysis of shame as the primal moral instinct affect our concepts of forgiveness and atonement? Does one *forgive* shameful

---

7. Kurt Riezler makes this observation especially in the case of sexual shame. "In sexual intercourse," he wrote, "without love, the companion becomes the observer. Shame decreases with increasing love, increases with decreasing love. It takes its leave when love reaches its peak and reappears when love takes its leave."

This observation is closely related to Riezler's equally insightful definition of love. Love, he says, is a relation "between human beings [in which] the I and the You build up a We as the whole of an intimate world in which they are obliged to be to themselves what they are to each other and are permitted to be to each other what they are to themselves (Riezler, 1943:461-62).

acts? Can *forgiveness* remove the shame anxiety and bring reconciliation? Certainly if we use the terminology of forgiveness in this way, it alters its accustomed meaning of release from a debt of guilt. Where sin is thought of as an act of transgression and the consequences are conceptualized as an objective debt (guilt), forgiveness is viewed as pardon or release from the debt. But where sin is conceived as an uncleanness, weakness, or blemish and its consequences devaluate the worth and self-esteem of the sinner (shame), then how shall we understand the meaning of forgiveness? Clearly both concepts are involved in the biblical diagnosis of the human situation, and the grace of God's forgiveness in Christ resolves both aspects of the problem. But the dynamics of forgiveness in the case of shame have not been so clearly articulated as they have for guilt. The problem can be stated simply. When guilt is objectified, the offender can be pardoned. When shame is objectified, the offender can only be excluded.

What does it mean to offer forgiveness to one who feels shamed for some moral failure? How can alienation be overcome and communication be restored? How can the impurity or failure be removed? Can it be atoned for without the removal of the offender? If the offender is not removed, must he or she continue to live in shame? The dilemma is no longer keenly felt in modern individualistic societies that have made values relative and made the individual the final arbiter. In the group-oriented cultures of Asia, however, this is still a live issue, and one becomes aware of much that has long since slipped into the subconsciousness of the troubled West.

In cultures like Japan, which have sometimes been described as "shame cultures,"[8] public exposure and exclusion are still important sanctions for regulating social behavior.[9] In such cultural settings the voluntary exposure and admission of a fault (confession) and forgiveness of that fault become highly complicated. Confession becomes a form of self-shaming and quickly turns into groveling. Forgiveness becomes problematic because to say "I forgive" implies that I affirm the other person's badness, and thus forgiveness reaffirms his or her shame. Thus it is far easier to overlook, excuse, or forget than to confess and forgive. Indeed, *yurusu*, the Japanese word translated "forgiveness," means to excuse, indulge, or permit.

The example of intimate associates tolerating and making excuses even for serious misdeeds of a comrade in order to protect him or her is well known.[10] In this way the web of inner group relationships is maintained by *indulging* the indiscretion. Where it becomes impossible to gloss over or hide such misdeeds the only recourse is exclusion, and in these cases there is virtually no possibility for reconciliation. And where the offender owns responsibility and excludes himself or herself in an act of atonement, there may be a certain moral resolution, but it is precisely the self-exclusion that justifies such a resolution. Therefore it cannot lead to reaffirmation of the former relationship. Indeed, suicide, which is the ultimate act of self-exclusion, epitomizes the dilemma.

An Athenian Example

This kind of psychological and moral dilemma is well-known in ancient cultures. Paul Ricoeur has made an observation about the ancient Athenian society in his book, *The Symbolism of Evil* (1967), that may be helpful in understanding contemporary concepts of offense and its annulment in shame-oriented cultures.

Strictly speaking, forgiveness and reconciliation of the offender in the biblical sense of these words was an impossibility in the ancient, prephilosophical Athenian society. Offenses were viewed as uncleanness which polluted the land, and there was no remedy for the impurity short of exile or execution of the defiling person. Only the exclusion of the offender could atone for the sin and cleanse the homeland of dishonor. Thus we can speak only of the annulment of sin, not of its forgiveness. So long as the defiling person remained in exile the sin was expunged from the homeland.[11]

---

8. Ruth Benedict in her analysis (1946) of the Japanese society has pinned this label on the culture. In a similar vein Wolfram Eberhard in his *Guilt and Sin in Traditional China* (1967) has analyzed the Chinese culture. Singer (Piers and Singer, 1971) has effectively pointed out, however, that such classifications depend very much on the author's definition of shame, and that in any case all cultures have elements of both. Eberhard recognizes this latter point.

9. These sanctions are effective because in these cultures social relationships and interpersonal dependencies continue to be of paramount importance. A respectful relationship is considered a higher moral value than legalities or ideological truth.

The most effective way to break relationships is to shame another person; therefore these sanctions must be used cautiously. When one has been shamed, there is little chance for reconciliation.

10. "If a man happened to make a mistake in his work his friends in the group would protect him. Even in a very serious case, where no reasonable excuse would justify his actions, they would protect him with the group power and fabricate some irrational and emotional justification. They are at all times firmly on his side, not necessarily because he is right but because he is one of them. His fellows know well enough that he has committed a fault and is in the wrong, but even so, they retain to a striking degree their tolerance and sympathy for him. . . . One could point to many cases in which a man had committed a serious error and had even broken the law (and would have lost his position in another society), but remained comfortably in his post in spite of social accusations on the part of the general public . . ." (Nakane, 1973:127-31).

Nakane goes on deftly to describe how this leads not to freedom and authentic acceptance in group relationships but to intrigue and manipulation even in the *uchi no* (inner) group. And she points out how this is related to the need for and indulgence in taverns and bars where the group socializes together.

11. "The exile is not simply excluded from a material area of contact; he is chased out of a human environment measured off by the law. Henceforth the exile will no longer haunt the human space of the fatherland; where the fatherland ends there his defilement also ceases. To kill a murderer in the territory of the Athenian fatherland is to purify it; to kill him outside of

So far as the offender was concerned, his or her physical removal to a new place, a new homeland, provided the only possibility for a new beginning. In the new homeland under the jurisdiction of new laws "he was given new purity," says Ricouer. This finding a new place where one can begin again with a new identity is just what the Christian doctrine of forgiveness and reconciliation proclaims. Paul says that we are removed from the old jurisdiction of the law and placed under grace. The idea is the same; only the figure of exile is changed to the figure of return to the father's house. We are *forgiven*.

The Biblical World

The cultural expression of shame is much more evident in the world of the Bible than most modern Western readers are aware. It is not only a question of how often the word shame is used, although there are significant instances. The concepts of ritual purity and uncleanness, rules for the segregation of social classes and foreigners, attitudes toward women and sexual relationships, views of disease and death, exile as a form of punishment—all point toward a shame rather than a guilt orientation. Thus to a greater extent than is often recognized, the problem of sin in Israel was the problem of purifying the nation of its pollution without permanently expelling the unclean person. The problem was resolved by a common confession of shame before God (Isa. 6:5) and a careful definition of the degrees of sinfulness and the manner in which it might be cleansed. (See, for example, the rules of Leviticus.) For most transgressions ritual offerings could cover the offensive, dishonorable behavior. But the extreme case required execution of the offender whose continued presence would compromise the people and pollute the land (e.g., Josh. 7:13, 16-26).

To suggest that New Testament writers, including Paul, also were thinking in these terms far more than post-Reformation biblical interpreters and theologians realized is not unreasonable. A guilty conscience was Luther's problem, not Saint Paul's (Stendahl, 1963:202ff.). In the first-century world the moral impact of sin was experienced to a great extent as shame, and this is clearly reflected in the New Testament. The ultimate revulsion to sin can be expressed as glorying in what is contemptible to God, or vice versa, falling short of and shaming the glory of God (Rom. 3:23; 1:22-25; 1 Cor. 1:26-31; Phil. 3:19).

The Cross and the Shame of Sin

The concept of shame as a moral category, of which the Bible has considerable evidence, has been almost entirely overlooked as a means of understanding the death of Jesus *on the cross*. Perhaps here Asian cultures, and specifically Japanese culture, can make a contribution to the theology of atonement.

Sin as Shame (Dehumanization)

Shame is related to the fact that we have fallen short of the image of God, and it constitutes the primal anxiety reaction growing out of our realization of sin. Or, to put it in current secular vocabulary, shame is related to the dehumanization both of ourselves and others. We have disappointed and dishonored God in that we have fallen short of the covenant goals which would have fulfilled the divine image, i.e., our own human self-realization. In reaction we experience the chagrin and pain of failure when we become aware of the loss and anguish we have foolishly and selfishly caused to ourselves and others.

Thus shame is related in a unique way to the breakdown of interpersonal relations in the human family—both among humans and between humanity and the God in whose image they are created. We try to compensate for our sense of inferiority through self-justification and avoidance of others. We lash out in competitive rage, projecting our own inadequacies onto others and blaming them for our failures. We even blame God or deny his existence—an extreme form of avoidance. Certainly this is the meaning of the Adam and Eve and Cain and Abel stories.

The Cross as the Agony of Shame

Shame and guilt are closely intertwined in human experience, and to distinguish and isolate them for analysis is difficult. Guilt, for example, is a prime motivator of shame. Thus in the experience of forgiveness and reconciliation to God both aspects need to be dealt with. However, in light of our contention that shame is the primal moral instinct, we shall first examine the relation of the cross to human shame.

We have noted the psychological observations that love banishes shame and that shame does not respond to the law of talion. This corresponds precisely with the biblical message that the cross of Jesus is the revelation of God's love, not, we may add, propitiation of his anger. The propitiation of God's wrath by a calculated payment of the debt to his justice, which is the inescapable implication of the concept of assuaging God's just wrath no matter how the theory is modified, is grounded on the law of the talion (lex talionis). An equivalent vengeance or, if we use the metaphor

---

that territory is to kill an Athenian. New rites of asylum and welcome in another place, under other eyes, within the jurisdiction of another legislation will be able to give him a new purity" (Ricoeur, 1967:40). Note that for certain heinous sins this remains the only option in the writings of Leviticus.

of the accounting office, equivalent payment to balance the debt to justice must be paid in order to satisfy the moral requirements of God's law. Traditional Protestant theology brings God's love into the picture by pointing out that God himself provides the payment. He satisfies himself. But, as we have seen, this way of expressing God's self-justification inevitably exalts his punitive justice over his love.

We must recall that the cross was designed above all to be an instrument of contempt and public ridicule. Crucifixion was the most shameful execution imaginable. The victim died naked, in bloody sweat, helpless to control body excretions or to brush away the swarming flies. Thus exposed to the jeering crowd, the criminal died a spectacle of disgrace. By Roman law no citizen could be so dishonorably executed. The cross was reserved for foreigners and slaves.

It seems clear that the Jewish authorities fully understood this when they called for Jesus' crucifixion. He was not to die as a heretical prophet by stoning but as a ridiculous, blaspheming messianic pretender on a Gentile cross. Their taunts, "He saved others, but cannot save himself," underscore the ridicule. His weakness, ineffectiveness, and apparent failure to fulfill his promises were all heaped abusively upon him. The familiar words of the old hymn, "The Old Rugged Cross," are quite literally correct: the cross was "the emblem of suffering and shame." It epitomizes human concepts of defilement and exclusion. The one who was thus whipped out of the city and executed was "accursed" (Gal. 3:13).[12] Jesus died "outside the city wall" shamed as a deceiver of the people whose cause he had espoused.

When we understand the cross in this context of shame rather than guilt, the concept of propitiation becomes inappropriate. Kazoh Kitamori's conception of God's anguish (*tsurasa* for which the English translator has used "pain") seems much more appropriate to describe the tragic moral pain God endures in order to overcome the shamefulness of our evil.[13] He defines *tsurasa* as that agony or anguish suffered in the tragic but necessary sacrifice of a son or daughter in the cause of right—a pain which is at once natural and moral. On the cross the moral agony of the infinite love of God is revealed to us (John 3:16).

God's anguish as portrayed by Kitamori is closer to the outrage of being betrayed, dishonored, and disappointed by what he has lovingly created than it is to a detached, rational anger at the offense of his justice and the moral compulsion to be justified in his holiness. It is the anguish of love for his desecrated creatures that "never gives up" (1 Cor. 13:7-8a). His love is characterized by commitment to achieve his original purpose, namely, to create creatures in his own image who reflect his own glory. The cross is the revelation of this purpose to create by means of the power of love (*agapē*).

This love of God expressed itself through his solidarity with us in Jesus and especially through his shameful death on the cross. Jesus identified with the "poor." He was born and raised among the lower classes, associated with outcasts, and chose artisans, fisher folk, and tax collectors for his disciples. He belonged to the multitudes whom the religious leaders pronounced "accursed because they know not the law" (John 7:49). He identified with the socially excluded and despised and shared the stigma of their inferiority. *The cross is the epitome of this identification with us in shame.*

---

12. In orthodoxy the "curse of the law" has become equated with legal penalty for guiltiness. However, in its original form in Deuteronomy the curse is the opposite of blessing (Deut. 11:27-28). The curse is the curse of God as expressed in the law, i.e., it is the expression of God's severe displeasure and abandonment to the evil consequences of those actions which are cursed.

Especially in the text in Deuteronomy 21:22-23, to which Paul refers in Galatians 3:13, the accursed one is a defilement of the land, and Israel was commanded not to bring shame on the land by allowing the "accursed body" to hang exposed through the night. Thus it seems more correct to associate the curse with the shame of defilement and ostracism than with legal penalties for guilt. While the word used in Galatians 3:13 is *epikataratos*, the related word *anathēma* used more often in the New Testament had definitely come to include the idea of exclusion by the first century A.D.

Paul clearly says that Jesus suffered thus *for us*, (*huper hēmōn*), a vicarious suffering, but he does not explain this "for us" as an objective legal transaction between Christ and God as orthodoxy has done. See Büchsel's article on *Ara* and its cognates (1964:44; pp. 8f.). Therefore it seems best to understand this concept of curse in the context of shame rather than legal guilt.

13. While Kitamori uses the usual word *itami* for pain in his title, the inner meaning of his concept comes through most clearly when he explains the meaning of *tsurasa* in the context of Japanese tragedy. He has an instinctive understanding of shame and the utter moral impossibility of refusing loyalty even in the face of death. God's loyalty is expressed in his love which conquers his pain (Kitamori, 1965:234ff.).

Moltmann's lack of comprehension of Kitamori's concept of pain when he compares it to Bonhoeffer's concept of the weak, suffering God "who allows himself to be pushed out of the world," is typically Western. He only comments, "These suggestions must be taken further" (Moltmann, 1947:47). Bonhoeffer's idea is really closer to Shusaku Endo's concept of Christ as the "do nothing," weak Messiah.

Chapter 13

How did Jesus die for us?

Jesus' Vicarious Identification with Us

We have examined the dimensions of Jesus' identification with us in the shamefulness of our sin. He was made to share our sinful existence and suffer the full consequences (Rom. 8:3). But how does Jesus' solidarity with us in our shameful condition effect our salvation?

We have observed that this identification is a loving, empathetic *communication* with us. As one who shares our weakness and yet overcomes, he is an enabling communication (word). Only as from one of the poor could his words, "Blessed are the poor," have authority to bless. Only insofar as he was identified fully with those suffering the debilitating stigma of shame could his own "despising the shame" enable them to live above the existential circumstances in which they were trapped. Only as the carpenter's son conceived out of wedlock from the lowly Galilean town of Nazareth could his own sense of worth as God's Son and his total trust in God as loving Father begin to change their perception of themselves as God's children. Only *as one of them* in whom the glory of God's image was personified could he communicate that glory to others. His identification with us in our shameful situation enables us to identify with him in his realization of the "glorious liberty of the children of God" (Rom. 8:21).

The Language of Vicarious Sacrifice

This is the experienced context in which we are to understand the language of vicarious sacrifice. Jesus bore the shame of our sin which included the undeserved penalty for blasphemy. If he was the true revelation of God, then his accusers who rejected this truth were themselves the ones worthy of condemnation. In this sense we can say that he suffered not his own punishment but that which his accusers deserved.[1]

And inasmuch as we include all humanity in this generic rejection and dishonoring of God, we must say also "the chastisement of our sins was upon him." But this is not the substitution of a legal penalty which pays our debt to God's justice. It is rather *the substitution of total identification which accepts responsibility for all the group. He took our place including the consequences of this identification.* Thus "he who knew no sin was made sin for us" (2 Cor. 5:21).

Representation as Substitution

We can speak of Jesus' self-sacrifice as vicarious in two ways. He bore the consequences of our sin in order to be our servant (Mark 10:45). There is a vicarious element in all service, especially that which is done for those who cannot help themselves. Something is done *for* and *instead of* them. Thus Jesus took the "form of a servant" and identified with the human family. But more, "he humbled himself and became obedient unto death . . . on a cross" (Phil. 2:7-8). Jesus was not merely a victim of circumstances. He deliberately chose to be identified with the "poor" and to be their representative. He stood in for them in the confrontation with the power elite.

Jesus did not separate himself in pharisaical fashion to protect his own moral purity and reputation. He accepted the crowds, justified them against their accusers, forgave them, and blessed them as the chosen of God (Matt. 5:3; Luke 6:20). He was one of them. Indeed, a real part of the accusation against him was his mingling with "publicans and sinners." In the eyes of his accusers he was contaminated by his intimate association with them. This representational intimacy gave the accusation of blasphemy much of its force. His identification with the multitudes underscored the absurdity and danger of his claims in the eyes of the leaders. It also made the crowds more vulnerable to his presumed delusions. Thus they concluded that he must die rather than have the whole nation perish in delusion (John 18:14). In this sense he took the place of the Jewish nation as a representative substitute.

Again, the apostolic witnesses extended this concept to include generic humanity. Jesus took the place of all humankind inasmuch as his revelation

---

1. Wolfhart Pannenberg carefully works through the logic of the language of substitution both in the original historical setting and as it may apply more universally. In a summary statement of this logic he writes: "Under the presupposition that there is an element of substitution active in all social relationships, one is permitted to understand Jesus' death as a vicarious event in view of the unique reversal that the one rejected as a blasphemer is, in the light of his resurrection, the truly just man, and his judges, in contrast, are now the real blasphemers" (1977:269). His total section (pp. 258ff.) is most insightful, and I am indebted to him.

is a universal one. As one totally identified with and representing humanity, he faced his destiny of death on the cross.

Dynamics of Vicarious Identification

Viewing Jesus' vicarious sacrifice in the context of shame also helps us to understand the dynamics of vicarious identification in effecting personal change. Theories of guilt (penalty) substitution focus attention on gratitude and obligation as the basic motivations for following Christ. These motivations may impel us to obedience and loyalty, but they are inadequate to account for the reorientation of life which the New Testament calls repentance (*metanoia*). Repentance includes a radical change in our self-image to conform to Christ as the image of God. And this change is not motivated simply by gratitude for pardon.

Christ's vicarious identification with us enables us to identify ourselves with him and thus gain a new perspective on our true situation and to realize a new self-identity as children of God. His compassionate, personal communication with us as the Son and true image of God sharing our existential shame enables us to emerge from our self-isolation and confess our failure, feelings of unworthiness, and despair. Thus the possibility of accepting him as the true image of God and identifying with him as a member of God's family is opened to us.

Exposing False Shame

Further, the *crucified* Christ not only effects the resolution of shame anxiety; he also reveals the normative ethical-social dimensions of shame. *The cross exposes false shame as an idolatrous human self-justification and, in exposing it, breaks its power to instill fear.* Paul says that on the cross Christ "made a spectacle" of these cosmic powers that had for so long dominated society (Col. 2:15). By the same token we learn what is truly shameful in God's sight.

Shame is expressed in the taboos, mores, and laws of society which define its ethical character.[2] In theological terms we can say that the expressions of shame are negative indicators of a society's concept of the *imago dei* (divine image) reflected in humanity. They define what is considered truly human. Thus when we say that the cross exposes false shame and reveals the true nature of human shame, we are saying that the crucified reveals God's authentic image for humanity. The *crucified* Jesus has demonstrated God's standard of right human relations and has become the truly universal norm for humanity (Rom. 3:25ff.). This is Paul's word in 1 Corinthians 1:26-30 where he says that God has chosen what is foolish and weak, the low and despised in the world, to shame the wise and strong, the high and honored values of the world. The saving word from the cross is that the *crucified* Jesus Christ has been made our wisdom, righteousness, and holiness.

Many social expressions of shame have been ethically misplaced and perverted. They represent our selfish and often ignorant human attempts to control and dominate others for our own purposes, and thus they foster fear, superstition, and bondage. For example, physical deformities such as blindness at birth or birth into a low social class, which were thought to be the result of *karma*, were considered shameful. Taboos about menstruation and childbirth effectively kept women excluded from full social and political participation. Ritual defilements such as touching a dead body or instruments that an "unclean" person had used, eating "unclean" meats, and the like excluded the masses of lower-class people who were unable to avoid them (John 7:49). They included also what might be called the pseudo-moral defilement of associating with the wrong kind of people such as "tax collectors and prostitutes" (Luke 7:39).[3] All societies have outcasts with whom so-called good people hesitate to associate. The shame of crucifixion epitomized such perversion of values. What one does, not what is done to the person, constitutes the defilement.

From Jesus' example and teaching we learn that such taboos do not define the real shamefulness in human society. Rather, evil intentions, selfish desires, deceit, and pride which come from the heart defile humankind. Dishonoring parents, fornication, theft, adultery, coveting, and the like are the truly shameful acts (Mark 7:21-23). And we should feel shame in the presence of God who sees the heart and knows the intention.

We might note here that Jesus did not shift the categories from defilement and shame to transgression and guilt but gave to shame an authentic moral content and internalized norm, namely, exposure to the eyes of the all-seeing, righteous, loving God. Indeed, he described the judgment of God as making public the shameful things that we have imagined were hidden from sight (Luke 12:1-3). This transfer from an external social standard to an internalized theological standard is important for Christian formation in societies which continue to depend upon the shame of public exposure as a primary sanction against undesirable conduct. If it is not accomplished,

---

2. So-called "shame cultures" have been defined by anthropologists and sociologists as cultures that rely on public exposure to regulate social behavior and put a premium on "saving face." This is contrasted to "guilt" oriented cultures which encourage the interiorization of standards. However, both shame and guilt are related to a standard understood to be external to the individual; *and the ethical character of that standard is the crucial issue.* There is false guilt as well as false shame, as voluminous psychiatric literature attests.

3. The Gospel accounts of Jesus' ministry include many references to such taboos. See for example Mark 2:15-17; 7:1-19; Luke 7:36-39. Also see Acts 10:9-16 and Colossians 2:20-23.

the conscience remains bound to relative authorities such as tradition and local social approval.

Removing the Alienation

"Despising the Shame"

Jesus' crucifixion was an act of human shaming. His accusers understood it to be exposure before God and the people—a judgment upon sin. But the real ignomy was in the falseness of the accusations and the execution itself. Jesus accepted their judgment (both in the sense of condemnation and punishment) and suffered the most shameful death that religious and civil law had devised in order to expose the extremity of sin's shameful consequences. Thus he "despised the shame" (Heb. 12:2), i.e., he exposed the despicable character of our humanly devised shame.

In the same act he also revealed the true nature of God's holiness as the holiness of love. From the cross he asked God's forgiveness for his executioners who in ignorance thus excluded and shamed him. He accepted this contemptuous death rather than compromise the loving will of God. In so doing, his true glory as the undefiled Son of God was revealed (John 8:28). Mark indicates this in the pagan centurion's recognition of him as the suffering Son of God (Mark 15:39).[4] And in the resurrection one sees God's great reversal of perverted human values (1 Cor. 1:18-25).

Thus we can say that Jesus both shared our shame and has borne the shame for all who through his disclosure of God's holy love find freedom from its dread and power. His identification and suffering with us as the truly pure and honorable one has potentially released all humankind from the authority of false standards of value which cause hostility and dehumanization.

In exposing the misplaced shame and lovingly revealing the true failure of us all, Jesus, the "friend of sinners," removed the stigma and hostility which alienates us from each other and God. He has affirmed our worth as children of God, foolish and wayward children to be sure, and has pointed us to the renewed possibility of being formed in his image. He has called us to share in his sufferings, to take up our crosses, and in identification with him and through him to find our true self-esteem and fulfillment. He has called us not only to be reconciled with God but with other people, finding our true unity in the new self-image which we have in him.

"Abolishing Dogmas"

The message of Ephesians and Colossians is that Jesus abolished the dogmas that defined shame in the ancient world. The central Ephesians passage (2:13-16) focuses on the Jewish ordinances which Paul likened to the barrier in the temple precincts forbidding Gentiles to come closer to the holy place. He refers to this as a "wall of hostility" made up of the rules and taboos, written and unwritten, which caused the Jews to exclude Gentiles as "unclean," i.e., unholy. He says that Jesus abolished these *dogmas*[5] which give a false sense of separate identity before God. And he did this "in his flesh" *on the cross.* Thus he brought the Gentiles near "in his blood" of the new covenant (v. 13). In this manner he reconciled humankind to each other, and together to God "in one body through the cross, thereby bringing the hostility to an end" (v. 16.)

The same concept is present in Colossians 2:14-15. Here Paul says that through the cross the legal demands of the Jewish law such as circumcision have been cancelled. God erased the authority of these kinds of dogmas ("touch not, taste not," v. 21) which belong to the "elemental spirits" or "primal religions" with their taboos of defilement (vv. 20-23). And he disarmed the powers that operate by their authority (v. 15).

In these passages explicit attention is focused on the cross, the "body of flesh," and the "blood of his cross," that is, the actual physical crucifixion thus indicating that in the event itself a significant change was initiated. The change, however, is not described as a legal settlement of guilt or penalty. It is better understood as the erasing of shame and cleansing of defilements which caused ostracizaton and hostility. The concept of our reconciliation as a restoration of "purity" and "holiness" or rededication to God (Col. 1:22-23) also fits better into this context. The old sacred taboos of the holy have been abolished, and we have been consecrated to the true God in whose presence we are "blameless and without fault." Of course this new holiness is genuinely moral after the image of God himself (Col. 3:5-11, Eph. 4:20-25).

The Cross and the Guilt of Sin

Thus far we have used the word shame in our analysis of Christ's vicarious work of forgiveness, but it should now be clear that guilt is also involved in this suffering *for us.* Subjectively, guilt is the recognition that

---

4. The taboos of defilement were associated with the sacred or holy. Thus Mark places this confession of the centurion in the context of the tearing of the temple curtain which marked off the holy place. Exclusion meant exclusion from the sacred place, from "God's country"—the Fatherland. In light of this the centurion's confession that Jesus was the "Son of God" indicates his recognition that in spite of human exclusion from the sacred place, Jesus remains in fact the truly holy one of God.

5. *Dogma* in general refers to decrees, requirements, rules, teachings. In Ephesians and Colossians the term clearly applies to both Jewish and pagan regulations and taboos. In these contexts they are the ceremonial regulations such as circumcision and taboos like "touch not, taste not" which separate and cause feelings of alienation (see Eph. 2:15; Col. 2:14, 20; Kittel, 1964:230-32).

one's shame is blameworthy. One is not simply the victim of an imposed embarrassment, but the shame is the result of an intentional offense—a breach of responsibility, an act of selfishness and hostility. How does Christ's death on the cross, that is, death by a human act of condemnation and execution, relate to this guilt?

Guilt as Blameworthiness

First, we must understand that guilt is not created by law or ultimately defined by it. Guilt is ontological, not merely legal.[6] As Paul says, an intrinsic relationship exists between sin and death, i.e., a relationship that is not defined by an assigned legal penalty (Rom. 5:12-14). Moral evil is by definition antihuman, anti-"life and peace" (Mal. 2:5). Thus the Deuteronomic choice is between life and death: "See, I have set before you this day life and good, death and evil. I have placed before you life and death, blessing and curse; therefore choose life ... loving the Lord your God, obeying his voice" (Deut. 30:15-20.)

Guilt is primarily experienced as a sense of *indebtedness* and *blameworthiness*. The "anticipation of punishment" is a secondary anticipation which already reflects the legal and social punitive sanctions. But the primary sanctions of guilt are the constraint of a still deeper, more primal sense of the consequences of our actions. This constraint grows out of the realization that one's act has caused damage to another which is not simply unintended or unanticipated damage for which one might feel shame and sorrow. Guilt reflects the recognition that one's action against others was intentional and inappropriate. Thus the sense of blameworthiness. Such blameworthiness is experienced as a kind of debt owed to the people whom one has harmed. It is the sense that the other person has a right to *demand* repayment, that restitution *ought* to be made. Recompense anticipated as a demand, especially when the offender is unable to redress the wrong, is the source of guilt alienation.

Equivalent Penalty?

This perception of guilt as a debt lies behind the language of Christ's merit for us, or payment of our debt—a language more appropriate than penalty, but still lacking the fully personal dimension. The imagery of penalty differs from that of debt in that penalty is the way in which the anger of the offended person is assuaged when restitution is impossible. In its baser form issuing a penalty is a reaction of rage and takes the form of unlimited revenge, or revenge to the full extent of the offended person's ability to afflict it. In its regulated forms it takes the shape of legally or socially prescribed equivalents, i.e., *lex talionis*. And this equivalent is named justice in dealing with the guilt of the offender.

The *lex talionis* is a way to restrain the reaction of anger and not the way of prescribing the reaction of love. Insofar as this constraint represents a giant step in the moral control of anger in society, it reveals something of the nature of God, but it in no way defines the ultimate necessity of his nature. Even in our highest human moral responses we recognize that the demand of a penalty is inappropriate. Love transcends the justice of the *lex talionis* to the full extent that the disclosure of God in Christ transcends the Law of Moses. Therefore the cross itself, seen in light of the resurrection, must be our principle of theological interpretation. We must understand the types and shadows of the law in terms of the reality of Christ himself.

The cross involved no equivalent compensation or payment of penalty demanded by God's anger. God is justified in forgiving us on the basis of his own holy love and not on the basis of an equivalent penal satisfaction which has been paid to him through the death of Jesus.[7] The cross itself as an act of solidarity with us is the divine ethical justification for forgiveness, and the resurrection of Jesus demonstrates the effectiveness of God's love in Christ to forgive and cleanse us from sin.

In our experience of forgiveness as an ethical pardon we are led to repentance and newness of life through the life and death of Jesus (Rom. 5). Repentance includes (1) remorse and shame caused by guilt for our past transgressions (*metamellomai*), (2) a complete change of mind about Jesus as the true image of God (*metanoia*), and (3) a determination to live in solidarity with him (*epistrephō*). Such repentance does not *pay* for the past sin; God's forgiveness remains an act of pure grace.

Therefore, when we speak of the work of Christ as an expiation or re-

---

6. Pannenberg (1968), following Von Rad (1962), points out that in Israel the consequences of evil were not primarily legal. Even Paul in the New Testament sees death not as legal punishment but as natural consequence. The right or good is intrinsically connected to life—both personal and physical life—and wrong or evil is antilife.

7. The language of penalty and satisfaction persisted in seventeenth- and eighteenth-century Protestant orthodoxy even though its leading advocates like Quenstedt (1617-88), a Lutheran, and Heidegger (1633-89), a Reformed representative, admitted that the words are not directly used in the New Testament (see Franks, 1962:esp. 414,435).

In the early twentieth century men like P. T. Forsyth and James Denny wrestled with the unsatisfactory extremes of the legal metaphor while at the same time maintaining a doctrine of atonement by the sacrifice of Jesus on the cross. They repudiated the idea that the sacrifice was a legal penalty to propitiate the justice of an angry Father. The cross itself represents both the holiness (Forsyth) and moral love (Denny) of God himself. For Forsyth it was Jesus' full obedience or honoring the holiness of God which was realized in the crucifixion. For Denny it was his solidarity with us, his willingness to suffer the full consequences and pain of sin, that reconciles us.

These are attempts to move from a *legal* to a *moral* ground for atonement, but neither makes use of the shame-alienation motif. (See Forsyth, 1910 and Denny, 1911 and 1918. See also McDonald, 1985:250-257, 272-278.)

moval of guilt we must stay by the category of moral responsibility. To say that he bore our guilt can only mean that he accepted solidarity with us in our responsibility for sin in the sense that he assumed the responsibility to correct the intrinsic consequences, namely, alienation and death. As the Fourth Gospel puts it, Christ did not come to condemn but to give eternal life (John 3:16-18). He did not disassociate himself from us and point an accusing finger, but he identified with us and saved us from perishing. His only judgment was that like the entrance of light he exposed the true nature of human evil and forced a decision (*krisis*) (see John 3:19-20; 12:48-49).

This taking of responsibility for our sin is to be understood as the purpose and work of Christ's whole life and ministry and not simply as a transaction effected on the cross. Certainly this is the implication of Philippians 2:5-11 where Paul describes the incarnation as Christ "emptying" himself of divine prerogatives and accepting the "form of a servant," humbling himself even to a death on the cross (cf. Isa. 5:12). This is the language of total commitment and involvement on our behalf.

Bearing Our Sins

Already in his earthly ministry Jesus was bearing our guilt (Matt. 8:17), forgiving our sins (Matt. 9:1-8), and healing our diseases (Luke 4:18; Mark 10:45). Even then he was the Savior, and the cross was simply the final and total expression of his bearing our sins (1 Pet. 2:21-24). Thus the cross becomes both the supreme act of his self-giving and the symbol of his complete solidarity with us in our behalf.

What then does this solidarity with us in guilt mean? Stated briefly: *In solidarity with us*, that is, fully living among us as one of us and *on our behalf*, Jesus obligated himself to live completely under the authority of God, fulfilling the covenant responsibility ("born under the Law," Gal. 4:4) even though it inevitably meant that he would suffer the full consequences of our guilty alienation, namely death.

Certainly, to say that Jesus accepted responsibility for our guilt does not mean that he declared us acquitted of guilt. We are guilty, and we must confess our guilt. Neither did he excuse or indulge our guiltiness. He did not excuse either himself or us from the command to love God with our whole being. Indeed, he fulfilled the commandment and thus fully acknowledged its authority. Rather, Christ calls all people to repent. But inasmuch as he was executed by humans as a result of their guilty alienation, he may be said to have suffered the liability of their guilt—not, however, in the sense that he paid an equivalent penalty in order to satisfy God's anger or justice.

Jesus fulfilled his responsibility *in our midst*, challenging our claim of faithfulness and the validity of our self-justification, even though it meant that humankind, stung by this exposure of their guiltiness, executed him as the offender. In a classic example of the human deflection of guilt, his judges in the guise of official responsibility projected their own fault upon him. Pilate who said, "I find no fault in him," evaded responsibility, washing his hands of the matter. Thus in effect he shifted the burden of guilt onto Jesus. And the Jewish authorities who accepted the moral responsibility for his execution, saying, "His blood be upon us," were intending to assert their own righteousness and Jesus' guiltiness before the law.

Nor is our contemporary situation much different. We continue both in our individual and social relationships to project our guilt onto others whom we punish in our continuing attempt to justify our own faults. For example, in our political and economic systems we continue to shift the guilt of violence onto the poor and oppressed, "the least of these" whom Jesus called "my brothers and sisters," who challenge the injustice of the system and threaten our unjustified advantage. Thus we must also confess that Christ bore our guilt as well as the guilt of the people in his own generation.

In Summary

We may say that the crucifixion of Jesus is related to our guilt in the following ways. First, the crucifixion of Jesus exposes the true nature of our sin as an act of self-contradiction motivated by our selfish anxieties and desires. Precisely in the extremity of the cross our shameful actions are seen to be blameworthy. Our fault is not merely an act against human legislation, mores, or taboos; it is an act against life itself.

Second, Jesus' crucifixion exposes the seriousness of human sin. In the grip of sin's blind perversity and stubborn self-justification we put to death the innocent and pure Son of God. These two theological insights are structured into the pattern of the Gospel narratives and are especially clear in the Johannine narrative. The self-contradictory defense of the religious system and the prerogatives of its leaders finally forced the death of one who challenged it with the authority of love.

Third, the crucifixion demonstrates that the true righteousness of God is the righteousness of love, a love which creates the new moral possibility by the gracious removal of the offense through unlimited self-giving. And, we may add, this is the nature of God's righteousness which we can share "by faith."

And fourth, somehow in the mystery of love this revelation of true righteousness moves us to repentance and reunion with God, the true source of our life. The cross is God's declaration that our faults are pardonable when and where Jesus is recognized as the authentic disclosure of God's will for our lives. In this gift of himself even unto death and "while we were yet sinners" we come to realize that we are indeed forgiven. In giving himself to us and for us he frees us to give ourselves to God and to live in the joyous expectation of resurrection to eternal life.

Chapter 14

Our Solidarity with Christ: Receiving Salvation

Christians claim that Jesus did something "for us" that changed our relationship to God and opened up new possibilities not only for this life but for eternity. These claims raise the question how we can participate today in this achievement of Jesus "for us." Assuming the full accuracy of the accounts of Jesus' life, death, and resurrection, what real difference does it make for life *today*? How does one man's life 2,000 years ago, even if that man was the "Son of God," make any significant difference for our lives in the twentieth century?

Such a question is not normally raised in connection with the contributions of other religious leaders. The example and personal influence of strong personalities is extended through their writings, and the events which they set in motion take their course for good or ill. To profit from the teachings of Moses or the Buddha, for example, one must simply obey them. To reap the benefits of the mystical philosophers and teachers one must learn their secret knowledge as a disciple and follow the disciplines prescribed.

But the nature of the claims made for Jesus raises the theological and moral questions of how we can "receive the benefits" of his life and death, to use Calvin's phrase. Indeed, the nature of the claims for him raises the question of our subjective or existential appropriation of his accomplishments to the level of the original question about his accomplishments. For if what Jesus was and did are not fully paradigmatic and transferable to our life in the world and ultimately to the world itself, then his life has only the interest and value of a novelty.

The answer to this question of how we receive the salvation of Jesus will, of course, be closely related to our understanding of what it means to be "saved," and varying answers have been given in the long history of the church. We cannot here follow these at length, but a brief review of the main types of motifs followed in answering the question will help to sharpen the issues for us.

Some Theological Models Used by the Church

The following review is schematic and for the purpose of clarifying the issues involved rather than giving a fully rounded historical description of each position. We will be describing general motifs rather than the position of any one theologian, and we should keep in mind that the motifs are not necessarily contradictory. Indeed, within each motif an attempt is made to give recognition to the different dimensions of the Christian's experience of salvation. However, real differences of theological emphasis and practice are present in the various traditions represented.

Belief: Intellectual Appropriation

According to our first motif Christ's benefits are appropriated by believing in his vicarious substitutionary atonement for us. This definition of faith in Christ as belief in the theological efficacy of his cross is the product of hundreds of years of theological development beginning with the Roman Catholic tradition. For example, the so-called Athanasian Creed which comes from the early Middle Ages ends its statement on the Trinity with these words: "Whoever, therefore, wishes to be saved, let him think thus concerning the Trinity." It should be added, however, that faith according to this tradition was also implicitly understood to include trust in the authority of the church and participation in its sacraments.

During the Reformation this connection with participation in the church was cut, and in the post-Reformation period the definition of faith as theological belief in Christ's atonement was made the sole connection between the cross as penalty for sin and the forgiven sinner. Contemporary Evangelicalism follows this pattern of Protestant orthodoxy.[1] Each of the positions which we shall briefly describe also claims the word "faith," but each gives the word its own nuance of meaning. The evangelical Protestant position defines faith as essentially *belief.*

The work of Christ is defined as a historical "once for all" event that potentially changed the relation of humankind to God. By his death and resurrection as a divine Savior Jesus made atonement to God for our sins. He propitiated the wrath of God and satisfied the demands of the law of God, and thus he changed the divine-human relationship. Through his "penal substitutionary" sacrifice humankind can be saved from the punishment due sin. And this salvation is received by simply believing in its reality "for us" and putting our trust in his "finished work." This act of belief is called faith, and by it we are justified in God's sight.

The significant distinction in this position is that faith is defined as belief, that is, an intellectual connection which in and of itself appropriates the reality of Christ's atoning work. Luther had given *trust* priority in his definition of saving faith. We might say that for Luther faith is believeful *trust*. Indeed, he virtually equated such trust with the experience of salvation by grace. Protestant orthodoxy, however, returned to the priorities of Roman Catholic orthodoxy and made belief in orthodox doctrine the basis of salvation. Of course a warm piety and "personal relationship" to Christ may and should also be cultivated.[2] But speaking in strictly theological terms, belief provides the saving connection between the "once for all" event of 2,000 years ago and the individual's life today.

Incorporation: The Mystical Approach

The earliest concepts of saving faith, of course, also included belief in the orthodox definition of Jesus as the God-man, but this belief did not focus so clearly on the cross as payment of a debt to justice which could be appropriated by belief. It focused rather on the incarnation of God for us. For example, Ignatius of Antioch (c. 35-107) said that Christ overcame demons, dissolved sorcery, and began the final conquest of death at his birth (Lightfoot, 1898:68). Justin Martyr (100-165), echoing Paul in Colossians, said that on the cross Christ broke the spell of devils and destroyed the principalities and powers (see Kelly, 1958:169). Irenaeus (c. 130-200) also spoke of Christ overcoming the powers of death for us in the resurrection, but he also viewed his life of perfect obedience as a reversal of the disobedience of Adam (humankind). He considered Jesus' passion and death on the cross to be the necessary and supreme expression of his full obedience to God. The cross and resurrection, he also said, were the final conflict of God with demonic powers in which the devil was vanquished. The resurrection was the heavenly *coup de grace* in which death was defeated. Thus in Jesus, the God-man, humankind has been given the opportunity to make a new start.

For Origen (c. 185-254) Christ's whole life was a conflict with the powers of darkness. He spoke of Christ's death specifically as a ransom paid

---

1. B. B. Warfield (1851-1921), Reformed theologian and teacher at Princeton Theological Seminary, whose books are still widely used, is a serious, scholarly representative of this position. See my brief biography (Kraus, 1981:198-201) for an introduction to Warfield.

2. This personal relationship was especially cultivated in the Pietistic movement within Protestantism as a balance to the formal orthodoxy of the seventeenth and eighteenth centuries.

to the devil who had gained the rights of ownership through humankind's rebellion against God. According to Origen the devil accepted the exchange of Christ for the sinners which he held in bondage, but he could not hold him in hell. Christ was raised from the dead, thus overcoming the demons in his resurrection. But however it was explained, and this is a bare outline of the theological theories of these men, Christ's work in our behalf changes the cosmic and human situation, making it possible for us to escape the power of death.[3]

According to this understanding of salvation the question is, How do we share in Christ's victory over death and Satan? And the answer comes clearly, namely, *by union with him in his mystical body, the church.* Already in the early first century Ignatius held that the church is a place of safety from the power of Satan and a place of cleansing from the defilement of sin. (In the church, he said, the bishop has the care of souls, and therefore one should faithfully respect and obey him.) But beyond this union with the church faith and love bring us into a mystical union with Christ himself. Ignatius understood this as a union with him in his suffering. He viewed martyrdom as a faith participation in the conflict and victory of Christ, and he sought to attain resurrection through a martyr union with Christ.

Irenaeus taught that in the incarnation God joined himself to humanity in union or solidarity with humankind. God became like us so that we in turn might become like God through incorporation into Christ. Thus solidarity with him in his mystical body is the way in which we share the results of Christ's obedience unto death.[4] We must be in mystical relationship with Christ, or participate in him, like we once participated in the sinful humanity of Adam. Through this participation of faith, which is a participation in the church, we receive the infusion of the Holy Spirit who gives us life and strength for the new holy works that Christ commanded.

This idea was developed by fourth-century Greek church fathers such as Gregory of Nyssa (c. 330-395), Gregory of Nazianzus (c. 330-389), and John Chrysostom (c. 347-407). The concept of Christ sharing our *flesh* was emphasized. Thus their concept is sometimes called the "physical theory" of Christ's saving work. Through the incarnation, death, and resurrection the divine life and victory over death became a possibility for all humans. Christ is the new beginning for humanity. By being joined to his humanity we also share in his divine accomplishment. J. N. D. Kelly says that "John Chrysostom explains that it is precisely because the Word has become flesh and the Master has assumed the form of a servant that men have been made sons of God" (Kelly, 1958:381). Of course this is not merely a physical process. Gregory of Nazianzus described it like this: "He takes me wholly, with all my infirmities, to Himself, so that as man He may destroy what is evil, as fire destroys wax or the sun's rays the vapours of the earth, and so that as a result of this conjunction I may participate in His blessing" (Kelly, 1958:381).[5]

In later Roman Catholic developments emphasis upon mystical communion in the body of Christ focused on the sacraments. The work of Christ was made effective for the individual's salvation through participation in the sacraments of the church, especially baptism and the Lord's Supper.

Through baptism "original sin," i.e., the sin and guilt with which one is born, is forgiven and the possibility of good works is restored. Through the supper, which was interpreted as a reenactment of Christ's eternal sacrifice on the cross for us, we are restored to mystical fellowship. In the sacramental acts of worship when believers receive the bread and wine they actually receive the mystical flesh and blood of Christ, and thus they participate in his body.

Imitation: the Moral Approach

Yet another recurring theme and variations may be seen in the history of theological explanations of Christ's relation to us. The theme or motif has generally been labeled *moral* or *subjective* because it emphasizes that Christ is a moral exemplar.

This motif was prominent in early attempts to explain the significance of Jesus' life and death, although it was seldom if ever the exclusive explanation. For example, the major emphasis of Clement of Alexandria (c. 150-213) was upon Christ as "Instructor," but he also spoke of Christ's death as a ransom which delivered sinners from the clutches of the devil; and he said that Christ as God forgave sin. Even as the "Instructor," Christ was not simply an exceptional rabbi. He was the incarnate Word of God. In his

-----

3. See Gustav Aulén, *Christus Victor* (1950), for a fuller description. Also R. H. Culpepper (1966) has a helpful chapter on the church fathers' interpretation. See also John Driver (1986).

4. John Kelly says, "The conclusion to which his argument leads is that humanity, which as we have seen was seminally present in Adam, has been given the opportunity of making a new start in Christ, the second Adam, through incorporation in His mystical body. The original Adam, by his disobedience, introduced the principle of sin and death, but Christ by His obedience has reintroduced the principle of life and immortality" (Kelly, 1958:173).

5. The conceptions of these early theologians was mythical and quasi-physical. For example, "spirit" was considered to be a highly refined substance that could permeate our bodies, giving them new life, or water, giving it the power of the sacrament. Jesus' work was conceived as making a "substantial" or ontological difference in the earthly-heavenly cosmos. Thus mystical solidarity was more than a pious or personal relationship.

The later Greek fathers clearly assumed the philosophical position of Plato called "realism." Accordingly each individual human being is simply part of one whole humanity so that the experience of a part can become the experience of the whole through a kind of infusion.

manhood we see the true image of God, and for Clement this image of God becomes our exemplar rather than Jesus' precepts, or even his example of martyrdom on the cross. Clement wedded Greek concepts of rational virtue and Christ's example in order to explain his significance to his own culture. He wrote:

> He is to us a spotless image; to Him we are to try with all our might to assimilate our souls. *He is wholly free from human passions wherefore also He alone is judge, because He alone is sinless.* As far, however, as we can, let us try to sin as little as possible. For nothing is so urgent in the first place as deliverance from passions and disorders, and then the checking of our liability to fall into sins that have become habitual (1925:210; emphasis mine).

So Clement sums up the moral approach in this manner: the Lord has come (1) to forgive our past sins, (2) to deliver us from the power of sin, and (3) to train us in virtue so that we may by his grace achieve the true image and likeness of God. Accordingly we receive this salvation through repentance and self-discipline following Christ's divine law.

In the work of Abelard (1079-1142), who is often associated with the moral-influence theory of atonement, the cross plays a larger role but not as ransom or sacrifice. Abelard was writing at a time when the crucifix with the suffering Christ hanging on it had become a central object of pious devotion. For him the death of Christ was the supreme demonstration of God's eternal love and atonement for sin. Its purpose was to move us to repentance and a true love for God. Since we know that Christ was truly God's Son and representative, his faithfulness unto death for our sakes frees us from our fear and hostility toward God. The love awakened in our hearts is the ground of God's forgiveness, and thus we are enabled to follow his example and teaching as the way of salvation.

A third example of this approach may be seen in the writings of Rudolph Bultmann (1884-1976) who insisted that the existential meaning of the cross for us is of sole importance. Bultmann, of course, is not moralistic, nor does he belong to the *imitatio Christi* tradition. But in the sense that he makes the effectiveness of the cross depend entirely upon a human existential moral response to Christ as exemplar, he can be classed in Abelardian tradition. He rejected as "irrational mythical doctrine" all talk of sacrificial atonement, ransom, and the like, and he viewed the cross as God's pronouncement of judgment upon the world's values. As he himself put it:

> Because a crucified one is proclaimed as Lord of the world it is demanded of man that he subject himself to God's judgment, i.e., to the judgment that all of

man's desires and strivings and standards of value are nothing before God, that they are all subject to death. If God has reconciled the world to himself through the cross, then this means that he has made himself visible in the cross and, as it were, says to man, "Here I am!" All of man's accomplishments and boasting are at an end; they are condemned as nothing by the cross (1960b:197).

Faith, then, is *submission* to this judgment of God, *renunciation* of boasting in human power and values, and *obedience* which Bultmann describes as "precisely the acknowledgment of the way of the cross as the way of life" (1960:199). In this faith-decision about one's own existence we find liberation from the domination of self and are given new life. This is the meaning of resurrection, for this decision to "surrender to death all that is one's own" includes trust in God who gives life to the dead. Again Bultmann writes, "For self-surrender through the cross means positively that the man who no longer wills to be for himself exists for others. Since what has been opened up to him in the cross is the liberating love of God, the love of Christ also compels him to serve his fellowmen (2 Cor. 5:14), and his faith is active in love (Gal. 5:6)" (1960:199).

According to Bultmann, then, Jesus becomes the supreme paradigm for our own personal decision about the true meaning of life. In Jesus we encounter "the God who is Creator and Judge, who claims man completely for himself and freely gives his grace to those who become nothing before him" (1960:201). Christ's life and death are the great exemplar of decision for God and others, and we appropriate his revelation by accepting his understanding of life as our own. This we do when we respond in faith to the proclamation of the gospel and commit ourselves in baptism to his way of life.

Solidarity with Christ: Personal Appropriation

Each of the previous motifs seeks to give a holistic interpretation of the subjective experience of salvation with special emphasis given to one aspect. Sometimes this special emphasis is explicitly corrective in nature as, for example, was Luther's emphasis on "faith alone." This Protestant emphasis on faith-belief was an attempt to correct a misplaced emphasis on salvation by self-effort (works) and reliance upon the sacramental means of grace offered by the church. These misplaced emphases had grown out of the early medieval insistence, quite right in its place, on the necessity of incorporation into the body of Christ for salvation. In turn the moral approaches, especially modern ones, have attempted to give existential decision and a real following of Christ more weight than did Protestant orthodoxy; certainly we must applaud this attempt.

Anabaptism too, while attempting a balanced interpretation, also took a self-consciously corrective stance. Its emphasis on *Nachfolge Christi* (discipleship or following Christ) at best demanded existential decision in the face of persecution, but it also sometimes eroded into moralism (see Friedmann, 1973). Its attempt at a balance between faith and works was sometimes less than perfect, with too much emphasis on works. However, at its heart the emphasis on faith as a living relationship and works as simply the product of regeneration reflects the stance of the original gospel. And its emphasis on salvation as life under the lordship of Christ, sharing his suffering, and bearing the cross still has much to teach modern Christians (e.g., Menno Simons, "The Cross of the Saints," in Wenger, 1956:581ff.).

Our question today as those who stand in the Anabaptist tradition by choice and conviction is how to enunciate this authentic insight in our contemporary context. For that I have chosen the concept of solidarity or *koinōnia* with Christ as the interpretive category. We have spoken of God's solidarity with us in Christ as the ethical ground of forgiveness (chap. 13). Now we must speak of our solidarity with Christ in the experience of grace as the stimulus to ethical response. For in this participation or sharing in the life and death of Christ are we being saved.

Pauline Concept

The concept of participation or *koinōnia* in Christ may be found in a number of Pauline texts, but it is nowhere more vividly described than in the portrayal of his own experience with Christ in Philippians 3:7-14. The language of the passage is well worth noting. The key phrase, "the knowledge of Christ Jesus my Lord"(TEV), which is found in verse 8 and repeated in verse 10, is described in the most experience-centered terms. This knowledge of Christ is no mere intellectual knowing about—either historical or philosophical. Neither is it a kind of mystical contemplation or emotion-centered attachment. Paul describes it as a possession of great advantage for which he was willing to give up the richness of a superior religious tradition in Judaism. The advantage possessed is Christ himself as "my Lord." This suggests that the advantage lies in coming under the authority and discipline of Christ in contrast to the former authority and discipline of the Mosaic law. And Paul makes this explicit when he describes being "in Christ" as attaining to the kind of righteousness which we see in Christ and which comes through him (v. 9). This is the true "righteousness from God."

Then in verses 10 and 11 Paul repeats his desire to "know Christ" and adds yet a new characterization of this knowledge. To know Christ means to have *koinōnia* (participation) in his suffering even to the point of dying a death like his, i.e., a *cross* death. And Paul desires this in the hope that he may also participate in Christ's resurrection. He wants even now to know the "power of that death" (cf. Eph. 1:19-20; Rom. 6:5-11). This is the pattern of solidarity or *koinōnia* with Christ, and it parallels point by point the description of Christ's solidarity with us in Philippians 2:5-11.

Such *koinōnia* may best be described as an actual participation in the life of another—a kind of embodiment in the experience of the other. Jesus was the embodiment, participation, or *koinōnia* of God in our human existence and for our salvation. And we in turn through *koinōnia* in Christ, i.e., in his Spirit and body, appropriate that salvation (see 1 Cor. 1:9; 6:17; 13:13; Phil. 2:1). His vicarious life and death was a life in solidarity with and for us. Now we are to take upon ourselves this same life and death with the hope that we will also receive resurrection.

The other Pauline phrase which suggests this concept of solidarity with Christ is the phrase "in Christ" or "into Christ." Again, this is not primarily a mystical incorporation but a life in the body and Spirit of Christ.[6] For example, to be in Christ according to Galatians 3:25-28 means to live beyond the barriers of social, economic, and sexual taboos in a Christ-like relationship to others. It is to live in a new order of creation (2 Cor. 5:17) beyond the old religious definitions. It means to receive the Spirit of Christ in the midst of his new community (Acts 2:38). Precisely in baptism—the rite of initiation into the body of Christ—are we united with Christ in death and resurrection (Rom. 6:3-4).

Again, to be in Christ means to have the mind of Christ (Rom. 12:1-2; Phil. 2:5) and to let the "fruit of his Spirit" be produced in our lives (John 15:4-5; Gal. 5:19-24). All this is summed up well in Romans 8:3-4 where Paul says that Christ who was made in the "likeness of sinful flesh" has made it possible for us to live a life of authentic righteousness as we "walk . . . according to the Spirit," or, if we may paraphrase, "as we live in solidarity with Christ."

In light of this New Testament concept we must, therefore, move beyond the categories of mystical piety. Especially in popular piety the language of mystical participation in Christ has been understood as a purely interior spiritual result of Christ's "finished work" of substitutionary sacrifice and unrelated, or at best indirectly related, to ethical behavior and life in the world.

---

6. The language of "Christ mysticism" was introduced into scholarly circles by Adolph Deissmann, *Die neutestementische Formel 'in Christo Jesu'* (1892), and given great popularity in the works of James Stewart—especially in *A Man in Christ: The Vital Elements of Paul's Religion* (1935). In Fundamentalist circles it was further popularized in a more radical form by L. E. Maxwell's *Born Crucified* (1945). Eric Wahlstrom in *The New Life in Christ* (1950) challenges this mystical view, pointing out the moral aspects of Paul's image.

Forgiveness the Test Case

Thus we must raise the question how this language of solidarity with Christ in his suffering and death relates to the language of vicarious substitution. Does the exclusiveness implied in substitution cancel out the inclusiveness of solidarity? If not, what did Jesus do for and instead of us that also involves us in radical attitudinal changes, restitution for past offenses, obedience following the example of Christ, and participation in his mission of salvation?

The test case is the experience of forgiveness. How is forgiveness through the cross of Christ related to solidarity with Christ? To use Paul's language, how does our experience of being forgiven involve us in sharing his "ministry of reconciliation"? Are these two separate experiences, namely, of being "saved" (justified) and then attempting to respond appropriately?

Or are we forgiven (saved) only as we forgive and share Christ's mission under his lordship? All that we have said up to this point leads us to conclude that the latter alternative is correct.[7]

Forgiveness is spoken of in the New Testament as an act of grace (*charizomai*) which frees or releases us (*aphesis*) from *past* obligations which we have failed to meet (debts). While the Christian concept clearly has been conditioned by the Hebrew concept of covenant law and may on occasion implicitly include the idea of release from the penal consequences of sin, *it goes far beyond juridical amnesty and speaks of the creation of a new order of personal relationships in which both the shame and guilt of sin are banished.*[8]

Forgiveness is a freeing from the burden of past failure experienced as both guilt and shame which inhibits our free, loving response to God and others. Thus to participate in Christ's forgiveness means not only receiving forgiveness through Christ; at the same time it is "forgiving one another, as God in Christ forgave you" (Eph. 4:32; Col. 3:13).

This sharing in the forgiveness of Christ is at the heart of the gospel as we should understand by the prayer, "Forgive us our debts as we forgive our debtors." The Prayer of St. Francis puts it eloquently: "It is *in forgiving* that we are forgiven."

Understanding salvation as solidarity with Christ in a new order of creation does not negate the grace of forgiveness; rather it gives us the subjective ethical content and basis of forgiveness. *Christian forgiveness is experienced as both ethical pardon and a stimulus to ethical response.* God wants our obedience and has freed us for obedience through participation in Christ. Where grace is cheap, that is, makes no claim on us, forgiveness lacks moral character.

The Experience of Solidarity with Christ

Finally, we must take a more detailed look at how salvation is appropriated through solidarity with Christ. We have already referred to the experience of Paul described in Philippians 3 and to the phrase, "in Christ," which expresses the concept of solidarity with Christ. Now we conclude with a more careful examination of the concept. Our solidarity with Christ includes the gift of the Spirit/spirit, or what may be called the *attitude* of Christ. Second, it includes the adoption of his *lifestyle* (discipleship). And last, it means participation in his *mission*.

Repentance: Adopting the Attitude of Christ

The salvation of Christ is appropriated in the experience of *repentance* (*metanoia*). Repentance is a change of attitude in response to the offer of forgiveness. It is the subjective process by which the results of Christ's life and death are made effective in one's own life. It can be defined as the act of entering into solidarity with Christ. It is an act also described as *conversion* (*epistrephō*) or turning around; and Paul describes it as being united with Christ in his death, burial, and resurrecton to new life (Rom. 6:3ff.). Or again, in Galatians (2:19-20) Paul refers to being "crucified with Christ" so that a new ego comes to life.

In still other language this solidarity with the attitude of Christ is

---

7. Many analyses of the psychology of forgiveness note that to define the dynamics of the experience is extremely difficult, if not impossible. Thus they begin by ruling out related but different concepts. For example, forgiveness is not forgetting. It involves us in an experience of actually resolving the personal consequences (hostility, anger, blame) of the misdeed even when the deed is not forgotten. The following are corrections to commonly held misconceptions.

a. Forgiveness is not an arbitrary or unconsidered act of mercy which the recipient experiences as simply a stroke of good fortune. Such a pardon requires no moral response from the recipient.

b. Forgiveness is not a self-serving mercy which lays a new demand or burden upon the one forgiven. Such an act of pardon does not radically change the relationship between the offended and the offender.

c. Forgiveness is not the same as toleration of faults. Toleration is a kind of permissiveness and is often the result of indifference. It overlooks the fault without dealing with its cause.

d. Forgiveness is not the same as indulgence of or excusing faults. This is a common meaning of *yurusu*. Such excusing is a psychological denial of the guilt and evasion of the shame which would normally be attached to wrongdoing.

e. Christian forgiveness is not merely immunity from the legal penalties attached to the fault. Such acquittal without a fundamental change in the situation may simply invite a recurrence of the offense.

8. In the New Testament the objects of forgiveness are transgressions and failures. In a text or two the objects are debts or obligations which we have failed to fulfill. But nowhere is explicit mention made of the legal penalties of sin as the objects of *aphesis*. Neither are we promised escape from the intrinsic consequences of our past sins nor release from restitution where that is possible.

described as receiving the Spirit/spirit of Christ or having the "mind of Christ." This spirit is not "the spirit of the world" but of God (1 Cor. 2:12-16). And the renewal of the mind changes the patterns of thinking and action to conform to Jesus (Rom. 12:1-2). A new attitude toward life and God frees us from legal obedience (Gal. 3:2-3). This new attitude is in one word the spirit of love, and both John and Paul agree that those who do not show this new attitude do not "belong to Christ" (Rom. 8:9; 1 John 3:14ff.). Or again, this new mind-set is described with the word *shalom* which Jesus said would be the hallmark of his presence with the disciples (John 14:27-31).

This is the shape of the individual's "participation in" or *koinōnia* of the Spirit—what is meant by the "Spirit of Christ in you" or "having the mind of Christ." One brings this mind-set or disposition to every level of life and human relationships. The gift of the Spirit of Christ is not simply a charismatic privilege accompanying salvation; it is the redeemed and redeeming, the reconciled and reconciling, the saved and saving posture which that Spirit represents.

Discipleship: Adopting Christ's Lifestyle

Participation in the Spirit of Christ is at the same time the experience of an enlivening presence and a controlling pattern or style (2 Cor. 5:14). "If we live by the Spirit, let us also walk by the Spirit," wrote Paul (Gal. 5:25).[9] The motivation and enablement to live according to a new pattern of relationships characterized by love is an essential element of Christ's salvation. Thus, "If anyone be in solidarity with Christ, there is a new order of creation; the old has ended and the new has begun" (2 Cor. 5:17).

The phrase "in Christ" does not indicate a mystical relationship, as we noted earlier, but a style of life. To be "baptized into Christ Jesus" (Rom. 6:3) is to become part of the social reality—"the body of Christ."[10] This new social body is characterized by a new order of relationships in which "neither circumcision nor uncircumcision (i.e., neither the taboos of Jewish law or pagan religious practices) any longer define human relationships. "In Christ" the legal and religious discriminations of sex, race, or social and economic standing can no longer be allowed to dominate relationships (Gal. 3:27-29; Col. 3:11). The work of Christ on the cross was precisely to reconcile the hostile factions of world society to God and to each other, thus creating one "new humanity." And as one becomes part of this one new humanity in the *koinōnia* of the Spirit of Christ, salvation from the old alienation and hostility becomes a reality. Indeed, the family metaphor, which Paul uses to describe our new relationship to God, communicates the new attitude and lifestyle which will characterize the family members. The sharp distinction between "standing" and "state" so characteristic of earlier dispensationalist theology is utterly misleading at this point. To be in the family of God means to adopt the lifestyle of his Son, Jesus Christ (cf. 2 Cor. 3:18; 1 John 3:2).

Clearly, then, solidarity with Christ means a new pattern of relationships in society. What the orthodox Protestant tradition has not seemed to recognize is that the changed pattern of relationships is an essential part of the gospel of salvation itself. On the other hand, the liberal tradition in its attempt to correct the imbalance too easily identified the reign of God and the new pattern of Jesus with the existing democratic institutions and ethical social reforms. This was especially true in the Ritschlian theology represented in America in the writings of Rauschenbusch. This genuine attempt to move to a more "biblical" norm than that of orthodoxy, which had incorporated much of the classical rationalism of Aristotle and Plato, ultimately foundered on the rocks of modern rationalism.

The mission of Jesus, our Savior-King, was to inaugurate a new social-spiritual order of human relationships under the authority of God. The pattern of this new order, which is also known as "the kingdom of God and his righteousness" (Matt. 6:33), is Jesus himself. Of course we are not suggesting a new primitivism which calls for literal imitation. That is why I have chosen the word *style*. That style is described as "taking up the cross and following [Christ]" (Mark 8:34). That style is also incorporated in the "new commandment" to love as Christ has loved and to serve one another as he served (Mark 10:45; John 13:16-17).

Christ's salvation has been appropriated where this pattern of relationships is realized and to the extent that it is realized among us.[11]

Solidarity with Christ in His Mission

The Protestant Reformers and orthodox theologians following them defined Christ's "vocation," what we have called mission, in contrast to that

---

9. The hortatory "let us walk" in this context does not indicate the possibility of "living by the Spirit" but not "walking by the Spirit." Rather, the point that is being made is that the life in the Spirit includes both attitude (Gal. 5:22-23) and conduct. We do not have life by the Spirit and then follow the law as our pattern (v. 18).

10. The phrase "in Christ before me" (Rom. 16:7) indicates "in the Christian movement." And the use of the figure of baptism in Romans 6 clearly indicates an initiation into the body or family of God (Acts 2:38; Eph. 2:19).

11. One can see reflected in the New Testament itself the struggle of the first churches to incorporate this new pattern. The principles are clearly enunciated, for example, in Galatians 3:25ff., Colossians 3:11, and Ephesians 5:21. A *modus vivendi* with contemporary social practices is sought in 1 Corinthians 11:1-16 and in Philemon, and it is obvious that different understandings and practices prevailed in different places. For example, note the difference between the attitude of the Pastorals and 1 Corinthians toward the place of women in the church program. Even if the Pastorals are actually from the hand of Paul, they most likely represent an attempt to deal with local cultural patterns and conditions. They should not be interpreted as his final, mature position even though they are late in composition.

of Christians. His vocation was to be the divine Savior. This was a specialized, divine calling "not of the world" but "for the world." In a limited sense the clergy who are called to preach the gospel may be said to participate in Christ's prophetic ministry, but the lay Christians' vocations are in and of the world, i.e., Christians must live as citizens of this world fulfilling the many public duties which that entails. That means that they must serve *in and according to* ethical patterns of the old order. They are to do such tasks, of course, motivated by *faith* in Christ's justifying death and their own *love* for the neighbor. This was their mission.

Further, Luther was careful not to interpret the Christian's suffering as a participation in the mission of Christ. Using the categories of *merit* and *penalty*, Luther could not include Christians' efforts and suffering, not even martyrdom for Christ's cause, as a part of the *satisfaction* for sin. He was too deeply involved in combatting the current notion that the "treasury of the church," which could be used to make satisfaction for sins, included the merits of the saints as well as those of Christ.[12]

The language of the New Testament concerning our relation to Christ's mission is far less reserved than this. The disciples were "baptized with" the Holy Spirit of Jesus precisely so that they could continue his mission (Matt. 28:19-20; John 20:22-23; Acts 1:8). This is the message of John 14—17 where Jesus includes the disciples in the continuance of his own mission in the most intimate terms. And, of course, the secret of identification is participation in the Spirit. Again, in Colossians Paul can even speak of "completing what was lacking in the sufferings of Christ" on behalf of the church (1:24).

In all of this there is no intention to detract from or nullify the "once for all" character of Christ's work. He has done what no one before or since has done or can do. He remains the unique source from which the reconciling influence comes. His life, death, and resurrection have reconciled us to God. He changed the human situation so that it can never be the same again. Certainly the Reformers were correct in again stressing the crucial point that what Christ did does not need to be repeated. But in what does the uniqueness of his role consist? And how are we related to it?

Speaking precisely, Christ's role was that of *initiator*. He was the "pioneer" of our faith righteousness. He was the "first born among many children." But a pioneer is honored precisely because he has opened the way for others to follow. Theologically we do not properly represent Christ's true uniqueness by assigning him a qualitatively different mission (vocation) from that of his disciples, but rather, by recognizing his continuing authority and control of the mission as Lord and giving proper credit to the enabling role of his Holy Spirit. Jesus himself promised that his disciples would do greater works than he himself had done (John 14:12), but that is only because he himself as the Spirit continues with them as the enabling power. This Spirit is the primary witness. The disciples are "also witnesses" as they participate in the Spirit (John 15:27). The church does not take Christ's place or inherit his authority as, for example, Elisha inherited the mantle of Elijah. The church operates under Christ's authority—sent by him on his mission to represent him. Perhaps this word *represent* best states the relationship of his witness and ours.

Solidarity with Christ in his mission means to represent him in acts of witness (*marturia*) that continue his witness to the Father. This witness is spoken of by Jesus as "taking up the cross and following after him" (Mark 8:34-35) and by Paul as sharing in Christ's suffering (Phil. 3:10). To participate in the mission one must share the style as a disciple calling all humankind to such a disciple style (Matt. 28:19-20). This includes—but is more than "proclamation" of—a message about the historical Jesus Christ and his saving death.[13]

Such suffering or bearing the cross is by no means a persecution complex. Rather, it denotes a stance or style of relationship and response to the world order which does not recognize the authority of the crucified Messiah. As the Apostles' Creed puts it, Jesus "suffered under Pontius Pilate"; that is, the opposition to Jesus came from the social-cultural order and not just from hostile individuals. John's Gospel refers to the specifically religious aspect of this order as "the Jews," that is, the religious leaders, and in its totality it is called "the world."

---

12. Not until quite late in his life did Luther seem to see that part of the problem with the Roman Catholic concept of the "merit of saints" is inherent in the concept of merit itself.

Insofar as the church claimed to control the sacramental grace and the flow of merit from the treasury to the sinner it claimed a participation in Christ's work of redemption. Luther rightly rejected this completely and insisted that Christ alone bore the guilt of sins and made satisfaction for us (see his commentary on Galatians, "Christ redeemed us from the curse . . ." (Luther, 1961:136-37).

As for the "cross and sufferings" of the Christian, Luther interprets them entirely as a discipline to "tame the flesh" (see Luther's Preface to Romans (1961:31).

In the beautiful passage in "The Freedom of a Christian" Luther says that we should each be "a Christ" to our neighbor. That is, we should serve the neighbor as Christ served in the freedom of love and not under the necessity of law. However, the point of this extended passage is not participation in the salvific mission of Christ, but only love's freedom from the law in the service of the neighbor following the example of Christ (Luther, 1961:73ff.).

13. Emphasis on the formal sermon and ceremonial sacraments as proclamation of Christ rather than emphasis on authentic representation of Christ's mission through the lifestyle of his followers is certainly a form of "cheap grace." Proclamation is important, but it needs to be kept in its proper order of relation to demonstration of the new reality (Luke 10:8-9). Here I am not speaking so much of a temporal sequence as existential priority which gives proclamation its authenticity. Solidarity with Christ in mission means participation in the power of the Spirit for an authentic representation of the original paradigm, namely, the "suffering" and "crucifixion."

Thus solidarity in the mission of Christ also can be properly spoken of as nonconformity to the world (Rom. 12:1-2). In our twentieth-century world perhaps one of the clearest examples of this kind of nonconformity in witness to Jesus may be seen in the suffering of those Christians who have refused cooperation with racism and militarism in the name of Christ. Such suffering is clearly what Peter refers to as "sharing Christ's suffering" (TEV) and "suffering as a Christian" (1 Pet. 4:13, 16).

Solidarity with Christ in his mission means espousing the patience and purpose of Christ in servanthood. The purpose of his mission is spoken of in a variety of ways, but if we express it in its most comprehensive form, the goal is nothing less than a "new heaven and earth wherein dwells righteousness" (2 Pet. 3:13; cf. Rom. 8) or as in Ephesians, "the reuniting of everything in Christ" (1:10). And the advent of Jesus means that this "new creation" or reconciliation has begun (2 Cor. 5:17; Eph. 2:11ff.). In Christ's cross God has already created one new humanity and has broken down the old walls of hostility between Jew and Gentile.

Christ's mission for the church then is to "make disciples of all nations" (Matt. 28:19); to exercise the "ministry of reconciliation" (2 Cor. 5:18-19); or as God's "chosen race, a royal priesthood, a holy nation" to declare God's wonderful deeds (1 Pet. 2:9-10). God's plan is that "through the church" the wisdom and power of God manifested in the cross of Jesus shall be made known to the rulers and authorities which dominate this present world (Eph. 3:10). This in no way excludes the witness to individuals, which is sometimes called "personal evangelism." But the mission of Jesus as the Messiah dare not be restricted to the narrower definition of evangelism as calling individuals out of the world which has already been prejudged to damnation.

Jesus himself refused to prejudge the world or to predict the "end" which is in the Father's hands. He simply bore faithful witness to the will of God for the world in both word and deed. In the same manner the church is called, not to prejudge the world to destruction and restrict the purpose of Christ's mission, but to be the instrument of God's offer of forgiveness to the world. This it must do even though that offer is spurned and the church must live a martyr existence under the sign of the cross. The mission is the mission of Jesus, the Messiah. The church has no authority to redefine the mission in ways which justify the world in its recourse to violent power and allow the church to escape martyrdom.

Thus, in conclusion, under the sign of the cross and in hope of the resurrection we are being saved by our solidarity with Christ. As we allow our minds to be renewed in his likeness, take up his style as our own, and participate in his mission under his lordship our lives take on new direction, integration, and purpose. Precisely as Jesus, the crucified, becomes our Lord can he be our Savior. And what is true for the individual is also true for the world as a whole. Christ, the crucified King, has been "lifted up" as the Savior of the world.

References Cited

Augustine, Aurelius
1902 "On Marriage and
       Concupiscence," Book 1, *A*
       Select Library of the Nicene and
       Post-Nicene Fathers of the
       Christian Church, Vol. V, *Saint*
       Augustine: Anti-Pelagian
       Writings, ed. by Philip Schaff.
       New York: Charles Scribner's
       Sons.

Aulén, Gustav
1950 *Christus Victor.* London:
       S.P.C.K.

Baillie, Donald MacPherson
1948 *God Was in Christ: An Essay on*
       Incarnation and Atonement.
       New York: Charles Scribner's
       Sons

Barrett, C. K.
1960 *The Gospel According to John.*
       London: S.P.C.K.

Barth, Karl
1949 *Dogmatics in Outline.* London:
       SCM
1956 *Church Dogmatics,* Vol. I, 2, ed.
       by G. W. Bromiley and T. F.
       Torrence. Edinburgh: T. & T.
       Clark.

Barth, Marcus
1969 "The Faith of the Messiah,"
       Heythrop Journal.

Beardslee, J. W., III, (ed.)
1965 *Reformed Dogmatics.* New York:
       Oxford.

Benedict, Ruth
1946 *The Chrysanthemum and the*
       Sword. Boston: Houghton and
       Mifflin.

Berkhof, Hendrikus
1962 *Christ and the Powers,* trans. by
       John Howard Yoder. Scottdale:
       Herald Press.
1979 *Christian Faith, An Introduction*
       to the Study of the Faith, trans.
       by Sierd Woudstra. Grand
       Rapids: Eerdmans.

Boettner, Loraine
1947 *Studies in Theology.* Grand
       Rapids: Eerdmans.

Bonhoeffer, Dietrich
1967 *Letters and Papers from Prison,*
       trans. by Reginald Fuller. New
       York: Macmillan Co.

Bowker, John
1970 *The Problem of Suffering in the*
       Religions of the World.
       Cambridge: University Press.

Brandon, S. G. F.
1967 *Jesus and the Zealots.* New York:
       Scribner.

Buber, Martin
1958   *I and Thou*, trans. by R. Gregor-
            Smith. New York: Scribner.

Büchsel, Friedrich
1964   "*Agorazō*, et al.," *Theological
            Dictionary of the New
            Testament*, ed. by Gerhard
            Kittel. Grand Rapids: Eerdmans.
1964   "*Ara*, et al.," *Theological
            Dictionary of the New
            Testament*, ed. by Gerhard
            Kittel. Grand Rapids: Eerdmans.
1965   "*Hilasmos*," *Theological
            Dictionary of the New
            Testament*, ed. by Gerhard
            Kittel. Grand Rapids: Eerdmans.

Bultmann, Rudolf Karl
1951   *Theology of the New Testament*,
            (2 volumes), 1955 trans. by
            Kendrick Goebel. New York:
            Scribner's.
1955   "Christ the End of the Law,"
            *Essays Philosophical and
            Theological*. London: SCM.
1960   *Existence and Faith: Shorter
            Writings of Rudolf Bultmann*,
            trans. by Schubert M. Ogden.
            Cleveland and New York: World
            Publishing Co.

Calvin, John
1960   *Institutes of the Christian
            Religion*, in *Library of Christian
            Classics*, XX, Vol. I, ed. by John
            T. McNeill, trans. by Ford Lewis
            Battles. Philadelphia:
            Westminster Press.

Campenhausen, Hans von
1964   *The Virgin Birth in the Theology
            of the Ancient Church*, trans. by
            Frank Clarke. Naperville, Ill:
            Alec R. Allenson.

Clement of Alexandria
1925   "The Instructor" *The Ante-
            Nicene Fathers: Translations of
            the Writings of the Fathers
            Down to A.D. 325*, Vol. II,
            Fathers of the Second Century,
            ed. by The Rev. Alexander
            Roberts, D.D., and James
            Donaldson, LL.D. New York:
            Charles Scribner's Sons.

Cook, Michael L., S.J.
1981   *The Jesus of Faith: A Study of
            Christology*. Ramsey, N.J.:
            Paulist Press.

Cullmann, Oscar
1950   *Christ and Time, the Primitive
            Christian Concept of Time and
            History*, trans. by Floyd V.
            Filson. Philadelphia:
            Westminster.
1956   *The State in the New Testament*.
            New York: Scribner.
1963   *The Christology of the New
            Testament*. London: S.C.M.
            Press. (Westminster published an
            American edition in 1964.)

Culpepper, R. H.
1966   *Interpreting the Atonement*.
            Grand Rapids: Eerdmans.

Davies, W. D.
1958   *Paul and Rabbinic Judaism:
            Some Rabbinic Elements in
            Pauline Theology*. London:
            SPCK (1st ed., 1948; 2nd ed.,
            1955).

Denny, James
1911   *The Death of Christ*, London:
            Hodder and Stoughton
1918   *The Christian Doctrine of
            Reconciliation*. London: Hodden
            and Stoughton; New York:
            Doran.

Diessmann, Adolph
1892   *Die neutestementische Formel
            'in Christo Jesu'*. Marburg.

Driver, John
1986   *Understanding the Atonement
            for the Mission of the Church*.
            Scottdale: Herald Press.

Dunn, James D. G.
1980   *Christology in the Making*.
            Philadelphia: Westminster.

Eberhard, Wolfram
1967   *Guilt and Sin in Traditional
            China*. Berkeley: University of
            California Press.

Eller, Vernard
  1981 *War and Peace from Genesis to Revelation.* Scottdale: Herald Press.
  1974 *The Most Revealing Book of the Bible: Making Sense Out of Revelation.* Grand Rapids: Eerdmans.

Endo, Shusaku
  1974 *Wonderful Fool,* trans. by Francis Mathy. Rutland, Vermont and Tokyo: Tuttle.
  1978 *A Life of Jesus,* trans. by Richard A. Schuchert. New York, Paulist Press.

Erickson, Eric
  1950 *Childhood and Society.* New York: W. W. Norton.

Forsyth, P. T.
  1910 *The Work of Christ.* London: Hodder and Stoughton
  1917 *The Justification of God.* London: Independent Press.

Franks, Robert S.
  1962 *The Work of Christ, A Historical Study of Christian Doctrine.* London: Thomas Nelson & Sons.

Friedmann, Robert
  1973 *The Theology of Anabaptism: An Interpretation.* Scottdale: Herald Press.

Fuller, Reginald H.
  1965 *The Foundations of New Testament Christology.* New York: Scribner's.

Griffiths, Bede
  1982 *The Marriage of East and West.* London: Collins.

Hahn, Ferdinand
  1973 *The Worship of the Early Church.* Philadelphia: Fortress Press.

Hengel, Martin
  1981 *The Atonement, The Origins of the Doctrine in the New Testament.* London: S.C.M.

Hermann, Wilhelm
  1971 *The Communion of the Christian with God,* (2nd English ed. trans. by J. Sandys Stranton and R. W. Stewart), ed. by T. Voelkel. Philadelphia: Fortress.

Hordern, William
  1964 *Speaking of God, The Nature and Purpose of Theological Language.* New York: Macmillan.

Jenni, Ernst
  1962 "Messiah," *Interpreter's Dictionary of the Bible,* ed. by George A. Buttrick. New York: Abingdon.

Jeremias, Joachim
  1964 *The Lord's Prayer.* Philadelphia: Fortress Press.

Johnson, Luke Timothy
  1982 "Romans 3:21-26 and the Faith of Jesus," *The Catholic Biblical Quarterly.*

Kaufman, Gershen
  1974 "The Meaning of Shame," *Journal of Counseling Psychology,* November.

Kaufman, Gordon
  1968 *Systematic Theology: A Historicist Perspective.* New York: Scribner's Sons.

Kelly, John Norman Davidson
  1958 *Early Christian Doctrines.* New York: Harper.

Kierkegaard, Soren
  1944 *Concluding Unscientific Postscript,* trans. by David F. Swenson and Walter Lowerie. Princeton: University Press.

Kitagawa, J. M.
  1966 *Religion in Japanese History.* New York: Columbia University Press.

Kitamori, Kazoh
  1965 *The Theology of the Pain of God,* Richmond: John Knox Press.

Kittel, Gerhard
1964 "Abba," *Theological Dictionary of the New Testament*, Vol. I. Grand Rapids: Eerdmans. 1964 "Dogma, et al.," *Theological Dictionary of the New Testament*, ed. by Gerhard Kittel. Grand Rapids: Eerdmans.

Klaassen, Walter
1981 *Anabaptism: Neither Catholic nor Protestant*. Waterloo, Ont.: Conrad Press.

Klaassen, Walter (ed.)
1981 *Anabaptism in Outline: Selected Primary Sources*. Scottdale: Herald Press.

Klassen, William, and Walter Klaassen (trans. and eds.)
1978 *The Writings of Pilgram Marpeck*. Kitchener, Ont., and Scottdale: Herald Press.

Kooiman, Willem Jan
1961 *Luther and the Bible*, trans. by John Schmidt. Philadelphia: Muhlenberg Press.

Koyama, Kosuke
1984 *Mount Fuji and Mount Sinai* London: SCM.

Kraus, C. Norman
1958 *Dispensationalism in America: Its Rise and Development*. Richmond, Va.: John Knox Press.
1976 "Toward a Theology for the Disciple Community," *Kingdom, Cross, and Community: Essays on Mennonite Themes in Honor of Guy F. Hershberger*, ed. by John Richard Burkholder and Calvin Redekop. Scottdale: Herald Press.

1979 *The Authentic Witness: Credibility and Authority*. Scottdale: Herald Press.
1981 "Benjamin Breckenridge Warfield," *A Cloud of Witness: Profiles of Church Leaders*. Harrisonburg, Va.: Eastern Mennonite Seminary.

Ladd, George
1975 *I Believe in the Resurrection of Jesus*. Grand Rapids: Eerdmans.

Lampe, G. W. H.
1972 "The Holy Spirit and the Person of Christ," *Christ Faith and History*, ed. by S. W. Sykes and J. P. Clayton. Cambridge: University Press.
1977 *God as Spirit*. Oxford: Clarendon Press.

Lightfoot, J. B.
1898 "Epistle of Ignatius to the Ephesians," *The Apostolic Fathers*. New York: Macmillan.

Luther, Martin
1960 "Preface to the Old Testament," *Luther's Works*, vol. 35, *Word and Sacrament*, ed. by E. Theodore Bachman. Philadelphia: Muhlenberg Press.
1961 *Martin Luther: Selections from His Writings*, ed. by John Dillenberger. Garden City, N.Y.: Doubleday.

Lynd, Helen
1961 *On Shame and the Search for Identity*. New York: Science Editions.

Machen, John Gresham
1932 *The Virgin Birth of Christ*. New York: Harper.

Mackintosh, H. R.
1927 *The Christian Experience of Forgiveness*. London: Nisbet.

Macquarrie, John
1966 *Principles of Christian Theology*. New York: Scribner's.
1967 *God-Talk, An Examination of the Language of Logic and Theology*. New York: Harper & Row.

Manson, T. W.
1963 *The Teachings of Jesus*. Cambridge: University Press.

Marty, Martin E. and Dean G. Peerman (eds.)
1967   *New Theology No. 4.* New York: Macmillan.

Maxwell, L. E.
1945   *Born Crucified.* Chicago: Moody Press.

May, Rollo
1969   *Love and Will.* New York: Norton.

McCarthy, Dennis J.
1962   "Blood," *Interpreter's Bible Dictionary,* Supplementary Volume (V). Nashville: Abingdon.

McDonald, H. D.
1985   *The Atonement of the Death of Christ, in Faith, Revelation and History.* Grand Rapids: Baker.

Melanchthon, Philipp
1965   *Melanchthon on Christian Doctrine: Loci Communes, 1555,* trans. and ed. by Clyde L. Manschreck. New York: Oxford University Press.

Moltmann, Jürgen
1974   *The Crucified God, the Cross of Christ as the Foundation and Criticism of Christian Theology,* trans. by R. A. Wilson and John Bowden. New York: Harper and Row.

Moule, C. F. D.
1977   *The Origin of Christology.* Cambridge: University Press.

Mueller, David L.
1969   *An Introduction to the Theology of Albrecht Ritschl.* Philadelphia: Westminster Press.

Nakane, Chie
1973   *Japanese Society.* New York: Pelican Books.

Neill, Stephen
1976   *Jesus Through Many Eyes.* Philadelphia: Fortress.

Newbigin, Lesslie
1983   *The Other Side of 1984: Questions for the Churches.* Geneva, Switzerland: World Council of Churches.

Niebuhr, Reinhold
1935   *An Interpretation of Christian Ethics.* New York and London: Harper.
1955   *The Self and the Dramas of History.* New York: Scribner's Sons.

Niebuhr, Richard R.
1964   *Schleiermacher on Christ and Religion, A New Introduction.* New York: Scribner.

Niesel, Wilhelm
1956   *The Theology of Calvin,* trans. by Harold Knight. Philadelphia: Westminster Press.

Outler, Albert (trans. and ed.)
1955   *Augustine: Confessions and Enchiridion,* (Library of Christian Classics, Vol. VII). Philadelphia: Westminster.

Pannenberg, Wolfhart
1968   *Revelation as History.* trans. by David Granskau, London: Macmillan.
1977   *Jesus—God and Man.* 2nd. ed., trans. by Lewis Wilkins and Duane Priebe. Philadelphia: Westminster Press (1st English ed., 1968).

Paton, Alan
1953   *Too Late the Phalarope.* New York: Scribner.

Perrin, Norman
1976   *Rediscovering the Teaching of Jesus.* New York: Harper and Row (1st ed., 1967).

Piers, Gerhart, and Milton B. Singer
1971   *Shame and Guilt—A Psychoanalytic and Cultural Study.* New York: W. W. Norton.

Porteous, Norman W.
1962 "Image of God," *The Interpreter's Dictionary of the Bible*. Vol. 2. Nashville: Abingdon.

Porteous, Alvin C.
1971 *In Search for Christian Credibility: Explorations in Contemporary Belief*. Nashville and New York: Abingdon.

Raitt, Jill
1977 "The French Reformed Theological Response [to the Formula of Concord]," *Discord, Dialogue, and Concord*, ed. by Lewis Spitz and Wenzel Lohff. Philadelphia: Fortress Press.

Rauschenbusch, Walter
1917 *The Theology of the Social Gospel*. New York: Macmillan Co.

Reischauer, Edwin O.
1971 *Japan: The Story of a Nation*. Tokyo: Tuttle.

Renan, Ernest
1904 *The Life of Jesus*. London: Watts & Co. (1st English ed., 1863).

Richardson, Alan
1941 *Creeds in the Making*, (2nd. ed.). London: S.C.M. Press.

Ricoeur, Paul
1967 *The Symbolism of Evil*, trans. by Emerson Buchanon. New York: Harper and Row.

Riezler, Kurt
1943 "Comment on the Social Psychology of Shame," *The American Journal of Sociology*, January.

Ringgren, Helmer
1956 *The Messiah in the Old Testament*. Chicago: Alec R. Allenson.

Ritschl, Albrecht
1966 *The Christian Doctrine of Justification and Reconciliation*, Vol. 3. trans. and ed. by H. R. Macintosh and A. B. Macaulay. Clifton, N.J.: Reference Books Publishers. (First published in Bonn, Germany, 1889.)
1972 "Instruction in the Christian Religion," *Three Essays*, trans. by P. Hafner. Philadelphia: Fortress.

Robinson, James M.
1959 *A New Quest of the Historical Jesus*, (Studies in Biblical Theology, No. 25). London: S.C.M. Press.

Rogers, Carl R.
1966 "The Necessary and Sufficient Conditions of Therapeutic Personality Change," *Counseling and Psychotherapy: Classics on Theories and Issues*, ed. by Ben N. Arn, Jr. Palo Alto, Calif.: Science and Behavior Books, Inc.

Samuel, Vinay, and Chris Sugden (eds.)
1983 *Sharing Jesus in the Two-Thirds World*. Bangalore, India: Partnership in Mission—Asia (also Grand Rapids: Eerdmans, 1984).

Schaeffer, Francis A.
1968 *The God Who Is There*. Downers Grove, Ill.: Intervarsity.

Seeberg, Rheinhold
1952 *Text-book of the History of Doctrines*, Book II. Grand Rapids: Baker Book House (1st ed., 1895, 1898).

Sheldon, Charles
1897 *In His Steps: What Would Jesus Do in Solving the Problems of Present Political, Economic and Social Life?* Chicago: Fleming H. Revell.

Sobrino, Jon, S.J.
1978 *Christology at the Crossroads, A Latin American Approach*. Maryknoll: Orbis Books.

Stendahl, Krister
1963 "The Apostle Paul and the Introspective Conscience of the West," *Harvard Theological Review.*

Stewart, James S.
1935 *A Man in Christ: The Vital Elements of Paul's Religion.* London: Hodder and Stoughton.

Stott, John R. W.
1985 *The Authentic Jesus: The Certainty of Christ in a Skeptical World.* Downers Grove, Ill.: Inter-Varsity Press.

Taylor, Vincent
1940 *The Atonement in New Testament Teaching.* London: Eppworth Press.

Thelle, Notto R.
1983 "Doing Theology in a Buddhist Environment," Part II, *Japanese Religions,* XIII:2, December.

Thielicke, Helmut
1977 *The Evangelical Faith,* Vol. 2: *Doctrine of God and Christ,* trans. by Godffrey W. Bromiley. Grand Rapids: Eerdmans.

Tupper, E. Frank
1973 *The Theology of Wolfhart Pannenberg.* Philadelphia: Westminster.

Turner, H. E. W.
1953 *Jesus, Master and Lord.* London: A. R. Mowbray Co.

Von Rad, Gerhard
1965 *Old Testament Theology,* trans. by O. M. G. Stalker. New York: Harper & Row.

Wahlstrom, Eric
1950 *The New Life in Christ.* Philadelphia: Muhlenberg.

Weber, Otto
1983 *Foundations of Dogmatics,* Vol. 2, trans. by Darrell L. Guder (from 1962 German edition). Grand Rapids: Eerdmans.

Welch, Claude, (ed.)
1965 *God and Incarnation in Mid-nineteenth Century German Theology* (A Library of Protestant Thought). New York: Oxford.

1972 *Protestant Thought in the Nineteeth Century,* Vol. 1. New Haven and London: Yale University Press.

Wenger, J. C.
1954 *Introduction to Theology: A Brief Introduction to the Doctrinal Content of Scripture Written in the Anabaptist-Mennonite Tradition.* Scottdale: Herald Press.

Wenger, J. C. (ed.) 1956 *The Complete Writings of Menno Simons,* trans. by Leonard Verduin. Scottdale: Herald Press.

Wesley, John
1954 *A Compendium of Wesley's Theology,* ed. by Robert W. Burtner and Robert E. Chiles. New York, Nashville: Abingdon.

Whale, J. S.
1941 *Christian Doctrine.* Cambridge: University Press

Yoder, John H.
1972 *The Politics of Jesus.* Grand Rapids: Eerdmans.

General Index

Index of Persons

Scripture Index

The Author

With his wife, Ruth, C. Norman Kraus served under Mennonite Board of Missions for seven years in Asia and Australia (1980-1987). It was during this time that the present book was written.

He has served on the Mennonite Board of Mission's overseas committee and has gone on teaching missions to churches in India, Indonesia, the Philippines, Taiwan, Hong Kong, Australia, and various East African countries. He was also a member of the Health and Welfare Committee of the Mennonite Board of Missions for five years.

Kraus has taught at the following seminaries in Asia: Serampore Theological College (1966-67) in India; Union Biblical Seminary (1983) in Pune, India; Eastern Hokkaido Bible School (1981-86) in Japan; and Baptist Theological College of Western Australia (1987).

Prior to this recent assignment in Japan, Kraus was a professor of religion and director of the Center for Discipleship at Goshen College. He was also book review editor of the *Mennonite Quarterly Review*. A student of both Anabaptism and Evangelicalism and its origins, he is the author of *Dispensationalism in America* (John Knox, 1958).

A native of Newport News, Virginia, Kraus earned graduate degrees from Goshen Biblical Seminary, Princeton Theological Seminary (Th.M.), and Duke University (Ph.D.). Aside from numerous articles, he is also the author of *The Healing Christ* (Herald Press, 1971), *The Community of the Spirit* (Eerdmans, 1974), *The Authentic Witness* (Eerdmans, 1979), and the editor of *Evangelicalism and Anabaptism* (Herald Press, 1979).

He is a Mennonite minister in the Indiana-Michigan Mennonite Conference, where he was ordained in 1950. He is married to the former Ruth Smith and they are the parents of five grown children.

At present he and Ruth are at home in Goshen, Indiana, where he is continuing his writing and doing short-term assignments for the Mennonite Board of Missions.